THE STRUGGLE IN BLACK AND BROWN

JUSTICE AND SOCIAL INQUIRY

SERIES EDITORS

Jeremy I. Levitt

Matthew C. Whitaker

The Struggle in Black and Brown

AFRICAN AMERICAN AND MEXICAN AMERICAN RELATIONS DURING THE CIVIL RIGHTS ERA

EDITED AND WITH AN INTRODUCTION BY
BRIAN D. BEHNKEN

UNIVERSITY OF NEBRASKA PRESS   LINCOLN & LONDON

The oral histories in chapter 2, "The
Movement in the Mirror: Civil Rights
and the Causes of Black-Brown Disunity
in Texas," appear courtesy University
of Texas–San Antonio Institute of
Texan Cultures. Chapter 4, "The
Neighborhood Adult Participation
Project: Black-Brown Strife in the War
on Poverty in Los Angeles," an excerpt
from *Race and the War on Poverty:
From Watts to East LA*, is reprinted
courtesy University of Oklahoma Press.

∞

Library of Congress Cataloging-in-
Publication Data
The struggle in black and brown:
African American and Mexican American
relations during the civil rights era /
edited and with an introduction by
Brian D. Behnken.
    p. cm.—(Justice and social inquiry)
Includes bibliographical references
and index.
ISBN 978-0-8032-6271-3 (pbk.: alk. paper)
1. African Americans—Civil rights—
United States—History—20th century.
2. Mexican Americans—Civil rights—
United States—History—20th century.
3. Civil rights movements—United
States—History—20th century. 4. African
Americans—Relations with Mexican
Americans—History—20th century.
5. United States—Race relations—
History—20th century. 6. United States—
Ethnic relations—History—20th century.
I. Behnken, Brian D.
E185.61.S9148 2011
305.800973—dc23   2011032970

Set in Sabon.

CONTENTS

ILLUSTRATIONS

ABBREVIATIONS USED IN THE TEXT

AAPQE	African American Parents for Quality Education
AWOC	Agricultural Workers Organizing Committee
ACLU	American Civil Liberties Union
AFL-CIO	American Federation of Labor and Congress of Industrial Organizations
AFSCME	American Federation of State, County, and Municipal Employees
AFPS	American Fund for Public Service
BBC	Black and Brown Coalition
Project BRAVO	Building Resources and Vocational Opportunities
CASA	El Centro de Accion Social y Autonomo
CSAC	Chicana Service Action Center
CPLC	Chicanos por la Causa
CIC	Commission on Interracial Cooperation
CAA	Community Action Agency
CAP	Community Action Program
CIO	Congress of Industrial Organizations
CORE	Congress of Racial Equality
PVL	Democratic Progressive Voters League
EYOA	Economic and Youth Opportunities Agency
EOA	Economic Opportunity Act
EOF	Economic Opportunity Federation
EEOC	Equal Employment Opportunity Commission
EODC	Equal Opportunity Development Corporation
Project FREE	Family, Rehabilitation, Education, Employment
FLOC	Farm Labor Organizing Committee
GLACAA	Greater Los Angeles Community Action Agency
HCCAA	Harris County Community Action Agency
HCCO	Harris County Council of Organizations
HUAC	House Un-American Activities Committee
INS	Immigration and Naturalization Service

JACL	Japanese American Citizen's League
LULAC	League of United Latin American Citizens
LDF	Legal Defense and Education Fund, Inc.
LAAFSNC	Los Angeles Area Federation of Settlements and Neighborhood Centers
MACHOS	Mexican American Committee on Honor Opportunity and Service
MAPA	Mexican American Political Association
MASO	Mexican American Student Association
MIWON	Multiethnic Immigrant Worker Organizing Network
NAACP	National Association for the Advancement of Colored People
NFWA	National Farm Workers Association
NAPP	Neighborhood Adult Participation Project
OEO	Office of Economic Opportunity
PSBC	Parent—Student Boycott Committee
PUHS	Phoenix Union High School
PASO	Political Association of Spanish-Speaking Organizations
PPC	Poor People's Campaign
PPE	Poor People's Embassy
SAISD	San Antonio Independent School District
SANYO	San Antonio Neighborhood Youth Organization
SER	Service, Employment, Redevelopment
SCLC	Southern Christian Leadership Conference
SNCC	Student Nonviolent Coordinating Committee
SDS	Students for a Democratic Society
TCRF	Texas Civil Rights Fund
TELACU	The East Los Angeles Community Union
UFW	United Farm Workers
UFWOC	United Farm Workers Organizing Committee
UOIC	United Organizations Information Center
UT	University of Texas
WLCAC	Watts Labor Community Action Committee
YCCA	Young Chicanos for Community Action
YSA	Young Socialist Alliance
YOB	Youth Opportunities Board

THE STRUGGLE IN BLACK AND BROWN

INTRODUCTION

BRIAN D. BEHNKEN

In October 1967 a large group of Mexican American and African American activists met in Albuquerque, New Mexico for the annual conference of the Alianza Federal de Pueblos Libres. Called together by Alianza leader and New Mexican activist Reies López Tijerina, the meeting explored the possibility of black and Chicano unity and collaboration.[1] Virtually every major Black Power organization sent a representative: Ron Karenga of the Us organization, James Dennis of the Congress of Racial Equality, Ralph Featherstone of the Student Nonviolent Coordinating Committee, Walter Bremond of the Black Congress, and Anthony Akku Babu of the Black Panther Party. The most important Chicano groups also sent leaders to the gathering. These included Tijerina, José Angel Gutiérrez of the Mexican American Youth Organization, Bert Corona of the Mexican American Political Association, David Sánchez of the Brown Berets, and Rodolfo "Corky" Gonzales of the Crusade for Justice. Never before in the history of the African American and Mexican American freedom struggles had so many activists from so many different civil rights groups met in an attempt to forge a cooperative, cross-racial alliance. Blacks and

Chicanos listened to speeches in Spanish and English, attended various meetings, chanted "Black Power," "Chicano Power," and "Poder Negro" at several gatherings, and ultimately produced a "Treaty of Peace, Harmony, and Mutual Assistance."[2]

While the meeting was unusual, the treaty proved extraordinarily unique. Representatives from all the different groups signed the seven-part pact. One of the most important aspects of the meeting and the treaty was an acknowledgement for the activists that "for the first time the old myth of coalition for mutual self-interest is exploded and we move into the area of mutual respect." Article I began with the words, "Both peoples (races) will consider this TREATY as a SOLEMN agreement, and subject to the Divine Law of the GOD of JUSTICE." Framing the treaty as applying to both blacks and Chicanos—whom the treaty writers' identified as individual races bound by religious law—situated browns and blacks within a similar racial, religious, and historical perspective. Further, Article I stipulated that "Both peoples do promise not to permit the members of either of said peoples to make false propaganda of any kind whatsoever against each other, either by SPEECH or WRITING." This statement began the process of unifying these different groups in a cooperative alliance that, if nothing else, ensured that each side would not denigrate the efforts of the other side.

Article II went further in illuminating the extent of black-brown cooperation envisioned in the treaty. It began, "both peoples (races) do promise, never to permit violence or hate, to break this SOLEMN TREATY between said peoples." This clause seemed to recognize a history of separation and animus shared by African Americans and Mexican Americans. Article III continued in this vein, noting that "both peoples, make a SOLEMN promise, to cure and remedy the historical errors and differences that exist between said peoples." In Articles IV and V, the treaty writers detailed exactly what interethnic unity might look like. "Let it be known," Article IV began, "that there will be a RECIPRIOCAL right to send an EMISSARY or DELEGATE to the conventions, Congresses, and National reunions of each of said peoples." This statement proposed that all the various organizations involved in the Alianza conference could continue to interact with each other, an important step in coalition building. Article V reiterated this arrangement, stating "let it be known that both peoples will have a political delegate to represent his interests and relations with the other." Again, the treaty writers foresaw what they hoped would become a collaborative relationship whereby the various groups would continue to work together. The treaty delegates also insisted that this relationship would continue into perpetuity: "this TREATY, will be valid between the two said peoples, as long as the Sun and Moon shall shine." [3]

The Albuquerque meeting and the subsequent "Treaty of Peace, Harmony, and Mutual Assistance" represented a curious moment in the history of race relations between Mexican American and African American people. Indeed, the treaty was a document that seemed to epitomize the often contradictory attitudes of black people toward those of Mexican origin, and of Mexican Americans toward African Americans. On the one hand, the effort to bridge two of the most powerful ethnic movements in the United States was an endeavor rooted in the activism of the time, one that recognized the potential strength of a united struggle, the similarities of two oppressed and segregated groups, and the power of the oppositional forces arrayed against the Black and Chicano Power movements. At the very least, the treaty and meeting represented an inchoate attempt at bridging differences between browns and blacks. On the other hand, one must wonder why a *treaty* was needed to smooth relations between these groups. Since nation-states usually write treaties, and they sign such accords to conclude longstanding disputes and end wars, this treaty seemed to recognize the territorial nationalism of these groups while simultaneously acknowledging that blacks and Chicanos had deeply felt disagreements and perhaps were even at war with each other. The document represented in one light a model of ethnic inclusion and in another showed the limits of interethnic cooperation. The treaty signified the willingness of each side to discuss unity, but ultimately produced no long-term unification of the black and Chicano civil rights movements.

As the Albuquerque meeting and the treaty revealed, black-brown relations in the United States, especially during the civil rights era, could be both conflicted and cooperative, contentious and collaborative. The field of comparative civil rights scholarship is new, and there are relatively few book-length works that explore the interactions of blacks and Chicanos during the civil rights period.[4] *The Struggle in Black and Brown* builds on this developing scholarship. The ten essays included compare the history of the African American and Mexican American civil rights movements in a variety of local settings in the Southwest in an effort to elucidate the nature of race relations between these two groups. The authors track black-brown relations from the 1940s to the 2008 presidential campaign, exploring a wide variety of topics and regions. This exploration includes a comparison of African American and Mexican American leaders in 1940s Texas, the unification of black and Chicano civil rights/labor groups in California, the divisions between African Americans and Mexican Americans generated by the War on Poverty, black-brown cooperation during the Poor People's Campaign, the cultural connections established by black and Chicano musicians during the civil rights period, and the ways in which politics and economics bifurcated these groups in the twentieth and early twenty-first centuries. What this book and its eleven contributors ultimately show is that collaboration and conflict often existed side-by-side in the Mexican American and African American civil rights struggles.

When Americans think about the civil rights movement, I would suggest they typically remember events in the South that

4

involved blacks protesting against Jim Crow segregation. They probably also recall well-known leaders like Dr. Martin Luther King Jr. and well-known protests such as the Birmingham Campaign of 1963 and the Mississippi Freedom Summer of 1964. Yet across the United States civil rights organizations and protests developed that did not involve Dr. King, the Deep South, and in many cases black people. Part of what *The Struggle in Black and Brown* shows is that numerous civil rights movements occurred throughout the United States involving African Americans, Mexican Americans, Native Americans, Asian Americans, European Americans, and in many cases combinations of a variety of these groups. The essays in this collection help to move the discussion of the civil rights movement beyond black and white and out of the South. In so doing, we hope to complicate the very meaning of the term "civil rights movement."

Scholars have been somewhat reluctant to tackle the issue of black-brown relations in the civil rights period. When they have explored instances of African American and Mexican American interaction, they have tended to simplify relations between these two groups as good or bad, typified by either conflict or cooperation. For example, in his book *The Presumed Alliance*, legal scholar Nicolás Vaca characterizes black-brown relations as "troubled," "conflicted," and "divided."[5] He also notes that "the ostensible moral and philosophical bases for coalition politics have largely fallen apart because of competing self-interests."[6] Finally, he castigates notions of black-brown unity as "the presumed ideological alliance" between African Americans and Mexican Americans.[7] Vaca's account rather simplistically reduces black-brown unity to a fiction, a contention that hardly jibes with reality.

Other scholars offer an overwhelmingly optimistic view of black-brown relations. Historian Carlos Blanton dismisses scholarship like Vaca's, as well as the burgeoning field of

Mexican American whiteness studies as pioneered by historian Neil Foley. Blanton argues that "the distance between the African American and Mexican American civil rights movements is less significant than historians have generally held and ultimately explained far better by factors other than whiteness alone."[8] He rejects whiteness as a Mexican American civil rights strategy as well as black people's reaction to this white racialization. Blanton oversimplifies a rather complex history and seems to view black-brown relations as unproblematic and rosy. The scholars who view black-brown relations as unproblematic—like those who look upon race relations between these groups hypercritically—make the mistake of seeing black-brown relations as a zero sum game, as either all good or all bad. As this book makes clear, black-brown relations during the civil rights period were complex, varied, and hardly as static as Vaca or Blanton aver.

The complexity of the problems African Americans and Mexican Americans confronted during the civil rights period almost single-handedly demonstrates the multifaceted nature of black-brown relations. Across the United States, but especially in the Southwest, Mexican Americans and African Americans encountered a persistent and pervasive Jim Crow order that denied persons deemed "nonwhite" of the full flower of American democracy, equality, and citizenship. Jim Crow customs and laws differed across the Southwest, but many states shared not only common laws but commonly held assumptions about blacks and Mexican Americans. For example, in Arizona, California, New Mexico, and Texas, Mexican American and African American children attended segregated schools. Voting for both groups was frequently circumscribed through a variety of disfranchisement measures, including the poll tax, the all-white Democratic primary, and voter intimidation. Blacks and Mexican Americans generally held low-wage, menial jobs, which forced them to live in communities that, if not segregated through de jure laws, were segregated along de facto lines because of economics. White business owners frequently denied both groups service, and signs reading "No Mexicans Allowed," "No Mexicans Served Here," "No Colored Served Here," "No Dogs, Negroes, Mexicans," or more simply "We Cater to White Trade Only" peppered store fronts across southwestern cities and towns. The broad variety of laws and customs ensured racial separation across the Southwest. This system of segregation should remind us that Jim Crow was a national issue, not solely a southern phenomenon.

More problematically, white people tended to regard Mexican Americans and blacks as racially inferior, degenerate, and suspect. Such conceptions allowed whites to underpin the segregation system with an understanding of racial difference that seemed natural, biological, and permanent. Thus any challenge to segregation violated a vaguely defined set of racial, moral, and religious beliefs. This is what historian George Fredrickson meant when he called racism a "scavenger ideology," because it allowed white people to pick and choose the various racist arguments that deterministically supported the Jim Crow system.[9] When fighting for civil rights, Mexican Americans and African Americans not only challenged segregation, they also confronted this host of racist assumptions that pigeonholed nonwhites as deficient. As both groups found out, desegregating restaurants and acquiring voting rights proved far easier than destroying the underlying racism to which many whites continued to cling.

Mexican-origin people had one advantage when challenging segregation. In many parts of the Southwest, and before the advent of the 1960s, Mexican Americans attempted to categorize themselves as white. In some cases this racial positioning involved simply what Mexican Americans called themselves and were called by other Americans. In New Mexico and Arizona, for example, Mexican-descent people often preferred the label Spanish American, which signaled a white heritage via Spanish birth. In Texas and California, Mexican Americans frequently called themselves Latin American, which also signaled European ancestry. Mexican Americans also rejected any designation of Mexican-origin people as nonwhite on the census, on birth and death certificates, on poll tax receipts, and on traffic tickets, among other forms of documents. This white racial positioning offended some African Americans, although it did not foreclose the chances for a united movement. While the essays in this collection do not universally deal with this whiteness issue, it is nonetheless necessary for us to understand as an important part of black-brown relations.[10]

Relations between Mexican Americans and African Americans tended to vary by region. Besides comparing blacks and browns and their experiences during the civil rights movement, this book opens a window onto regional differences and similarities shared by states such as Texas, California, New Mexico, and Arizona, and more broadly the Southwest and West. Region proves important because of the differing character of racial oppression in different parts of the country. In Texas, for example, longstanding racial animosities between blacks and browns bifurcated the two movements and set the stage for divisions between blacks and Mexican Americans. In California, by contrast, African Americans and Mexican Americans unified groups such as the Student Nonviolent Coordinating Committee and the National Farm Workers Association in order to battle against racial segregation of blacks and for equal economic rights for Mexican farm workers.

Population also frequently moderated race relations between blacks and browns. The relative strength of each group was frequently determined by its population. For example, in New Mexico and Arizona blacks constituted a small proportion of the state's population and they had a relatively weak civil rights movement. African Americans consequently joined the protests of Mexican American civic groups on several occasions in order to bolster their own civil rights struggle. In Texas, blacks and browns both had significant populations and strong civil rights movements. Since each group fought for their own community, and since they won many victories separately, the need for unification was lessened. In New Mexico and Arizona blacks and browns occasionally unified their movements while in Texas unity eluded these groups.

Context also offers an explanation for unity and disunity during the black and Mexican American civil rights struggles. Specific protests, for instance, seem tailor-made for generating either unity or disunity. Labor struggles in Texas, California, and elsewhere frequently produced black-brown coalitions. When African American and Mexican American activists moderated the divisive power of race by focusing on economics, they recognized the shared oppression of each group. In order to win better wages, hours, and working conditions, blacks and browns cooperated with each other. Other aspects of the civil rights era generated competition, distrust, and disunity. War on Poverty programs bear this point out. The War on Poverty in many instances provided federal monies to distinct groups—blacks, Chicanos, Indians, Asians—with little thought as to how groups receiving fewer funds might react. In numerous southwestern communities, African Americans and Mexican Americans came into conflict over the perception that one group received preferential treatment from the government. As such, browns and blacks became competitors for War on Poverty funds, and this competition frequently degenerated into outright hostility and animosity.

A host of other factors demonstrate the multifaceted nature of Mexican American–African American relations. Leaders, for example, proved important for generating either harmony or acrimony. In Texas, educator and activist George Sánchez frequently spoke highly of the black civil rights movement and occasionally reached out to black civil rights leaders. In Arizona, prominent African American leader Lincoln Ragsdale often worked with Mexican Americans to eliminate segregation. And in California, white activist Mike Miller attempted to unite Anglos, blacks, and Mexican Americans. But in other areas, the actions of important leaders generated friction and hostility. In California, antipoverty activist Opal Jones seemed to favor poor blacks over poor Chicanos, which angered the Mexican American community in Los Angeles. Similarly, Texas leader Felix Tijerina rebuked the idea of black-brown unity and castigated anyone wishing to align the two movements. Like leadership, culture had the potential to both unite and fragment Mexican Americans and blacks. Music, for instance, tended to bridge racial and ethnic differences. African American and Mexican American musicians frequently borrowed from one another, creating syncretic forms of music that spoke to the activism and protests of each group. But culture could also fragment these groups. Cultural nationalism came to be a major component of the more radical Black Power and Brown Power movements. But cultural nationalism often divided browns and blacks since some activists viewed separation as a natural method of exploring cultural traditions. In sum, black-brown relations in the civil rights period were varied, complicated, and dynamic.

The essays in this collection highlight areas of both conflict and cooperation, explore the attitudes and opinions of both groups, position civil rights struggles and race relations within the larger framework of social justice, and thereby nuance the broader discussion regarding black-brown relations. The objective of *The Struggle in Black and Brown* is to compare specific moments of protest in local contexts, to underscore instances of cooperation and conflict, and to explain the reasons for the unity that occurred in various moments during the period and the disunity that also frequently marred the efforts of African American and Mexican American civil rights activists. The civil rights era offers a particularly advantageous viewpoint for examining race relations between these groups. By studying a time period when cooperation and conflict coincided, *The Struggle in Black and Brown* reveals both the problematic nature of black-brown relations in the United States while simultaneously exposing instances of coalition building and collaboration. More important, this book helps explain why African Americans and Mexican Americans chose to join forces in certain instances, while at the same time illuminating the causes of black-brown disunity.

In the first chapter Lisa Ramos, in "Not Similar Enough," explores the relationships of Mexican American and African American civil rights leaders in 1940s Texas. In the early 1940s, Mexican American civil rights leader and nationally recognized education expert George Sánchez began making overtures to the American Civil Liberties Union (ACLU). Sánchez also considered joining the Mexican American civil rights effort with the National Association for the Advancement of Colored People, having heard of NAACP attorney Thurgood Marshall's legal struggles on behalf of African Americans in Texas. But, unlike with the ACLU, he concluded not to pursue this possibility. Ramos explores what drove Sánchez to reach out to the ACLU and not to the NAACP. She demonstrates that Sánchez feared unity with the NAACP might damage both the black and Mexican American struggle.

In the second chapter, "The Movement in the Mirror," Brian D. Behnken examines the causes of African American and Mexican American disunity in Texas and demonstrates that a number of factors contributed to the development of two separate civil rights movements. The racial geography of Texas, class issues, strategic and tactical differences, and dissimilar leaders and leadership styles all generated disunity between Mexican Americans and African Americans. Most important, racial prejudices on both sides reduced the chances for cooperative ventures between these two groups. Black and Mexican American racial and racist perceptions of each other drove these movements apart. Behnken shows that while both struggles in Texas had numerous similarities, blacks and browns largely failed to unite their movements.

In chapter three Lauren Araiza explores the relationship between the Student Nonviolent Coordinating Committee (SNCC) and the National Farm Workers Association (NFWA) in the chapter entitled "Complicating the Beloved Community." When Cesar Chavez and the farm workers began their first strike against grape growers in Delano, California in September 1965, the union immediately called on African Americans for assistance. The SNCC readily answered this call. Araiza shows that the resulting alliance, which lasted for two years, was the first instance of a multiracial coalition between organizations of the black civil rights and Chicano movements in California. She explores the NFWA's motivations for pursuing interethnic alliances and SNCC's reasons for entering the alliance with the farm workers. Araiza ultimately demonstrates the success of this alliance, but also that the SNCC-NFWA coalition ended by 1967 as a result of SNCC's adoption of a black nationalist ideology.

In the fourth chapter, "The Neighborhood Adult Participation Project," Robert Bauman examines the War on Poverty and black-brown relations in Los Angeles. In the mid-1960s the Los Angeles Neighborhood Adult Participation Project (NAPP) attempted to eradicate poverty in Los Angeles. NAPP was the only antipoverty program that emphasized citizen participation and it became embroiled in significant controversies, most of which centered on racial divisions and tensions between African Americans and Mexican Americans. Bauman shows that from the creation of NAPP, Mexican Americans questioned its racial configuration, especially in regard to the location of most of the neighborhood centers and the numbers of Mexican American versus black employees. Because of the racial divisions within NAPP, and the economic competition for War on Poverty programs more generally, blacks and Chicanos downplayed interethnic cooperation and dismissed unification as a tactic for obtaining poverty aid. Bauman concludes that many blacks and Mexican Americans involved in NAPP came to see each other as competitors rather than allies.

In chapter five William Clayson shifts the focus on the War on Poverty to Texas. In "'Mexican versus Negro Approaches' to the War on Poverty" Clayson traces conflicts between Mexican American and African American community leaders in Texas over control of programs funded by the Office of Economic Opportunity (OEO), the agency created by Lyndon Johnson to fight his War on Poverty. In communities across the state, African American and Mexican American groups vied for a greater share of OEO funding, often complaining about neglect caused by an undue emphasis on the needs of the other group. Clayson demonstrates that leading Mexican American figures expressed particular frustration with the OEO for its neglect of Mexican American poverty. At the same time, depending on the locale and which group had the smaller population, African Americans and Mexican Americans complained that attention paid to the larger group (blacks in Houston, Mexican Americans in El Paso) eclipsed their concerns. Clayson demonstrates that the ascension of group interest above consensus and cooperation created an adversarial relationship between blacks and browns, both of whom came to see the other as a competitor for limited War on Poverty funds.

In the sixth chapter Jorge Mariscal explores the potential for a relationship between Dr. Martin Luther King Jr. and Cesar Chavez in one month in 1968. In "Cesar and Martin, March '68" Mariscal shows the immense personal struggles that afflicted both leaders as they attempted to adhere to the philosophy of nonviolence while exploring the idea of unifying blacks and browns. While Chavez and King never met and only communicated by telegram, their coming together would have resulted in a significant alliance of two powerful movements. While

Mariscal imagines what might have been, he also describes the stressful period through which both men moved. He compares the philosophy and organizing practices of two key leaders and how their movements overlapped at a critical juncture in the 1960s. In March 1968, shortly before King's assassination, both men were aware of each other but the plans that might have led them to collaborate had only just begun. Mariscal debunks much of the popular understanding of Chavez and King, an understanding that links the two men in a united struggle that never occurred.

In chapter seven, "Black, Brown, and Poor," Gordon Mantler examines black-brown relations in the Poor People's Campaign (PPC). Martin Luther King developed the PPC in an effort to transform the black freedom struggle into a national class-based coalition of the poor. King did not live to see the campaign develop, nor did his survivors witness a recognizable coalition emerge from it. Nonetheless, Mantler demonstrates that the campaign proved to be a transformative moment for Mexican American activists who went to Washington. Mantler shows that the campaign substantially contributed to the Chicano movement's increasing sophistication and strength by building and deepening relationships among Mexican American activists. Ironically, the last crusade of Martin Luther King, the most prominent leader of the black freedom struggle, became a key building block for the nationalist unity and rhetoric of the Chicano movement.

In the eighth chapter Luis Alvarez and Daniel Widener probe the words, sounds, and cultural expressions of prominent African American and Chicano musicians in the 1960s. In "Brown-Eyed Soul" Alvarez and Widener analyze the connections and conflicts between black and brown musicians who drew from similar cultural influences, political conditions, and working-class sensibilities in the urban neighborhoods of Southern California. Focusing largely on popular music, they show that

cultural production and consumption spawned an array of social and political relationships among African Americans and
Chicanos. Musical groups like War, El Chicano, and Sunny and
the Sunliners fostered a cultural politics that linked the experiences of Chicanos and blacks with one another. Alvarez and
Widener demonstrate that the multiethnic and cross-racial cultural expression of Chicanos and African Americans became a
central part of the movements for social change and ethnic nationalism of the era.

In chapter nine Abigail Rosas investigates African American and Mexican American residents' pursuit of civil rights and
economic opportunity in South Central Los Angeles from the
1970s to 2000. In "Raising a Neighborhood" Rosas details the
work of two female activists in South Central, Elena Santiago
and Ruth Smith.[11] Elena and Ruth both immigrated to South
Central at roughly the same moment in the 1940s. But they
came from different communities—Ruth from the Deep South
and Elena from Mexico. In South Central they forged a bond
as community mothers to watch over children and protect the
neighborhood from drugs and violence. Rosas argues that the
civil rights struggles of Mexican American and African American women in South Central complicate the narrative of black-
brown relations. She shows that local residents chose to work
across racial and gender lines in order to cope with this region's
social problems, which included economic restructuring, immigration, and dehumanizing governmental services and policies.

In the final chapter Matthew Whitaker explores the legacy
of black-Latino relations and more recent interactions among
these two groups in the late twentieth and early twenty-first
centuries. In "A New Day in Babylon" he examines the social,
economic, and political impact of black and Latino relations
on various communities across the United States. Whitaker explores three fundamental aspects of African American and Mexican American relations: the positive and negative perceptions

that members of each group have toward the other, the issues that have proven the most divisive for blacks and Chicanos, and the instances in which the two groups have cooperated to secure social justice and greater political power. He shows that while both groups have often had a contentious history of race relations, geographical proximity, a shared experience of economic inequality and political marginality, and dreams of a more equal and just society all serve as a common ground upon which to forge substantive unions.

Taken together, the ten chapters presented in this book demonstrate the multifaceted nature of black-brown relations in the United States. Both the Mexican American and African American civil rights struggles have their own unique histories. The point of this book is to show instances of unity and disunity as they occurred between both movements. While cooperation and conflict existed during this period, these terms were certainly not mutually exclusive and they unfortunately flatten a varied and exciting history. This book is intended to unflatten this history. My hope is that, if nothing else, *The Struggle in Black and Brown* complicates our understanding of both civil rights struggles and the nature of black-brown relations during the civil rights period. Perhaps with increased scholarly attention, Mexican Americans and African Americans will indeed find a unity, as the writers of the "Treaty of Peace, Harmony, and Mutual Assistance" had hoped, that will last "as long as the Sun and Moon shall shine."

Notes

1. Throughout this introduction I use the terms "black" and "African American" to denote people of African heritage. For Mexican-origin people, the terms "Mexican American," "Mexican descent," "Mexican origin," "Chicana/o," and "Latina/o" are used to describe this group. For whites I use "white" and "Anglo." The authors of the ten chapters in this book each chose the ethnic or racial designations they preferred for African Americans, Mexican Americans, and European Americans.

2. For discussion of the meeting and treaty, see George Mariscal, *Brown-Eyed Children of the Sun: Lessons from the Chicano Movement, 1965–1975* (Albuquerque: University of New Mexico Press, 2005), 191–95.

3. "Treaty of Peace, Harmony, and Mutual Assistance," October 1967, copy in author's possession. My special thanks to Dr. Jorge Mariscal for voluntarily sharing his copy of the treaty with me. Mariscal continues a time-honored tradition of sharing research material with his fellow scholars, and his generosity is greatly appreciated.

4. Most of the recent works on black-brown relations during the civil rights period have come from unpublished dissertations. See Ramona Allaniz Houston, "African Americans, Mexican Americans, and Anglo Americans and the Desegregation of Texas, 1946–1957" (PhD diss., University of Texas, 2000); Mark Brilliant, "Color Lines: Civil Rights Struggles on America's 'Racial Frontier,' 1945–1975" (PhD diss., Stanford University, 2002); Lauren Araiza, "For Freedom of Other Men: Civil Rights, Black Power, and the United Farm Workers, 1965–1973" (PhD diss., University of California, Berkeley, 2006); Brian D. Behnken, "Fighting Their Own Battles: Blacks, Mexican Americans, and the Struggle for Civil Rights in Texas" (PhD diss., University of California, Davis, 2007); Gordon Mantler, "Black, Brown, and Poor: Martin Luther King Jr., the Poor People's Campaign, and Its Legacies" (PhD diss., Duke University, 2008). For the few books comparing blacks and Mexican Americans during the civil rights era, see Matthew C. Whitaker, *Race Work: The Rise of Civil Rights in the Urban West* (Lincoln: University of Nebraska Press, 2005); George Mariscal, *Brown-eyed Children of the Sun: Lessons from the Chicano Movement, 1965–1975* (Albuquerque: University of New Mexico Press, 2005); Laura Pulido, *Black, Brown, Yellow, and Left: Radical Activism in Los Angeles* (Berkeley: University of California Press, 2006); Michael Phillips, *White Metropolis: Race, Ethnicity, and Religion in Dallas, 1841–2001* (Austin: University of Texas Press, 2006); Neil Foley, *Quest for Equality: The Failed Promise of Black-Brown Solidarity* (Cambridge MA: Harvard University Press, 2010); Mark Brilliant, *The Color of America Has Changed: How Racial Diversity Shaped Civil Rights Reform in California, 1941–1978* (New York: Oxford University Press, 2010); Brian D. Behnken, *Fighting Their Own Battles: Mexican Americans, African Americans, and the Struggle for Civil Rights in Texas* (Chapel Hill: University of North Carolina Press, 2011). For a more politically oriented look at black-brown relations, see Bill Piatt, *Black and Brown in America: The Case for Cooperation* (New York: New York University Press, 1997); Tatcho Mindiola, Yolanda Flores Nieman, and Nestor Rodriguez, *Black-Brown: Relations*

and Stereotypes (Austin: University of Texas Press, 2002); Stephen J. Herzog, *Minority Group Politics: A Reader* (New York: Holt, Rinehart and Winston, 1971); Harriett D. Romo, ed., *Latinos and Blacks in the Cities: Policies for the 1990s* (Austin: University of Texas Press, 1990).

5. Nicolás C. Vaca, *The Presumed Alliance: The Unspoken Conflict Between Latinos and Blacks and What It Means for America* (New York: Rayo, 2004), 4, 8.

6. Vaca, *The Presumed Alliance*, 188.

7. Vaca, *The Presumed Alliance*, 2.

8. Carlos K. Blanton, "George I. Sánchez, Ideology, and Whiteness in the Making of the Mexican American Civil Rights Movement, 1930–1960," *Journal of Southern History* 72, no. 3 (August 2006): 603. Blanton specifically criticizes Neil Foley's essay, "Becoming Hispanic: Mexican Americans and the Faustian Bargain with Whiteness," *Reflexiones* (1997).

9. George M. Fredrickson, *Racism: A Short History* (Princeton: Princeton University Press, 2003), 8–9.

10. See Steven H. Wilson, "*Brown* over 'Other White': Mexican Americans' Legal Arguments and Litigation Strategy in School Desegregation Lawsuits," *Law and History Review* 21, no. 1 (2003); Foley, "Becoming Hispanic"; Neil Foley, "Straddling the Color Line: The Legal Construction of Hispanic Identity in Texas," in *Not Just Black and White: Historical and Contemporary Perspectives on Immigration, Race, and Ethnicity in the United States*, ed. Nancy Foner and George Frederickson, 341–57 (New York: Sage, 2005); Neil Foley, "Partly Colored or Other White: Mexican Americans and Their Problems with the Color Line," in *Beyond Black and White: Race, Ethnicity, and Gender in the U.S. South and Southwest*, ed. Stephanie Cole, Allison Parker, and Laura F. Edwards, 123–44 (College Station: Texas A&M University Press, 2003); Clare Sheridan, "'Another White Race': Mexican Americans and the Paradox of Whiteness in Jury Selection," *Law and History Review* 21, no. 1 (2003); Thomas A. Guglielmo, "Fighting for Caucasian Rights: Mexicans, Mexican Americans, and the Transnational Struggle for Civil Rights in World War II Texas," *Journal of American History* 92, no. 4 (2006); Tomás Almaguer, *Racial Fault Lines: The Historical Origins of White Supremacy in California* (Berkeley: University of California Press, 1994).

11. To protect the confidentiality of these activists, "Elena Santiago" and "Ruth Smith" are pseudonyms.

ONE

Not Similar Enough

Mexican American and African American Civil Rights Struggles in the 1940s

LISA Y. RAMOS

On July 6, 1948, University of Texas professor George I. Sán-chez penned a letter to Thurgood Marshall, special counsel for the National Association for the Advancement of Colored Peo-ple (NAACP).[1] At the time, Sánchez was a scrappy and stubborn forty-one-year-old scholar-activist who had worked on improv-ing the social and economic conditions of Mexican Americans since his days of teaching in the rural mountains of his native New Mexico.[2] Marshall was a forty-year-old distinguished and courageous attorney from Baltimore, Maryland, in charge of the NAACP's Legal Defense and Education Fund, Inc. (LDF).[3] In his letter to Marshall, Sánchez expressed unqualified support for the NAACP's campaign to end segregation. He wrote: "I would be very happy to give you whatever cooperation I can."[4] Sán-chez was referring to Marshall's request for the affidavits of var-ious academics and researchers in the *Delgado et al. v. Bastrop et al. Independent School District* (1948) school desegregation case, in which ten Mexican-descent parents and grandparents sued four central Texas school districts, a county superinten-dent, the state superintendent of public education, and the state board of education on behalf of their twenty Mexican American children. The families brought suit because these local school districts and state officials refused to allow Mexican-descent children to attend Anglo schools, even if an Anglo school was closer to their homes, and for compelling the Mexican-descent children to attend the Mexican School.[5]

Now that these two key leaders within the Mexican American and African American civil rights community had connected, why did they not discuss merging their antidiscrimination efforts?[6] Both were, after all, in the middle of school desegregation legal campaigns. This failure to join the black and Mexican American civil rights struggles prior to the social revolution of the 1960s has become the center of much debate. According to one side of this debate, Mexican American leaders were wedded to whiteness, meaning they possessed a strong identification with the white race and especially the idea of white racial supremacy over other racial groups.[7] This phenomenon demonstrates why no joint black-brown civil rights effort emerged prior to the 1960s. Some scholars argue that politically active Mexican Americans did not abandon a white race identity in favor of a minority status until the late 1960s or early 1970s.[8] For instance, legal scholar Ian Haney López writes, "[S]ince the 1930s, members of the Mexican community had insisted, in the face of a strong presumption by Anglo society to the contrary, that Mexicans were white."[9] He suggests that many Mexican Americans embraced this identity until the late 1960s when Mexican American youth began to assert a Chicano, nonwhite (brown race) identity.[10] Historian Guadalupe San Miguel buttresses this view when he writes that prior to the 1970s "activist Mexican Americans in Houston and throughout the country had viewed themselves as part of the white or Caucasian race in order to obtain social justice and equal educational opportunity."[11] These scholars distinguish between a pre-1960s white race identification and a post-1960s Chicano identification among Mexican American activists.

1. George I. Sánchez, professor at the University of Texas at Austin, in the 1940s. Nettie Lee Benson Latin American Collection, University of Texas Libraries, the University of Texas at Austin.

21

2. Thurgood Marshall, attorney for the NAACP, 1957. Library of Congress, Prints & Photographs Division, Visual Materials from the NAACP Records, Reproduction no. LC-DIG-ppmsc-01271.

Rather than enveloping themselves completely in white race claims in the pre-1960s period, I argue that key Mexican American middle class leaders, specifically Professor George I. Sánchez, demonstrated an awareness of the limits of whiteness and understood that African American discriminatory experiences shared common traits with their own experiences. Some African American activists, in particular Thurgood Marshall, also understood that the Mexican American and African American legal civil rights struggles could draw upon similar legal arguments and strategies.[12]

While it would be an exaggeration to suggest that the Mexican American and African American legal civil rights struggles were intimately linked prior to the 1960s, it would not be wrong to say that beginning in the 1940s each group realized that the other group had valuable theories, strategies, and experiences that could benefit its own struggle. Indeed, George Sánchez reached such a conclusion by the 1940s. In 1942, while professor of history and philosophy of education at the University of Texas at Austin and having recently completed a stint as president-general of the civic and patriotic League of United Latin American Citizens (LULAC), Sánchez resolved to bring an end to segregated Mexican schools and general anti-Mexican discrimination through class-action lawsuits.[13] Sánchez's recent leadership of LULAC, which emphasized assimilation into U.S. society and rectifying civil rights infringements against Mexican Americans, as well as his recent publication of a book on the governmental neglect and mistreatment of Mexican-descent people in New Mexico, *Forgotten People* (1940), provided the catalysts for this decision.[14]

Seeking new solutions, Sánchez branched out from LULAC to make connections with the American Civil Liberties Union (ACLU). He knew that LULAC, though it was a major Mexican American organization in Texas with dozens of councils by 1942, was a regional group with very few financial resources, while the ACLU was a nationally recognized organization with greater finances and ties to other major organizations.[15] As Sánchez noted in 1941 in a letter to U.S. Senator Dennis Chavez (D-NM), "both the League and the members of the committee are poor."[16] LULAC had relatively few successes ending segregation before the 1940s in part because of limited finances.[17] Sánchez hoped to change that.

To pursue his new goal of an invigorated and more active civil rights struggle, Sánchez met with Will W. Alexander, head of the War Manpower Commission's Minority Groups Branch, in late 1942. Sánchez and Alexander likely knew each other because of their ties to the Rosenwald Fund, a philanthropic organization which was most famous for building elementary schools for black children in the early 20th century.[18] Sánchez had worked for the Julius Rosenwald Fund as a research associate from 1935 to 1937, an experience that exposed him to the similarities between the segregation of black and Mexican American school children.[19] Alexander served as a member of the Rosenwald Fund Board of Trustees from 1930 to 1948 and vice-president from 1940 to 1948. He had other experiences in the field of minority civil rights, including serving as executive director of the Commission on Interracial Cooperation (CIC). The commission was founded in 1919 by white southerners who hoped to educate the public about race relations. When the two men met in late 1942, Alexander suggested that Professor Sánchez seek the assistance of the ACLU in order to bring a legal campaign on behalf of Mexican Americans.[20]

The ACLU was officially founded in January 1920 to defend the constitutional rights of individuals in the United States, as well as to use the defense of civil liberties to bring about radical social change.[21] It was one of the few organizations willing to attack racism in the early twentieth century. Roger N. Baldwin, the ACLU's executive director, had led the organization since its inception.[22] He came from a Brahmin Boston family and became involved in public service in part because of the influence of his relatives, such as his uncle William Henry Baldwin Jr., who was a dedicated and well-connected social reformer, and his aunt Ruth Standish Baldwin, who helped found the National Urban League.[23] Under Roger Baldwin's leadership, the ACLU became "a complex mixture of liberal social reform impulses and conservative reverence for the Bill of Rights."[24] In other words, the ACLU was both traditional and activist, with its emphasis on defending the basic tenets set out in this country's founding documents—the Declaration of Independence, the Constitution, and the Bill of Rights—and its emphasis on protecting the rights of the downtrodden and the oppressed.

Alexander thought that the Mexican American struggle against segregation was similar to the African American civil rights cause, which the ACLU already supported.[25] Roger Baldwin, in fact, had played a direct role in advancing the NAACP's legal civil rights struggle. In 1922 he urged Charles Garland to create the American Fund for Public Service (AFPS), which Baldwin later headed as chief administrator. The AFPS's purpose was to assist workers and minority groups. From 1925 to 1929, the AFPS provided the NAACP with $31,500 for its legal campaign against segregation. The NAACP would continue to receive funds from the AFPS throughout the late 1930s.[26] In the 1920s, the NAACP and the ACLU had also come to an agreement whereby the NAACP managed suits involving nonwhites, the ACLU directed litigation of whites, and they each kept abreast of the other's efforts.[27] Because of Baldwin's immense influence on the African American civil rights struggle, Alexander's advice that Sánchez approach Baldwin for aid appeared ripe with potential.

Sánchez heeded Alexander's recommendation and on September 15, 1942 he wrote to Baldwin (the two had already met a few years prior). The time to do battle in the courts for Mexican American rights, proclaimed Sánchez, had finally arrived.[28] He implored the ACLU to take up the Mexican American cause, declaring: "There is no organization that has ever assumed the sponsorship of these matters. These people are, institutionally, an orphan people. A few individuals like myself have been carrying the burden alone. The government agencies, like Dr. [Will] Alexander's [War Manpower Commission's Minority Groups Branch] . . . division, are in no position to do anything on these questions. . . . Do you think that the [A]CLU could expand its interests to include this area [Mexican American rights]?"[29]

Baldwin immediately responded to Sánchez and indicated a piqued interest in the Mexican American situation, but Baldwin also admitted that he "had not known that the [segregation] practices [against Mexican Americans] were so general."[30] He nonetheless offered the legal assistance of the ACLU. "We should be very glad to consider any legal tests attacking discrimination and we would be very happy to have your recommendations," Baldwin wrote.[31]

Baldwin and Sánchez would maintain a steady correspondence through the mid-1950s, and Baldwin's assistance proved vital in the Mexican American legal civil rights struggle.[32] Among other contributions, Baldwin helped Sánchez obtain funds from the Robert Marshall Civil Liberties Trust in the mid-1940s. In forming this new alliance, the ACLU hoped that Sánchez would lead the effort to end Mexican American discrimination.[33]

Sánchez was ambitious, and he imagined linking the Mexican American struggle with other prominent organizations. He considered reaching out to the other organization with vast experience in attacking minority civil rights through the courts: the NAACP. The NAACP was on the cutting edge, having already argued several cases before the Supreme Court addressing discrimination.[34] It also had the financial capabilities to bring several civil rights test cases; in the 1940s, its budget was in the hundreds of thousands.[35] In his initial letter to Baldwin in September 1942, Sánchez conveyed what he viewed as several commonalities between African American and Mexican American discrimination. "In the main, discriminatory practices [for the Mexican American] follow the same pattern observed in . . . [the] Negro field," he wrote.[36] By the same pattern, he meant that both groups faced exclusion or segregation from public facilities, workplaces, and private institutions.[37] Sánchez also noted that while both Mexican American and African American discrimination were of "the same pattern," local and state laws sanctioned segregating African Americans from white (Anglo) people, but did not require segregating Mexican Americans from white people.[38] Despite no law allowing segregation of Mexican-descent people from white people, white officials and residents of numerous communities had extended segregation to Mexican Americans anyway, and separation of Mexicans and Anglos had become the local custom in many Texas communities.[39] Thus, Mexican American discrimination was largely de facto (by custom) while African American discrimination was de jure (by law). For the Mexican American legal civil rights struggle, then, the challenge was not simply to prove that segregation laws were unconstitutional but to prove that segregation of Mexican Americans even existed. The fact that Mexican American segregation was de facto and therefore not formally acknowledged helps explain why Mexican American leaders sought to go to court. In the minds of Sánchez and other activists, the only way to eliminate de facto segregation against Mexican-descent people was to first get the courts to formally recognize this practice existed, and to *then* get the courts to outlaw anti-Mexican discrimination.

Despite the differences in African American and Mexican American segregation, Sánchez believed that the African American and Mexican American legal civil rights campaigns both had the same end goal. In his September 1942 letter, Sánchez argued that aligning a proposed Mexican American segregation case involving real estate with the NAACP's cases on real estate discrimination would benefit both the African American and Mexican American civil rights causes. He felt that uniting the two struggles with "their [NAACP's] very high powered lawyers" would produce good results and perhaps a victory. Sánchez proclaimed to Manuel C. Gonzáles, LULAC's national executive secretary, "I am confident that we can get their [NAACP's] fullest cooperation so that whatever action we take will dovetail with their plans and experience."[40]

Upon learning of Sánchez's idea of uniting Mexican American and African American civil rights campaigns, however, ACLU director Baldwin quickly dashed Sánchez's hopes of creating a unified black-brown legal civil rights struggle.[41] Baldwin advised Sánchez that if the Mexican American campaign brought the NAACP into their real estate lawsuit, the NAACP should only serve as a consultant. Baldwin explained that "the [black] race discrimination laws have a considerable history and a recognized status, while no such arguments can be invoked for discrimination against Spanish Americans."[42] Baldwin claimed that members of the Mexican American civil rights movement, on the other hand, had to prove that Mexican American discrimination was a persistent and entrenched problem of its own.

In the 1940s, African Americans had a clear and systematic pattern of antiblack discriminatory laws that they could cite as evidence of discrimination. Numerous state and local Jim Crow laws came into being in the late nineteenth century, with the most infamous being *Plessy v. Ferguson* (1896), which declared separate facilities for black and white people legal as long as those facilities were equal.[43] After this seminal decision, many states passed laws legitimizing systematic separation between black and white people.[44] *Plessy* did not directly apply to those of Mexican origin; Mexican Americans, instead, turned to historic treaties or legal precedents to demonstrate their legal white racial status in order to obtain full U.S. citizenship rights.[45]

In the *Delgado* case Mexican Americans also relied on the

argument that they, in part, belonged in the white race. This claim to a legal white racial status did not always lead to beneficial results, however. The group learned that claiming whiteness did not necessarily mean an end to discrimination, and proving anti-Mexican bias became a difficult task. They had no specific Jim Crow laws to challenge in order to achieve equality. Instead, the Mexican American legal civil rights struggle had to provide other evidence of persistent patterns of Mexican American exclusion or segregation in courts, schools, and other institutions. Mexican American civil rights activists sometimes asked Mexican Americans to testify about the extent and impact of anti-Mexican discrimination, but they did not know if Anglo judges or juries, who might hold anti-Mexican prejudices, would accept this testimony as valid or reliable.[46] Another option was to call Anglo superintendents and other local officials to testify in order to explain the nature of segregation in their communities, such as segregated education, and the rationale for separating Mexican-descent people in their communities.

The success of any Mexican American civil rights test case faced an extra hurdle—providing concrete proof that anti-Mexican discrimination even existed—that the African American legal civil rights campaign did not have to overcome. This is not to say that African American segregation was easier to defeat than Mexican American segregation; this was hardly the case, as African Americans had to continue returning to the Supreme Court when white officials found loopholes in antidiscrimination legal decisions or ignored these decisions altogether.[47] But Mexican American reformers had to establish a trail of proof while African Americans could turn to state and local documents filled with antiblack laws as proof. By claiming white race membership and nonwhite discrimination, Mexican Americans became entangled in a catch-22 dilemma, which proved to be the true Achilles' heel of Mexican American civil rights efforts.

Besides different discrimination patterns, the Mexican

American community's legal civil rights struggle, furthermore, was a nascent one just getting off the ground thanks to Sánchez, while the NAACP's legal battle against discrimination had begun in the late 1910s.[48] Because the African American civil rights movement was older, Baldwin thought that African American and Mexican American civil rights activists could not simply join forces.[49] Baldwin believed that African Americans did not have much too gain through a black-brown legal civil rights alliance in the early 1940s. He was emphatic that Mexican Americans would have to come up with their own legal civil rights strategies in the federal courts and could not depend predominantly on African American tactics. Baldwin in essence believed that Mexican Americans could not rely on African Americans to prop them up.

Though Baldwin made it clear that he thought joining the African and Mexican American legal civil rights struggles was the wrong path, Sánchez certainly did not have to follow his advice. Yet, Sánchez did just that. His motivations for complying with Baldwin's advice likely had to do with the virulently racist and strongly conservative political setting in Texas. Growing anti-communist sentiments in Texas in the early 1940s made it more difficult for minority civil rights activists to achieve political and social changes. Governor Wilbert Lee "Pappy" O'Daniel played upon Texans' fears of Communism, Nazism, and other radical ideologies as part of his reelection campaign in 1940, even writing President Franklin D. Roosevelt that he believed a fifth column existed in Texas. O'Daniel won his reelection bid in part because he tapped into Texans' fears of change and the unknown.[50]

Texas played a leading role in national anti-Communist efforts in the late 1930s and early 1940s as well. Martin Dies, congressman from southeast Texas, headed the House Un-American Activities Committee (HUAC) from 1938, its year of inception, to 1944. During Dies's tenure as HUAC chair, he turned over a list of organizations he claimed were traitorous to the United States because they worked on behalf of foreign governments. At the top of that list, Dies named the ACLU.[51] Dies also believed Communist infiltrators were spreading the message of social and racial equality among the African American community.[52] Dies and O'Daniel helped spearhead the formation of the Texas Regulars in the 1940s, a faction made up of former Democrats who vehemently opposed President Franklin D. Roosevelt's New Deal and proclaimed states' rights and white supremacy as their primary platforms.[53] In such an extremist climate, any person or organization who challenged the status quo in Texas, including civil rights activists like Sánchez or Marshall, faced the possibility of serious repercussions.[54]

Sánchez encountered fierce criticism for supporting radical organizations before. In early 1939, while a professor at the University of New Mexico, he came under attack for offering to play host to a meeting of El Congreso del Pueblo de Habla Española (Congress of Spanish-Speaking People). University officials may have even threatened to dismiss Sánchez. Opposition to the event came from as far away as Washington DC, with HUAC accusing El Congreso of promising to return the U.S. Southwest to Mexico. This vehement opposition led the organizers to move the gathering from New Mexico to California. The fallout from the event became one of the reasons Sánchez left New Mexico for Texas in 1940. His deep involvement in promoting the interests of oppressed minority groups had left Sánchez with several powerful enemies in New Mexico's political and business scenes.[55] He left his native state because he no longer believed that he could be an effective leader there.

Three years later in Texas, Sánchez found himself in a similar predicament. On the one hand, he acted boldly if not desperately by reaching out to the ACLU when no other major group, as he claimed, was helping the Mexican American civil rights cause. On the other hand, he had been scarred by his previous failed attempts to attack discrimination in New Mexico and now treaded cautiously. Sánchez did his best to minimize knowledge of the ACLU's role in the Mexican American legal civil rights struggle. He created the Texas Civil Rights Fund (TCRF) in 1943 as a central body that would help individuals and other organizations, like LULAC, fight anti-Mexican discrimination in the courts.[56] As Sánchez envisioned the goals of the TCRF, it would serve as a grievance and review board as well as a source of financial support. Based on his long history of fighting for civil rights, he believed it was more beneficial for the TCRF to remain in the background. He summarized this feeling when he stated, "I believe that this arrangement will receive wide approval, will attract substantial members, and will impress donors with the fact that this group is not a biased vested interest but a group of serious-minded, public-spirited leading citizens who wish to serve the cause of American rights."[57]

Sánchez needed outside donations to sustain the TCRF's work, another reason that explains the group's secretiveness. He knew that he could not hope to gain greater support in Texas if the agency seemed politically motivated rather than objectively structured. TCRF members agreed and decided not to announce their efforts since, they too believed, public knowledge of their efforts on behalf of Mexican American civil rights might set the organization back.[58] Prominent LULAC member John J. Herrera lent weight to this sentiment, recalling that in the 1940s, "LULAC had to be very careful then because even though the National Association for the Advancement of Colored People (NAACP) had gone openly into civil rights cases they [Anglo officials] were always ready to lop our heads off."[59] By forming a quiet alliance with the ACLU, creating a modest organization to assist Mexican American civil rights in the TCRF, and rejecting an open and intimate alliance with the African American civil rights struggles after consulting Baldwin, Sánchez may have been acting cautiously, but he did so because when he acted more boldly, as he did in New Mexico, he found himself without allies or resources. In Texas, where racism and political conservatism formed the bedrock of state politics, Sánchez believed he had to craft a civil rights organization that was small and modest in order to succeed.

Despite Baldwin's suggestion that Sánchez abandon any hopes of a joint African American and Mexican American civil rights alliance and Sánchez's acquiescence to Baldwin's advice, these facts did not prevent each minority group from occasionally reaching out to the legal strategists and advisors of the other group. In the mid-1940s, Thurgood Marshall became aware of Mexican American efforts to dismantle discrimination. He realized that Mexican Americans had created certain theories and strategies in their own lawsuits that might aid the African American cause. For example, he became aware of the *Mendez et al. v. Westminster et al.* (1946/7) case, in which district and federal courts declared segregation of Mexican-descent youngsters illegal as well as a denial of their rights under the equal protection clause of the Fourteenth Amendment.[60] Thurgood Marshall and the NAACP LDF staff wrote an amicus curiae brief for the appellate phase of the *Mendez* case in which their overarching argument posited that the practice of separate but equal was unconstitutional, something they would later argue in the famous U.S. Supreme Court case *Brown v. Board of Education* (1954), which dismantled the separate but equal precedent established under *Plessy v. Ferguson* (1896).[61]

The *Delgado et al. v. Bastrop Independent School District* lawsuit also drew Thurgood Marshall's attention.[62] Viewing the *Mendez* lawsuit's success in California, Sánchez urged lawyer Gus García to tackle the issue of the segregation of Mexican-descent children in Texas through the *Delgado* case.[63] García and Sánchez hoped to go beyond the *Mendez* decision. In *Mendez*, the Mexican-descent plaintiffs sued local school districts, trustees, and superintendents. In *Delgado*, however, the plaintiffs sued not simply local school officials and districts but also the state superintendent of public instruction and the state board of education.[64] The *Delgado* case held state school officials as responsible as local school officials for any illegal segregation of Mexican-descent children. The *Delgado* case judge, Ben H. Rice, agreed with the plaintiffs and declared the segregation of Mexican-descent children arbitrary and illegal. Most important, Judge Rice agreed that state school officials could be held culpable for unlawful segregation practices across Texas.[65]

In July 1948 Marshall and the LDF were in the process of bringing a lawsuit in Hearne, Texas, on behalf of an African American girl named Doris Fay Jennings due to the inferior and unequal school facilities provided African American schoolchildren there. Marshall wrote Sánchez asking for copies of some of the affidavits in the *Delgado* case.[66] Marshall hoped to benefit from the Mexican American legal victories in *Delgado* and *Mendez*. The Mexican American school desegregation campaign was tackling issues at the elementary and secondary school level, such as ordering state school officials to remove the accreditation of school districts who refused to integrate their schools and bringing in social scientists to explain the negative by-products of segregation. The LDF, with its historic emphasis on obtaining equal educational curricula, facilities, and teachers for black schoolchildren had only begun to explore different legal strategies, such as direct attacks on the unconstitutionality of segregation, in the mid-1940s.[67] Even though the Mexican American legal civil struggle was younger, Marshall understood it still had lessons to offer the African American civil rights struggle.

Sánchez agreed to send Marshall the affidavits of expert witnesses used in *Delgado* but cautioned that they were likely not useful in the Jennings case since the plaintiff's complaint in *Delgado* was that school officials discriminated against Mexican-descent children based on the children's putative poor English-speaking abilities. This focus on language segregation would not assist African Americans. Marshall's team needed affidavits that spoke more to the inequalities perpetuated by race-based segregation. Nothing more substantive was made of the Marshall-Sánchez connection in 1948, however, because the NAACP abandoned the Jennings case following the Hearne school board's refusal to obey the judge's order in the case, which called for greater parity between black schools and white schools.[68]

Even before Marshall reached out to him in 1948, Sánchez, too, had strongly believed that the Mexican American legal civil rights struggle was on the cutting edge of dismantling segregation and had something to offer other civil rights movements. While Sánchez failed to join the Mexican American and African American civil rights in 1942, by 1947, he thought that the nascent Mexican American legal civil rights struggle had lessons and strategies that could benefit the African American movement. In a letter to Clifford Forster, acting director of the ACLU in May 1947, Sánchez painstakingly explained why Mexican American legal efforts could benefit similar efforts by African Americans. Sánchez believed that Mexican American efforts and strategies might benefit the LDF's *Sweatt v. Painter* case.[69] In *Sweatt*, Heman Sweatt sued the University of Texas (UT) and its president Theophilus Painter for refusing to admit him to the UT law school. In the first phase of this case, a Texas court ruled that rather than admit Sweatt to UT, the university had six months to create a black law program for Sweatt that paralleled that offered white students. When UT finally set up the black law program, it showed few signs of being equal to the law program offered for whites. The black program was to be housed in the basement of a downtown Austin building, and it contained neither a law library nor extracurricular activities such as a law review or moot court.[70]

To prove discrimination, the LDF lawyers turned to a strategy they had first used in the *Mendez* case. As former LDF lawyer and director-counsel Jack Greenberg recalls, the LDF lawyers in Sweatt "built on an approach developed by Bob Carter in a 1946 friend-of-the-court brief that attacked segregation of Mexican Americans in California [the *Mendez* case] by documenting the psychological consequences of segregation."[71]

Sánchez had other ideas of the potential of the *Sweatt* case. He believed that while the *Sweatt* case offered hope for ending African American de jure discrimination, it would not have wider impact. Mexican American de facto school segregation cases, on the other hand, he argued could lead to the dismantling of school segregation and have a wider impact on other minority groups. Sánchez asserted:

> [E]ven if that case [*Sweatt*] were won on all counts, the situation for "Mexicans" would not be affected. Please remember that there is no authorization whatsoever in law for the segregation of the "Mexican," and the legality or lack of legality of the laws segregating Negroes is immaterial in this other field for the "Mexicans" are already in the position legally that the Sweatt case would put the Negro in if that case were won. This means that, while the winning of the Sweatt case has no effect on "Mexicans," the winning of a "Mexican" case would have the most fundamental bearing on the education of Negroes. So far from waiting on the Sweatt case, the "Mexican" case should be pushed with the utmost vigor as rapidly and as forcefully as possible.[72]

In the above analysis, Sánchez saw the Mexican American legal civil rights struggle as part of a larger civil rights struggle. He noted that the de facto discrimination of the "Mexican" population was the reality that the "Negro" population would have to face once the de jure discrimination of blacks was dismantled. The problem, as he understood it, was not simply eliminating biased laws but about forcing Anglo officials to integrate institutions. Sánchez's words proved prophetic, as seen by the *Brown v. Board of Education* (I, 1954) decision.

This case overturned the premise of "separate but equal" institutions. The lack of compliance with the Supreme Court's decision in *Brown* (I, 1954), however, led the Supreme Court to issue *Brown v. Board of Education* (II, 1955), which specifically ordered local school districts and district courts to put in motion desegregation efforts.[73] In 1947, therefore, Sánchez already anticipated that the battle to end de jure discrimination would not be the end of the African American civil rights struggle but would move African Americans into the de facto position that Mexican Americans occupied, one in which local segregation practices and customs, unsanctioned by law, would have to be addressed.

Sánchez was so eager to come up with strategies in which the two minority groups could find ways to once again find commonalities and possibly assist each other that he wrote Forster at the ACLU expressing his wish to get together with ACLU's Southern California branch lawyer A. L. Wirin and the NAACP's Thurgood Marshall. He professed:

> I have been trying for years to get a group of lawyers to sit down and analyze this issue and agree upon the best possible procedure. I think this issue is a fundamental one which has far reaching implications to all the other cases on segregation (particularly of Negroes), as I have pointed out above. It seems to me that one of the wisest things that could be done would be to bring together, for a day or two, the various lawyers whose interests are involved. There we could thrash out all questions and agree on a procedure. I would be more than happy to participate in such a conference.[74]

The Sánchez papers do not reveal whether such a conference ever materialized. The fact that Sánchez once again considered how the Mexican American and African American civil rights struggles could work together and that he responded willingly to Marshall's own inquiries for aid in the Jennings case demonstrated that Sánchez considered the African American legal civil rights effort as important to the Mexican American effort.

Sánchez's belief that he participated in a common cause with African Americans is important because it suggests that a key participant in the Mexican American legal civil rights struggle had the ability to look beyond whiteness claims and imagine alternate avenues to equality. Sánchez's interpretations of the *Delgado* and the other Mexican American court cases in which he was intimately involved demonstrated a deeper understanding of the purpose of civil rights struggles before the courts. He did not see the cases as simply ones that would reaffirm Mexican American's status as white people. Rather, he viewed them as having the potential to end any type of discrimination against any group of people.[75]

While the Mexican American and African American legal civil rights struggles borrowed from each other rather than uniting in a joint black-brown legal civil rights struggle, it would be inaccurate to portray them as purposefully distant due primarily to Mexican American leaders' embracing of antiblack racism. Rather, practical reasons, historical experiences, and the conservative politics of the time prevented a more formal and lasting union. Anglo officials and communities had mistreated, neglected, and excluded these two groups in different ways, and because they had been treated differently, they had to argue differently before the courts. Scholars should look at this period as one that symbolized a growing awareness, interest, and even outreach among civil rights leaders instead of simply another moment in which Mexican American embraced white supremacy and continued to reject African Americans.

Notes

1. Mark Tushnet, *Making Civil Rights Law: Thurgood Marshall and the Supreme Court, 1936–1961* (New York: Oxford University Press, 1994), 18–19, 21.

2. Lynne Marie Getz, *Schools of Their Own: The Education of Hispanos in New Mexico, 1850–1940* (Albuquerque: University of New Mexico Press, 1992), 49; Michael Welsh, "A Prophet Without Honor: Bilingualism in New Mexico," *New Mexico Historical Review* 69, no. 1 (1994): 21.

3. Michael D. Davis and Hunter R. Clark, *Thurgood Marshall: Warrior at the Bar, Rebel on the Bench* (New York: Birch Lane, 1992), 100–105; Tushnet, *Making Civil Rights Law*, 18–21; Mark Tushnet, *The NAACP's Legal Strategy against Segregated Education, 1925–1950* (Chapel Hill: University of North Carolina Press, 1987), 45–48, 100; Jack Greenberg, *Crusaders in the Courts: How a Dedicated Band of Lawyers Fought for the Civil Rights Revolution* (New York: BasicBooks, 1994), 19; Mark Tushnet, ed., *Thurgood Marshall: His Speeches, Writings, Arguments, Opinions, and Reminiscences* (Chicago: Lawrence Hill, 2001), 426.

4. Letter from George I. Sánchez to Thurgood Marshall, July 6, 1948, George I. Sánchez Papers, Box 24.8–Thurgood Marshall, 1948, 1955, Benson Latin American Collection, General Libraries, The University of Texas at Austin (hereafter GIS Papers, BLAC).

5. *Minerva Delgado et al. v. Bastrop Independent School District et al.*, Civil Action No. 388 (W.D. Tex. June 15, 1948); Letter from George I. Sánchez to Roger N. Baldwin, April 15, 1948, GIS Papers, Box 2.18–American Civil Liberties Union (ACLU), Roger Baldwin, 1946–1949, BLAC; Guadalupe San Miguel, *"Let All of Them Take Heed": Mexican Americans and the Campaign for Educational Equality in Texas, 1910–1981* (Austin: University of Texas Press, 1987), 123–28; Richard Valencia, *Chicano Students and the Courts: The Mexican American Legal Struggle for Educational Equality* (New York: New York University Press, 2008), 49–52.

6. For a discussion of another Mexican American activist and Thurgood Marshall, see Guadalupe Salinas, "Gus García and Thurgood Marshall: Two Legal Giants Fighting For Justice," *Thurgood Marshall Law Review* 28, no. 2 (2003): 145–75.

7. From the 1930s through the 1950s, many Mexican American activists understood the phrase "white race" to mean people whose ancestors came from European countries and people who identified strongly with their European heritage. Many of these activists embraced this identity not just to celebrate their Spanish ancestry but also to claim the privileges and rights only afforded to members of the "white race" in the early twentieth century United States. See Tomás A. Garza, "LULAC: A Future Power," *LULAC News*, 1, no. 7 (1932): 13, BLAC; "Are Texas-Mexicans 'Americans?'" *LULAC News* 1, no. 9 (1932): 7, BLAC; Rodolfo A. De La Garza,

"Who Are You?" *LULAC News* 2, no. 1 (1932): 1, BLAC; Alonso Perales, "El México Americano y la Politica del Sur de Texas: Comentarios" (San Antonio: Artes Gráficas, 1931), 3, in J. T. Canales Papers, Series IV, Subseries IV, Box 437.4, South Texas Archives, James C. Jernigan Library, Texas A&M University—Kingsville; Letter from Dr. Hector P. García to *Lubbock Morning Avalanche*, July 18, 1956, Dr. Hector P. García Papers, Box 221.28, Special Collections, Bell Library, Texas A&M University at Corpus Christi (hereafter HPG Papers, TAMU-CC); George I. Sánchez, "The American of Mexican Descent," Box 89.30, HPG Papers, TAMU-CC.

8. Haney López's words seem to ring true when one considers that in 1930 the Bureau of the Census implemented a method for solidifying Mexican Americans' racial position in the United States. That year it employed a "Mexican" racial category for the first time. The influx of thousands of Mexican immigrants (many of whom were poor, Catholic, and dark-skinned and thus clearly different from the majority white population) since the 1910s provided the impetus for this new category. Protests by Mexican American communities across the United States in the 1930s led the Bureau of the Census to return Mexican-descent people to the "white" race category for the next decennial census. Because they had almost lost their legal status as whites, claims to membership in the white race by Mexican Americans became more common after 1930. Haney López does note that recent Mexican immigrants, darker-skinned Mexican Americans, and Mexican American pachuco youth (a subculture with its own dress style and language) were some of the groups who chose not to embrace a white race identity prior to the 1960s. Ian F. Haney López, *Racism on Trial: The Chicano Fight for Justice* (Cambridge MA: Belknap, 2003), 1–2. See also Thomas A. Guglielmo, "Fighting For Caucasian Rights: Mexicans, Mexican Americans, and the Transnational Struggle for Civil Rights in World War II Texas" *Journal of American History* 92, no. 4 (2006): 1212–18, 1231–36; Neil Foley, "Becoming Hispanic: Mexican Americans and the Faustian Pact with Whiteness," in *Reflexiones 1997: New Directions in Mexican American Studies*, ed. Neil Foley (Austin: Center for Mexican American Studies, 1998), 61; Clara Rodriguez, *Changing Race: Latinos, the Census, and the History of Ethnicity in the United States* (New York: New York University Press, 2000), 82–83; Mario García, "Mexican Americans and the Politics of Citizenship: The Case of El Paso, 1936," *New Mexico Historical Review* 59, no. 2 (1984): 187–204.

9. Haney López, *Racism on Trial*, 2–3.

10. The following is not an exhaustive list, but one that references some of the major books and essays that have made such a claim in the last fifteen

years. Foley, "Becoming Hispanic," 54, 65–66; Ariela J. Gross, *What Blood Won't Tell: A History of Race on Trial in America* (Cambridge MA: Harvard University Press, 2008), 289–91; Haney López, *Racism on Trial*, 77, 205–10; Guadalupe San Miguel, *Brown, Not White: School Integration and the Chicano Movement in Houston* (College Station: Texas A&M University Press, 2001), xi; Clare Sheridan, "'Another White Race': Mexican Americans and the Paradox of Whiteness in Jury Selection," *Law and History Review* 21, no. 1 (2003): 128–29, 135–37; Steven Wilson, "Brown over 'Other White'": Mexican Americans' Legal Arguments and Litigation Strategy in School Desegregation Lawsuits," *Law and History Review* 21, no. 1 (2003): 145–46.

11. San Miguel does note that a Chicano identification, with its emphasis on cultural nationalism, also made a black-brown coalition difficult, at times, in the post-1960s period. San Miguel, *Brown, Not White*, xi, 170–72, 207–8.

12. For a different perspective on the Marshall-Sánchez correspondence, see Neil Foley, *Quest for Equality: The Failed Promise of Black-Brown Solidarity* (Cambridge MA: Harvard University Press, 2010), 94–139.

13. Mario T. García, *Mexican Americans: Leadership, Ideology, and Identity, 1930–1960* (New Haven: Yale University Press, 1989), 253; Moises Sandoval, *Our Legacy: The First Fifty Years* (Washington DC: LULAC, 1979), 84–85.

14. Richard Griswold del Castillo, "Civil Rights on the Home Front: Leaders and Organizations," in *World War II and Mexican American Civil Rights*, ed. Richard Griswold del Castillo (Austin: University of Texas Press, 2008), 81–82; David Gutierrez, *Walls and Mirrors Mexican Americans, Mexican Immigrants, and the Politics of Ethnicity* (Berkeley: University of California Press, 1995), 77–78; San Miguel, *"Let All of Them Take Heed,"* 71–72; George I. Sánchez, *Forgotten People: A Study of New Mexicans* (Albuquerque: University of New Mexico Press, 1940).

15. Letter from George I. Sánchez to Roger N. Baldwin, September 15, 1942, GIS Papers, Box 2.17–ACLU, Roger Baldwin, 1942–45, BLAC; García, *Mexican Americans*, 33, 37; Gutierrez, *Walls and Mirrors*, 78, 81–82; Benjamin Márquez, LULAC: *The Evolution of a Mexican American Political Organization* (Austin: University of Texas Press, 1993), 10, 39; Cynthia Orozco, "The Origins of the League of United Latin American Citizens (LULAC) and the Mexican American civil rights movement in Texas with an analysis of women's political participation in a gendered context, 1910–1929," (PhD diss., University of California–Los Angeles, 1992), 6–7;

Samuel Walker, *In Defense of American Liberties: A History of the* ACLU, 2nd ed. (Carbondale and Edwardsville: Southern Illinois University Press, 1999), 112–14, 162–63; Box 1.10–Transcript translations of articles published in El Paladín, February-July, 1929, Oliver Douglas Weeks Papers, LULAC Archives, BLAC.

16. Letter from George I. Sánchez to Honorable Dennis Chavez, October 17, 1941, GIS Papers, Box 22.11–League of United Latin American Citizens (LULAC): 1941–47, BLAC.

17. Carlos K. Blanton, "George I. Sánchez, Ideology, and Whiteness in the Making of the Mexican American Civil Rights Movement, 1930–1960," *Journal of Southern History* 72, no. 3 (2006): 574; ACLU Bulletin #1078, May 31, 1943, and ACLU Minutes, Board of Directors, June 14, 1943, ACLU Records, The Roger Baldwin Years, reel 225, v. 2607: Correspondence–General–Spanish Americans, 1944, Public Policy Papers, Dept. of Rare Books and Special Collections, Princeton University Library (hereafter ACLU Records, RBSC, Princeton).

18. Hasia R. Diner, *In the Almost Promised Land: American Jews and Blacks, 1915–1935* (Baltimore: Johns Hopkins University Press, 1995), 175–76.

19. Blanton, "George I. Sánchez," 574.

20. Wilma Dykeman and James Stokely, *Seeds of Southern Change: The Life of Will Alexander* (Chicago: University of Chicago Press, 1962), 185, 253; Gunnar Myrdal, *An American Dilemma: The Negro Problem and Modern Democracy* (New York: Harper & Brothers, 1944), 842–43; George I. Sánchez, "George I. Sánchez Biography," 1, GIS Papers, Box 1.6–Biographical Data, 1943–65, BLAC; Letter from Sánchez to Roger N. Baldwin, September 15, 1942; Joel Williamson, *A Rage for Order: Black-White Relations in the American South Since Emancipation* (New York: Oxford University Press, 1986), 256–57.

21. Gloria Garrett Samson, *The American Public Fund for Public Service: Charles Garland and Radical Philanthropy, 1922–1941* (Westport CT: Greenwood, 1996), 12, 12n34, 16–17.

22. Samuel Walker, *In Defense of American Liberties: A History of the* ACLU (Carbondale: Southern Illinois University Press, 1999), 37, 46–47.

23. Robert C. Cottrell, *Roger Nash Baldwin and the American Civil Liberties Union* (New York: Columbia University Press, 2000), 1; Benjamin Quarles and Vincent P. Franklin, *The Negro in the Making of America*, 3rd ed., rev. (New York: Simon & Schuster, 1996), 231; Walker, *In Defense of American Liberties*, 37, 46–47.

24. Memo from Roger N. Baldwin to Peggy Lamson on Patriotism, July 1974, Peggy Lamson Collection on Roger Baldwin, Box 1.20, Public Policy Papers, RBSC, Princeton; Walker, *In Defense of American Liberties*, 30.

25. Letter from Sánchez to Baldwin, September 15, 1942.

26. Tushnet, *The NAACP Legal Strategy*, 2–5, 2n3, 5n12, 18; Samson, *American Fund*, 51. Another source argues that the ACLU worked with the NAACP in filing lawsuits and took on those lawsuits that the NAACP would or could not assume. See Walker, *In Defense*, 53.

27. Samson, *American Fund*, 51.

28. Letter from George I. Sánchez to Roger N. Baldwin, September 15, 1942; Letter from George I. Sánchez to Charles Bunn, September 15, 1942, GIS Papers, Box 8.19–Charles Bunn, 1942–48, BLAC.

29. Letter from Sánchez to Baldwin, September 15, 1942; Letter from George I. Sánchez to Manuel C. Gonzáles, October 2, 1942, GIS Papers, Box 17.10–Manuel C. Gonzáles, 1942–43, BLAC. Sánchez had reached out to Nelson Rockefeller, Coordinator of Inter-American Affairs, in 1941 for assistance in ending anti-Mexican discrimination, to no avail. Letter from George I. Sánchez to Nelson Rockefeller, December 31, 1941, GIS Papers, Box 31.9–Nelson A. Rockefeller, 1941–44, 1961, BLAC; Gutierrez, *Walls and Mirrors*, 131.

30. Letter from Roger N. Baldwin to George I. Sánchez, September 18, 1942, GIS Papers, Box 2.17–ACLU-Roger Baldwin, 1942–45, BLAC.

31. Letter from Baldwin to Sánchez, September 18, 1942.

32. See GIS Papers, Box 2.17–2.20–ACLU, Roger Baldwin, 1942–57, BLAC.

33. Letter from Roger Baldwin to George I. Sánchez, July 6, 1948, GIS Papers, Box 2.18–ACLU, Roger Baldwin, 1946–49, BLAC; Memo on Mexican American Civil Rights Organization, Roger Baldwin, August 16, 1951, GIS Papers, Box 2.19–ACLU, Roger Baldwin, 1950–52, BLAC.

34. Among the civil rights cases the NAACP brought were *Guinn v. United States* 238 U.S. 347 (1915), which declared that the grandfather clause, which excluded most African Americans from voting, was unconstitutional; *Buchanan v. Warley* 245 U.S. 60 (1917), which declared racially restrictive residential zones a violation of the fourteenth amendment; *Moore v. Dempsey* 261 U.S. 86 (1923), which held that several black men accused of murder had been denied their fourteenth amendment rights; *Corrigan v. Buckley* 271 U.S. 323 (1926), which made racially restrictive housing covenants legal; *Nixon v. Herndon* 273 U.S. 536 (1927), which declared the white primary unconstitutional on fourteenth amendment grounds; *Nixon*

v. Condon 286 U.S. 73 (1932), which declared the Texas Democratic Party State Executive Committee's attempt to prohibit blacks from voting as illegal under the fourteenth amendment; *Hollins v. Oklahoma* 295 U.S. 394 (1935), which held that the exclusion of black people from juries violated the fourteenth amendment; *Grovey v. Townsend* 295 U.S. 45 (1935), which declared that political party representatives could limit voting to whites in primaries; *Hale v. Kentucky* 303 U.S. 613 (1938), which, like the Hollins case, declared that exclusion of blacks from juries was illegal; and *Missouri Ex Rel. Gaines v. Canada* 305 U.S. 337 (1938), which declared that black people must be allowed to attend the state university's law school, which dealt a blow to the idea of separate but equal. Abraham L. Davis and Barbara Luck Graham, *The Supreme Court, Race, and Civil Rights* (Thousand Oaks CA: Sage, 1995), 60–79.

35. Greenberg, *Crusaders in the Courts*, 14–15.

36. Letter from Sánchez to Baldwin, September 15, 1942.

37. Patrick J. Carroll, *Felix Longoria's Wake: Bereavement, Racism, and the Rise of Mexican American Activism* (Austin: University of Texas Press, 2003), 24–27; Neil Foley, *The White Scourge: Mexicans, Blacks, and Poor Whites in Texas Cotton Culture* (Berkeley: University of California Press, 1997), 208–10; David Montejano, *Anglos and Mexicans in the Making of Texas, 1836–1986* (Austin: University of Texas Press, 1987), 160–62, 167–68.

38. The term "Anglo" or "Anglo-American" was used by Mexican American activists to refer to a person of white, European descent, except for those of Spanish descent.

39. The laws and practices in California, New Mexico, Arizona, and Colorado varied. Martha Menchaca, *Recovering History, Constructing Race: The Indian, Black, and White Roots of Mexican Americans* (Austin: University of Texas Press, 2001), 285–90.

40. Letter from Sánchez to Manuel C. Gonzáles, September 15, 1942, GIS Papers, Box 17.10–Manuel C. Gonzáles, 1942–143, BLAC. As historian Carlos Blanton notes, the correspondence between Thurgood Marshall and George I. Sánchez in the 1940s and 1950s also supports the idea that the two groups did not always fight separate battles. Blanton, "George I. Sánchez, Ideology, and Whiteness," 571.

41. Letter from Sánchez to Baldwin, September 15, 1942.

42. Letter from Baldwin to Sánchez, September 18, 1942.

43. *Plessy v. Ferguson* 163 U.S, 537 (1896).

44. Garna L. Christian, *Black Soldiers in Jim Crow Texas, 1899–1917*

(College Station: Texas A&M University Press, 1995), xv; Bruce A. Glasrud and Merline Pitre, *Black Women in Texas History* (College Station: Texas A&M University Press, 2008), 104; Michael J. Klarman, *From Jim Crow to Civil Rights: The Supreme Court and the Struggle for Racial Equality* (New York: Oxford University Press, 2004), 137, 177, 180, 199, 205.

45. See for instance Articles VIII and IX, Treaty of Guadalupe Hidalgo, February 2, 1848, http://avalon.law.yale.edu/19th_century/guadhida .asp (accessed July 8, 2009) and *Independent School District et al. v. Salvatierra et al.*, 33 S.W. 2d 795 (Tex. Civ. App.—San Antonio 1930), cert denied, 284 U.S. 580 (1931). While the treaty did not explicitly refer to Mexican-descent people as white people, it did refer to them as capable of becoming citizens of the United States. Because only "free white persons" could obtain U.S. citizenship prior to 1868, the treaty's acceptance of Mexican-descent people as U.S. citizens appeared to legally equate if not transform them into "free white persons." See also Ian Haney López, *White By Law: The Legal Construction of Race* (New York: New York University Press, 1996), 31; and "Transcript of 14th Amendment to the U.S. Constitution: Civil Rights (1868)," The House Joint Resolution proposing the 14th amendment to the Constitution, June 16, 1866, Enrolled Acts and Resolutions of Congress, 1789–1999, General Records of the U.S. Government, Record Group 11, National Archives, http://www.ourdocuments.gov/doc .php?doc=43&page=transcript (accessed May 24, 2010).

46. See, for example, the testimonies from school officials and school-children in *Independent School District v. Salvatierra, Delgado v. Bastrop ISP*, and *Mendez et al. v. Westminster School District et al.*, 64 F. Supp. 544 (D. Cal. 1946), aff'd, 161 F.2d 744 (9th Cir. 1947).

47. See for instance the legal decisions regarding voting rights, *Nixon v. Herndon* 273 U.S. 536 (1927), which declared the white primary unconstitutional on fourteenth amendment grounds; *Nixon v. Condon* 286 U.S. 73 (1932), which declared the Texas Democratic Party State Executive Committee's attempt to prohibit blacks from voting as illegal under the fourteenth amendment. Black voting rights would once again come up in 1944 in *Smith v. Allwright* 321 U.S. 649 (1944) and in 1953 in *Terry v. Adams* 345 U.S. 461 (1953). Thus, the courts were certainly not a panacea for ending Jim Crow; they simply gave leverage to African American civil rights activists when the courts ruled in their favor.

48. Tushnet, *The NAACP's Legal Strategy*, 4–5; Samson, *American Fund for Public Service*, chaps. 8, 11, and 21.

49. Letter from Roger Baldwin to George I. Sánchez, July 6, 1948, GIS

Papers, Box 2.18–ACLU, Roger Baldwin, 1946–49, BLAC; Memo on Mexican American Civil Rights Organization, Roger Baldwin, August 16, 1951, GIS Papers, Box 2.19–ACLU, Roger Baldwin, 1950–52, BLAC; Letter from Baldwin to Sánchez, September 18, 1942.

50. George N. Green, *The Establishment in Texas Politics: The Primitive Years, 1938–1957* (Norman: University of Oklahoma Press, 1984), 38–42.

51. Green, *The Establishment in Texas Politics*, 69–71.

52. Haynes Johnson, *The Age of Anxiety: McCarthyism to Terrorism* (Orlando FL: Harcourt, 2005), 115–16.

53. Zaragosa Vargas, *Labor Rights are Civil Rights: Mexican American Workers in Twentieth-Century America* (Princeton: Princeton University Press, 2004), 115.

54. Green, *The Establishment in Texas*, 72; Montejano, *Anglos and Mexicans*, 274–75.

55. Mario T. García, *Memories of Bert Corona: The Life and Narrative of Bert Corona* (Berkeley: University of California Press, 1995), 109–10; García, *Mexican Americans*, 149. Sánchez had also been involved in a scandal surrounding a survey on Anglo-Hispano (Mexican-American) relations in the mid-1930s. This time it was members of his own Hispano community who accused Sánchez of creating racial tension by supporting a survey that they found extremely offensive. The survey was an attempt to understand Anglo attitudes toward the Hispano population. It was to be answered only by Anglos and included twenty statements ranging from the more positive "Spanish-speaking people have the highest ideals in the Southwest" and "I have only the highest regard for all Spanish-speaking people of my acquaintance" to the more negative "No matter how much you educate Spanish-speaking people, they are nothing but greasers" and "It is glaringly obvious that the Spanish-speaking people are inferior." Sánchez saw his standing at the University of New Mexico diminish after this incident. He would finally leave the state for Texas in 1940. "Questionnaire on Attitude Toward Spanish Speaking People Stirs Row," *Albuquerque Journal*, April 27, 1933, Antonio A. Sedillo Papers, 1932–37, Center for Southwest Research (CSWR), University Libraries, University of New Mexico at Albuquerque. See also Phillip B. Gonzáles, *Forced Sacrifice as Ethnic Protest: The Hispano Cause in New Mexico & the Racial Attitude Confrontation of 1933* (New York: Peter Lang, 2001), 91–92, 126–28, 174–80.

56. Letter to Roger Baldwin from J. O. Loftin, March 31, 1944, ACLU Records, roll 225, v. 2607, ACLU Records, RBSC, Princeton.

57. Letter from George I. Sánchez to Roger N. Baldwin, September 18, 1943, GIS Papers, Box 2.17–ACLU, Roger Baldwin, 1942–45, BLAC.

58. Letter from Charles Bunn to George I. Sánchez, n.d. (ca. January 1942), 1–2; Letter from Sánchez to Bunn, September 15, 1942, 1; and Letter from George I. Sánchez to Charles Bunn, March 29, 1945, 2, all in GIS Papers, Box 8.19–Charles Bunn, 1942–48, BLAC.

59. Sandoval, *Our Legacy: The First Fifty Years* (Washington DC: LULAC, 1979), 36.

60. Gilbert G. Gonzáles, *Chicano Education in the Era of Segregation* (Philadelphia: Balch Institute, 1990), 28; Vicki Ruiz, "Tapestries of Resistance: Episodes of School Segregation and Desegregation in the Western United States," in *From the Grassroots to the Supreme Court: Brown v. Board of Education and American Democracy*, ed. Peter F. Lau (Durham NC: Duke University Press, 2004), 61–62.

61. Vicki L. Ruiz, "We Always Tell Our Children They Are Americans: *Mendez v. Westminster*," *The Brown Quarterly* 6, no. 3 (2004), http://brownvboard.org/brwnqurt/06-3 (accessed June 4, 2009); Valencia, *Chicano Students and the Courts*, 32.

62. *Delgado v. Bastrop*.

63. Valencia, *Chicano Students and the Courts*, 50n102.

64. During the *Delgado* case, the Texas State Board of Education presented a motion asking that it be dropped from the lawsuit. The district judge sustained the motion. Thus, the only state official held culpable was the state superintendent of public instruction. Final Judgment, *Delgado v. Bastrop*, 3; Final Judgment, *Westminster v. Mendez*, 1.

65. Final Judgment, *Delgado v. Bastrop*, 1–3. Letter from George I. Sánchez to Clifford Forster, May 16, 1947, GIS Papers, Box 3.2– ACLU, General Correspondence A–Z, 1945–65, BLAC. Unfortunately, the *Delgado* decision lost any weight when Texas replaced the State Superintendent of Education with a newly appointed Commissioner of Education by June 1949. The first commissioner, J. W. Edgar, was expressly chosen for not believing in forcing school districts to comply with desegregation. See San Miguel, "*Let All of Them*," 129; Valencia, *Chicano Students and the Courts*, 52; Lupe S. Salinas, "Gus Garcia and Thurgood Marshall: Two Legal Giants Fighting for Justice," *Thurgood Marshall Law Review* 28, no. 2 (2003): 145–76.

66. Letter from A. L. Wirin to George I. Sánchez, July 1, 1948, GIS Papers, Box 62.15–A. L. Wirin, 1947–50, BLAC. For a different view of this case, see Foley, *Quest for Equality*, 111–13.

67. Jorge C. Rangel and Carlos M. Alcala, "Project Report: De Jure

Segregation of Chicanos in Texas Schools," *Harvard Civil Rights–Civil Liberties Law Review* 7, no. 2 (1972): 338–39; Letter from Sánchez to Marshall, July 6, 1948; Tushnet, *The NAACP's Legal Strategy*, 106–9; Tushnet, *Thurgood Marshall*, 146.

68. Amilcar Shabazz, *Advancing Democracy: African Americans and the Struggle for Access and Equity in Higher Education in Texas* (Chapel Hill: University of North Carolina Press, 2004), 58–59.

69. Letter from George I. Sánchez to Clifford Forster, May 24, 1947, GIS Papers, Box 3.2–ACLU, General Correspondence A–Z, 1945–65, BLAC.

70. Shabazz, *Advancing Democracy*, 65–73, 102–7.

71. Greenberg, *Crusaders in the Courts*, 64.

72. Letter from Sánchez to Forster, May 24, 1947.

73. The Oyez Project, *Brown v. Board of Education (II)*, 349 U.S. 294 (1955) available at: http://oyez.org/cases/1950–1959/1954/1954_1 (accessed on June 28, 2009).

74. Letter from Sánchez to Forster, May 24, 1947.

75. Letter from Sánchez to Forster, May 24, 1947.

TWO

The Movement in the Mirror

Civil Rights and the Causes of
Black-Brown Disunity in Texas

BRIAN D. BEHNKEN

Shortly after the U.S. Supreme Court declared segregated schools illegal in *Brown v. Board of Education*, local and state government in Texas began examining ways to prolong separate education. The American G.I. Forum, one of the most important Mexican American civic organizations in the Southwest, hoped to halt these efforts. But when G.I. Forum executive secretary Ed Idar Jr. sent out a bulletin that vaguely promoted the unification of African American and Mexican American civil rights groups to fight for school integration, others in the forum firmly rebuffed his idea. For instance, G.I. Forum official Manuel Avila feared that Idar's proposal might damage the Mexican American civil rights struggle. "I only hope this does not hurt our cause," Avila wrote, "but I can already hear the Anglos saying, 'those nigger lovers, look it came out in their official organ with their blessing.'" Avila told Idar that "anybody reading it [the bulletin] can only come to the conclusion we are ready to fight the Negroes' battles." "To go to bat for the Negro as a Mexican-American," he added, "is suicide."[1]

Manuel Avila's comments helped to divide African Americans and Mexican Americans during the civil rights era in Texas.

He was not alone in airing such statements. Indeed, shortly after his letter, Felix Tijerina, the national president of the League of United Latin American Citizens (LULAC), the premier Mexican American civil rights group in Texas, also rejected the concept of black-brown unity, declaring "let the Negro fight his own battles." Blacks also refused to unify with Mexican Americans. Reverend D. Leon Everett of the National Association for the Advancement of Colored People (NAACP) disclaimed unification with Mexican Americans because, "there is every reason to believe they are anti-Black." Repeating the sentiments of Avila and Tijerina, Everett stated, "let them fight their own battles."[2]

Numerous African Americans and Mexican Americans reacted negatively to the concept of black-brown unity during the civil rights movement in Texas. Mexican Americans and African Americans had a long history of civil rights activism in Texas and they won many significant victories during the civil rights era. Yet, their efforts were rarely unified. Comparing both civil rights movements and exploring relations between African American and Mexican American remains a relatively understudied aspect of civil rights scholarship.[3] But, such a comparison can offer many new insights on American race relations and civil rights scholarship. Comparing movements and groups illuminates the level of political development in each community, the evolution of racial formation, and the character of two civil rights struggles disconnected from the Deep South and the Southwest.

This chapter explores the main causes of African American–Mexican American disunity during the civil rights era in Texas. A number of factors led to the development of two separate movements. These included the impact of Jim Crow segregation on race relations, the importance of geographical distance, the use of divergent tactics, and differences in leaders and leadership groups. Most important, racial animosities bifurcated these civil rights movements. Racism reduced the chances for cooperative ventures between these two groups. All of these factors contributed to the development of two civil rights struggles.

The segregation of Mexican Americans and African Americans helped separate these two movements. Both groups fought to defeat a similar form of Jim Crow segregation. Anglo racism allowed for the development of a dual racial caste system in Texas. Jim Crow meant the denial of services in public facilities, disfranchisement, neighborhood segregation, and segregated schools.[4] While "colored only" and "white only" signs were visible throughout the South, in Texas "No Mexicans Allowed," "No Mexicans Served Here," "Hombres Aqui" (men here), "No Mexicans Hired," "No Mexicans Need Apply," "No Dogs or Mexicans Allowed," and "No Chili, Mexicans Keep Out" were also commonly displayed.[5]

In addition to these statewide aspects of segregation, many local communities also implemented laws to shore up the Jim Crow system. For instance, ordinances in Houston segregated streetcars in 1903. Other local statutes kept the races separated at city hospitals, libraries, and swimming pools.[6] In Dallas and San Antonio, local custom guaranteed that blacks and Mexican Americans could only live in certain portions of these cities, attend segregated schools, and have access to low wage jobs. Austin's city government prevented Mexican Americans and African Americans from utilizing the city's main library and the downtown hospital.[7] Since much of the Jim Crow system was based on local custom, African Americans and Mexican Americans ultimately suffered both de jure and de facto forms of segregation.

Of the extralegal forms of Jim Crow, the most oppressive proved to be lynch "justice." Throughout the nineteenth and twentieth centuries, whites used lynching to maintain social, economic, racial, and sexual hegemony in the state. Anglos usually lynched African Americans for alleged sexual crimes—usually false claims of rape made by white women against black men.[8]

Mexicans also faced death at the hand of lynch mobs. Texas ranked third in the nation in total lynchings with 493. Although mobs murdered 352 blacks between 1882 (the first year records were kept) and 1968, 141 whites were also killed by lynch mobs. Historians William Carrigan and Clive Webb have determined that at least fifty of the 141 whites, and probably more, were of Mexican descent. Anglos usually killed these individuals for thefts. "More than other Americans," Carrigan and Webb note, "blacks and Mexicans lived with the threat of lynching."[9]

Given the similarities in the Jim Crow system, the persistence of segregation and racism that both African Americans and Mexican Americans endured, and the fact that each group experienced extralegal lynching, it might seem ironic that these groups did not significantly unite to battle racism and segregation in Texas. Paradoxically, segregation itself assisted in the development of two distinct civil rights movements. Jim Crow separated African Americans and Mexican Americans from whites, but also each other. Segregated spaces were set aside for blacks, whites, and Mexican Americans. For instance, while in many cases all three groups lived in neighborhoods side by side, they did not usually live in the same neighborhoods. White neighborhoods were for Anglos, Negro sections of town were for blacks, and Mexican barrios for Mexican Americans. Rarely did anyone "cross the tracks" to participate in protests with another community. Similarly, many locales had a tripartite education system with schools for whites, Mexican Americans, and blacks. Local governments frequently located schools in the neighborhoods of each ethnic group. For example, the San Antonio Independent School District (SAISD) operated Mexican Schools in the city's largely Mexican/Mexican American west side. To the east of the city, a predominately African American area, SAISD ran segregated school for blacks. In the other parts of the city where Anglos predominated, SAISD established schools for white children. When protesting segregated schools, each community tended to fight for itself because of the education system's racial lines. Indeed, school segregation—combined with neighborhood segregation—created a powerful impetus for groups not to join forces.[10]

The broader racial geography of the state also separated African Americans and Mexican Americans. For example, most black Texans lived in towns in East Texas, the Black Belt of the state, or major cities such as Dallas and Houston. Mexican-origin people predominated in the south and southwest part of the state, and in major cities such as San Antonio and Corpus Christi. As such, when civil rights struggles began the largest concentrations of each group, and by extension each movement, were separated by many miles and by the perception that geographical distance mandated separation. For example, in 1960 African American youths initiated sit-ins in the farming town of Marshall in East Texas.[11] Local police arrested numerous protestors and the local fire department attacked African Americans with fire hoses.[12] After several days of sporadic sit-ins, the protests ended.[13] Very few Mexican Americans lived in or near Marshall. Less than 1 percent of a total population of nearly twenty-four thousand in 1960 was of Mexican origin. This meant Marshall had a Mexican American population of around two hundred people.[14] Local leaders, including the Southern Christian Leadership Conference's Harry Blake and Cuthbert Simpkins, did not call on this group for support. Nor did they encourage Mexican Americans from other parts of the state to join the protests in Marshall. The result was hardly surprising: no Mexican Americans participated in the sit-ins.

A few years later, blacks organized similar protests in the nearby Black Belt community of Huntsville. The prominent African American activist Booker T. Bonner engineered demonstrations in Huntsville when the city refused to integrate after the passage of the Civil Rights Act of 1964. Unlike Blake and Simpkins, Bonner did appeal to Mexican Americans for support. Only Gilbert Campos of Houston responded to this call. The police constantly harassed Campos. When local authorities began to arrest protestors, they singled him out. As a Mexican American, local whites told Campos he had no reason to protest and that he should "get the hell out [of town]." When he refused, police arrested Campos.[15] The protests in Huntsville were almost as short-lived as those in Marshall. And although Booker Bonner called for Mexican American support, he received very little.

Mexican Americans also failed to encourage blacks to join their demonstrations. At about the same time as the Marshall and Huntsville demonstrations, Mexican Americans in South Texas began to organize voting and poll tax drives. These efforts commenced in the small town of Crystal City in 1963. Businessman Andrew Dickens and Juan Cornejo initiated a voting drive in order to replace the all-white Crystal City government. They hoped to encourage Mexican-origin people to vote and remove the Anglo power elite. Their poll tax drive proved phenomenally successful. When city council elections were held in 1963, Mexican Americans won all five seats, including Cornejo, who was elected mayor.[16] Alas, these victories proved short lived— the five were voted out of office in the next election cycle.

Few African Americans lived in or near Crystal City. The town had a total population of nearly ten thousand, but blacks comprised only 2 percent, or less than two hundred, of these residents. As in Marshall, Mexican American leaders in Crystal City made no real effort to appeal to blacks for support. They also did not encourage African Americans from other parts of the state to join the protests. As a result, not only did blacks not vote for the Mexican American candidates, they voted for the Anglo incumbents. One black Crystal City resident commented on his place in the city and with the election, saying, "this is one place where I'll never be in the minority." Clearly he was part of the minority, but he was not a part of the Mexican American

3. Throughout the civil rights era, black Texans vigorously protested discrimination. Here, Fort Worth activists participate in the 1965 "Alabama Sympathy March," which demanded increased voting protections from the federal government. These marches occurred simultaneously in almost every major Texas city. Although they too fought for political rights, few Mexican Americans participated in these marches. Courtesy of *Fort Worth Star-Telegram* Collection, Special Collections, the University of Texas at Arlington Library, Arlington, Texas.

community. For him, problems in Crystal City were specific to Mexican Americans, not blacks. Mexican Americans did not invite this individual to join the protests, he did not include himself as part of the Mexican American struggle, and other African Americans probably felt similarly.[17]

A few years after the Crystal City protests, Mexican Americans from the Rio Grande Valley engaged in a massive labor strike to push for the establishment of a uniform minimum wage. Part of this strike involved a huge march from the Valley to Austin. On July 4, 1966, this Minimum Wage March commenced with thousands of marchers. This time, the strike's organizers issued a call for activists from across the state to join the protests. After a rigorous search, I have determined that one African American joined the march for its duration. Moses LeRoy, a well-known radical labor organizer from Houston, marched the entire route.[18] He also spoke at many of the rallies the marchers held along the way to Austin. But LeRoy acted independently. Although a few blacks joined the march when it arrived in Austin, including Booker T. Bonner, Andrew Young, and Barbara Jordan, most blacks did not participate.[19]

The racial geography of the state, then, contributed to African American–Mexican American disunity. The distance between the protests discussed above certainly makes the lack of black involvement in Crystal City and Mexican American involvement in Marshall somewhat understandable. These East and South Texas communities are over 600 miles apart, a difficult distance to travel even today. But the lack of African American–Mexican American involvement from individuals who lived in or near these cities proves more difficult to explain. As the African American youth from Crystal City noted, the protests in each community only benefited the other group. Blacks did not usually invite Mexican Americans to join demonstrations, and vive versa. As a result, neither group participated in the protests of the other.

Much like geographical distance, labor and class issues also worked to separate African Americans and Mexican Americans in their civil rights struggles. While both groups were historically poor, black and Mexican-descent individuals viewed and experienced poverty differently. Most Texans saw the black poor as a ghettoized population that lived primarily in cities and worked in the unskilled labor pool as construction workers, railroad workers, or domestic servants. A small black professional class of ministers, lawyers, and doctors also served the black community. Texans perceived Mexicans and Mexican Americans as the rural poor—a mass of unskilled, low-wage migrant farm laborers. But Mexican Americans also performed a variety of urban jobs, including work in railroads, shipyards, and refineries. Like blacks, the Mexican American community also had a professional class of doctors, lawyers, and restaurateurs.[20]

Labor in Texas was constructed along a Deep South, black-white binary. Whether skilled or unskilled, white Texans viewed African American and Mexican American labor through the prism of race. Throughout the state, certain jobs were for Negroes, while only Mexicans did other jobs. As historian Neil Foley has shown, if a Mexican American or an Anglo did work deemed solely for black people (agricultural wage labor, for instance), those individuals would appear closer to blacks on the racial hierarchy of the state. Since Mexicans and Mexican Americans often worked jobs viewed as ethnically or racially Negro, their racial position in the state often fell closer to that of black people. This caused considerable discomfort for some Mexican Americans because, to them, blackness connoted second-class citizenship. These labor issues caused nonblacks to distance themselves from the African American community, which served to strengthen the black-brown divide.[21]

Ethnic leadership also assisted in dividing the African American and Mexican American movements. Leaders in each group differed in important ways. For example, the leadership of the black civil rights movement came primarily from the ministry. Baptist and Methodist leaders, the two denominations most openly supportive of black civil rights, viewed the struggle as biblically mandated and ordained by God.[22] Many of the preachers who led the black freedom struggle in the 1950s and 1960s began their activism by preaching the message of civil rights from the pulpit in previous decades. This type of preaching gave ministers the chance to join the struggle without participating in protests. Prominent ministers, such as Ernest Estell of Dallas, Lee H. Simpson and Moses L. Price of Houston, and Claude Black of San Antonio, all began their careers in the 1930s by preaching civil rights. They educated the next generation of leaders. For example, Rev. H. Rhett James, one of the leaders in Dallas's movement, began preaching in the church of E. C. Estell. These ministers not only opened a discourse about race and rights, they encouraged and frequently led demonstrations.[23]

Mexican Americans did not find as much support from their religious leaders. Mexican-descent people came primarily from the Catholic faith, and the Catholic Church largely ignored the Mexican American struggle for rights until the 1960s. Catholic leaders viewed protests in a negative light and they generally saw civil rights as a secular concern, not a religious matter.[24] It took until the mid 1960s for Texas's Catholic leaders to get involved in the Mexican American civil rights movement. Two factors explain this change in position. The first was a growing sense of social justice emanating from third world Catholic leaders, an idea eventually known as Liberation Theology and one embraced by the Church in Rome after the Second Ecumenical Council of the Vatican and after a general conference of Latin American churches held in Medellin, Colombia, in 1968.[25] The second factor proved to be a developing activist consciousness on the ground among Catholic priests. These individuals came to believe that their sacred vows, especially the vow of poverty, made priests beholden to their underprivileged congregants. These activist priests looked to nonviolent direct action as a way to bring about social and racial change that would benefit the poor. Much like their black counterparts, priests such as Robert Peña and Sherrill Smith of San Antonio, Patricio Flores and Antonio Gonzalez of Houston, and Lonnie Reyes of Austin all became involved in Chicano protests.[26]

Differences in religious leadership contributed to the African American–Mexican American divide. Black religious leaders generally led black churches, which meant they did not directly focus on problems in the Mexican American community. Once

Mexican American priests became concerned with the plight of the poor, they also tended to focus on Mexican Americans. As such, each group assisted its own constituents. Additionally, black ministers engaged in all manner of civil rights activism, from lawsuits to sit-ins to marches. Chicano priests tended to get involved in different protests, usually labor demonstrations and community outreach programs. These differences discouraged black-brown unity.

In addition to religious leaders, African American and Mexican American leaders also came from the business community. This also affected black-brown relations. Some Mexican American business leaders resisted black civil rights in order to protect their own interests. For example, restaurateur and LULAC president Felix Tijerina actively opposed the black sit-in movement that aimed to force business owners to integrate. He also refused to integrate his businesses until after the passage of the Civil Rights Act of 1964. Tijerina feared, as did other businesspeople, that integrating his restaurants might offend Anglo clients who would then take their business elsewhere. But such a stance hindered cooperation and coalition building with African Americans who supported the sit-in activists and their goals. Similarly, African American business owners who were also civil rights leaders had difficulty working with Mexican Americans. Black businesses traditionally did not have nonblack clientele, such as Mexican Americans. This made developing a dialogue with Mexican Americans less likely.[27]

For Mexican American and African American leaders, power sharing prevented further collaboration. To leaders in both communities, cooperative ventures and unification meant sharing power. Power sharing could lead to a lessening of each group's influence. Since both groups had a very fragile hold on power, they were less likely to share positions of influence. As San Antonio activist Harry V. Burns remembered, blacks did not want to join forces with Mexican Americans because "it would

cause some of the benefits to be split . . . they would be competing with us."[28] Similarly, former state representative Lauro Cruz
commented on competition, power sharing, and divisions between blacks and browns: "I think that what's at the bottom of
it [the black-brown divide] is the fact that, that the overall community, the total community usually is only willing to give up
so much of the pie."[29] To ensure the strength of a leader's pow-
erbase, Mexican American and African American leaders did
not unite.

Like leaders, African American and Mexican American leadership groups did not frequently unite their civil rights efforts.
Interestingly, similarities between civil rights organizations assisted the movements' bifurcation. For example, groups like
LULAC and the NAACP paralleled each other. They both essentially had the same structure and both fought through the government and courts for change, although the NAACP became more
protest oriented in the early 1960s. Other groups also mirrored
each other. Political organizations such as the Political Association of Spanish-Speaking Organizations (PASO) and the Harris County Council of Organizations (HCCO) and the Democratic Progressive Voters League (PVL) all supported voting
rights. But PASO fought for Mexican Americans while the HCCO
and PVL were black voting leagues. Other groups also demonstrate a similar division. The Mexican American Youth Organization, Advocating Rights for Mexican-American Students,
the Progressive Youth Association, and the Student Nonviolent Coordinating Committee—all militant youth organizations
formed in the 1960s—had tactical and organization similarities
and all fought primarily for their own ethnic group. Because
of their similarities, no real reason existed for black and Mexican American civil rights organizations to unify. Indeed, these
groups worked so well on their own that black organizations
frequently refused to work with other black groups and Mexican American civic organizations failed to join forces with other

Mexican American groups. If African Americans did not unite with African Americans, and Mexican Americans did not unite with Mexican Americans, what hope was there for cross-racial unification? Leaders in these groups simply saw no need to unify and so they did not.

While parallel organizations contributed to the lack of unification between blacks and browns, intergroup animosities also led to disunity. For example, leaders in LULAC and the G.I. Forum generally disliked black protest activism. When African Americans youths began sit-ins in 1960, LULAC president Tijerina rebuked their activism. "Sit-downs may be melodramatic," Tijerina stated, "but when they . . . antagonize a large segment of the other population, they automatically setup larger and more difficult obstacles in the path of their progress."[30] A few years later, league president Paul Andow vilified the black civil rights movement. He told the attendees at the 1963 LULAC convention that neither protests nor "joining forces with questionable civil rights groups [a veiled reference to the NAACP]" would lead to change.[31] Such vitriolic statements not only insulted black activists, they separated Mexican Americans and their civic groups from African Americans.

While black civil rights organizations did not denigrate Mexican American civil rights activism, the leaders of these groups did very little to unify with Mexican Americans. Indeed, black leaders, civil rights organizations, and the Negro press almost universally ignored the Mexican American movement. African American leaders in groups like the NAACP and SNCC seemed generally unfamiliar with Mexican American civil rights activism. For example, Dr. David Williams, an NAACP field secretary in West Texas recalled, "[I]n West Texas I never saw a Mexican at all at any kind of meeting for civil rights—period."[32] Such an assertion flies in the face of Mexican American civil rights efforts, which were concentrated, sustained, and successful in West Texas. Similarly, Dallas newsman and NAACP leader Marion Butts castigated the Mexican American community in Big D because "they didn't really come in to fight and help." Butts simultaneously ignored the activism of Mexican-origin people in Dallas while indicting them for not assisting African Americans.[33] Finally, Austin political activist Ada Anderson admitted, "Hispanics weren't considered [by blacks] at all."[34] These sentiments troubled Mexican Americans, who felt ignored and neglected by blacks, and rightfully so. Such ignorant statements distanced blacks and their civil rights groups from Mexican Americans.[35]

Strategic differences further divided the African American and Mexican American movements. Each struggle often utilized similar strategies in dissimilar ways. For example, when blacks engaged in sit-ins, pickets, and boycotts in the late 1950s and early 1960s, they used tactics that many Mexican American leaders found distasteful. When Mexican Americans engaged in direct action, they often did so by utilizing labor strikes to protest low wages, poor working conditions, and the general discrimination Mexican-descent people experienced on the job. Indeed, Mexicans and Mexican Americans had a long history of labor activism in the region. But most Texans saw these strikes as something distinctly Mexican. Blacks, therefore, did not often join forces with Mexicans and Mexican Americans to protest labor conditions. These strategic differences and the perception of dissimilarity forestalled close cooperation between these two groups.[36]

All the factors mentioned thus far reduced the chances for cooperation between African Americans and Mexican Americans. But race caused the most problems between groups and presented efforts aimed at cross-ethnic cooperation with their most formidable challenge. In particular, Mexican American white racial formation damaged relations with black people. Through the 1950s, Mexican Americans fought for civil rights by positioning themselves as members of the white race. This meant that Mexican Americans challenged discrimination by insisting that segregation should not apply to them since they were not black.[37]

In the United States race has generally operated as a binary, with blacks on one side and whites on the other. Even though many Mexican-descent individuals were not phenotypically white, they could recognize the power that came with white racial status. As historian Guadalupe San Miguel has noted, "[I]t is interesting, and probably in keeping with their desire to assimilate, that most members of the Mexican American Generation viewed themselves as members of the Caucasian or white race, although they were primarily a racially mixed or mestizo group."[38] San Miguel alludes to what historian Eric Avila calls the "racial ambiguities underlying the historical construction of Chicana/o identity" and what anthropologist Martha Menchaca refers to as "the Mexican American people's Indian, White, and Black racial history."[39] While San Miguel, Avila, and Menchaca correctly note the various racial roots of Mexican-descent people, many Mexicans and Mexican Americans distanced themselves from their nonwhite lineage. Jim Crow segregation and the black-white binary taught Mexican Americans the value of pushing for white rights.

Whiteness proved an advantage to Mexican Americans in a variety of ways. For example, in lawsuits like *Del Rio Independent School District v. Salvatierra* and *Delgado v. Bastrop Independent School District*, Mexican American attorneys argued that segregation violated the rights of Mexican Americans because they were white. During the 1930 *Salvatierra* case, Mexican American attorneys asserted that the Del Rio district planned to "affect [and] accomplish the complete segregation of the school children of Mexican and Spanish descent from the school children of all other white races in the same grades. . . ."[40] The judge concurred, although the decision was overturned on appeal. In 1948, during the preparation for the *Delgado* case, education expert George Sánchez argued that Mexican Americans should "be admitted to the white schools on the ground that Mexicans are Caucasians."[41] The attorneys and the state supreme court agreed, banning the segregation of Mexican American children on the grounds that they were white. It should be noted that, while victorious, many school districts refused to integrate Mexican-origin students.

Numerous other instances of Mexican Americans fighting for white rights abound. For example, throughout the 1930s, 1940s, and 1950s, leaders and individuals protested classification as nonwhite on census forms, city directories, poll tax receipts, traffic tickets, birth and death certificates, hospital forms, and other public documents. These efforts continued into the 1960s. For instance, in that decade, Mexican American leaders protested classification as nonwhite on military induction and hospital forms. Even in the 1970s, when Chicano activists had begun to argue that Mexican-origin people constituted a distinct minority group, some Mexican Americans continued to focus on acquiring white rights.[42] In short, whiteness was a commonly used strategy throughout the twentieth century.

Not all Mexican Americans favored the whiteness strategy nor opposed the black movement. But by arguing for whiteness, those Mexican Americans who did focus on whiteness fought to make Jim Crow more palatable. They wanted integration for Mexican Americans only. Since blacks fought to destroy Jim Crow, Mexican American efforts differed. This made them in some ways adversaries of the black civil rights struggle. As NAACP leader C. Anderson Davis remembered, "Mexican-Americans considered themselves white a long time." Davis noted that Mexican Americans did not want to ally with blacks because they understood this might damage efforts at white racial formation.[43] David Williams noted similarly that Mexican Americans "chose to be neutral [because] . . . a clean, quote, unquote, Mexican, could eat in a restaurant with whites; African-American

[sic] could never eat in the restaurant." While Williams speaks in code, he seems to imply that whiteness, which he equates with cleanliness, offered Mexican Americans advantages that blacks did not receive.[44] Whiteness offended these black activists, which distanced them from Mexican Americans.

Perhaps school integration best exemplifies how whiteness divided Mexican Americans and African Americans. As noted, Mexican American civic groups fought to eliminate segregated Mexican Schools on the basis that Mexican-origin pupils were white. They made little mention of the segregation of African Americans in black schools. When the Supreme Court handed down the *Brown v. Board* decision, Mexican American civic groups barely took notice. They continued to insist that their children be admitted to white schools. And when the state legislature began passing laws to prolong segregation, the most prominent Mexican American organizations sided with the state government and not African Americans. For example, some in LULAC debated the idea of joining forces with the NAACP to defeat the flood of racist bills coming from the legislature in 1957. League president Tijerina dismissed this idea. Similarly, LULAC's legal advisor, Phil Montalbo, explained to Tijerina, "[A] stand taken by you on such bills would tend to admit to our anglo-american (sic) friends that we considered ourselves separate and apart from the majority of American citizens."[45] Montalbo reminds us once again that, as whites, Anglos were the Mexican Americans' allies.

Numerous LULACers, and Mexican Americans more generally, agreed with this stance. For instance, A. G. Ramirez stated succinctly, "[M]y district does not want our people and our beloved LULAC to be affiliated with the Negroes. We are white and furthermore re[garding] the bills which were passed are unconstitutional."[46] Similarly, Dallas newsman Pedro Ochoa berated anyone wishing black-brown unity, explaining that many Mexican Americans "do not accept the integrant [integrationist] precept at public schools, and perhaps at churches and housing projects."[47] Ochoa also warned Mexican Americans to "preserve your white race, vote against integrationists, don't look to a black future."[48]

Such statements hurt Mexican American relations with black people. While a number of Mexican American leaders disagreed with Tijerina, Montalbo, and Ochoa, the damage was done. African Americans continued to fight against the segregationist legislation and for school integration, but they did so alone. Mexican Americans also continued to battle school segregation. They found that in many cases whiteness did very little to destroy segregated Mexican Schools, which meant that they not only failed to unify with blacks but also picked a losing strategy for integrating schools.

In the late 1960s and early 1970s, during the more radical Chicano movement, Mexican Americans discarded whiteness in favor of brownness. They argued that Chicanos constituted an identifiable minority group—they were brown people. A separate racial status gave Mexican Americans the ability to more forcefully utilize the Fourteenth Amendment to the Constitution, especially for school integration purposes. Blacks still had a hard time working with Chicanos. In dismissing whiteness, many Mexican Americans assumed that blacks and Chicanos would unite now that they both constituted racial minorities. African Americans, remembering the long history of Mexican American whiteness, saw things differently. They viewed brownness as another tactic, one that many African Americans saw as disingenuous and opportunistic. These opinions certainly did not endear Chicanos to blacks.[49]

Brownness did begin to win some benefits that whiteness did not. It gave Mexican Americans access to burgeoning affirmative action programs, allowed them to mobilize voters along ethnoracial lines into new Chicano political groups, and even helped generate Mexican American school desegregation protests. For example, in 1970 school districts in Houston, Dallas, San Antonio, Austin, and elsewhere began attempting to "desegregate" schools by integrating Mexican American students and blacks. Since these districts classified Mexican-origin students as white, they achieved integration without integrating the schools. Chicanos began a sustained boycott against these schemes, uniting the community around the rallying call of brownness.[50] While these protests ultimately convinced districts in Houston, Dallas, San Antonio, and elsewhere to implement a tri-ethnic integration program, they distanced Mexican Americans from African Americans. Many blacks feared that Chicanos simply did not want their children to attend schools with African American students. As historian San Miguel has noted, some blacks "believed that the boycott [against schools in Houston] was a racist reaction to integration; others did not trust the Mexican American community and believed that they were 'Johnny-come-latelies.'"[51] San Miguel suggests a growing resentment between blacks and browns in the late 1960s and early 1970s. Legal scholar George Martínez has characterized this resentment as follows: "Mexican-Americans have been free riders. African-Americans fight for civil rights; Mexican-Americans ride their coat tails and share in the benefits."[52] Such sentiments certainly did now win many Mexican American friends. Indeed, it seems likely that many Chicanos regarded black perceptions of these school protests as hurtful, hypocritical, or both. This further damaged chances for coalition building.

There were examples of African American and Mexican American cooperation in Texas, but in most cases these tended to be short lived. For example, in 1957, when LULAC, the G.I. Forum, and other groups rejected cooperating with blacks to stop the state's segregationist legislation, state Senators Henry B. Gonzalez and Abraham Kazen Jr. swung into action and filibustered the bills. In a show of support for black-brown cooperation, and lambasting the likes of Tijerina and Avila, Gonzalez

4. The Chicano boycott of Houston schools proved enormously successful. Here, a group of protestors picket the school administration building in 1970. Although school integration issues deeply affected black Texans, few African Americans joined the Chicano protests against the school district. Houston Metropolitan Research Center, Houston Public Library, Houston, Texas.

said, "I don't care what anyone thinks, this bill is odious to any free society and I am going to continue opposing it just as long as I can."[53] "For whom does the bell toll?" Gonzalez asked at one point, "[Y]ou, the white man, think it tolls for the Negro. I say, the bell tolls for you! It is ringing for us all, for us all."[54] Blacks wholeheartedly supported Gonzalez and Kazen, although the two could not prevent most of the segregationist bills from passing. But once the crisis over this segregative legislation passed, no real unity among African Americans and Mexican Americans remained. Gonzalez won a seat to the U.S. House in 1961, and removed himself as a key ally of the black freedom struggle from local activism in Texas.

Other examples of cooperation proved equally as brief. In 1963, for instance, blacks, Mexican Americans, and liberal whites attempted to unite in a political coalition that would work for the election of sympathetic white and minority politicians. African American and Mexican American leaders widely supported this Democratic Coalition. But once they realized that operating in the group meant sharing power, the Democratic Coalition disintegrated. Eventually a few leaders in San Antonio managed to cobble together the remnants of the Democratic Coalition into the Bexar County Coalition, which serviced only the San Antonio area.[55] Similarly, in 1970 African Americans and Chicanos in Houston attempted to establish a group dedicated to implementing a tri-ethnic integrated school system. The Black and Brown Coalition (BBC) drew together all minority groups concerned with school segregation. In a widely distributed flyer, the BBC stated: "We believe that the failure of our school system in educating our children academically and morally is the direct result of school officials' refusal to acknowledge and help minority group children . . . following the successful methods of Christ, Gandhi, King, and Chavez, the Black and Brown Coalition pledges to fight our cause with every available mean, and to promote the concept of human brotherhood." Much like the Democratic Coalition, however, the BBC foundered on the rocks of power sharing and the intransigence of the local school district. It dissolved after barely a year in operation.[56]

The failure of coalition groups reveals a great deal about the black-brown divide. While in several cases African Americans and Mexican Americans did attempt to unite, the few examples where some measure of unity occurred usually ended in failure. Each group feared sharing power and seemed to distrust the motivations of the other group. Combined with the unyielding nature of white racism in the state, especially within governmental bodies like school districts and the legislature, the failure of these coalitions hardly surprises. Indeed, the ephemeral and tepid nature of these coalitions taught hard lessons to blacks and browns. They did not work, and throughout the civil rights era did not seem likely to ever work.

In contrast to the few instances of cooperation and coalition building, examples of black-brown conflict in Texas abound. Throughout the civil rights period, the unification of these two movements proved largely impossible for African Americans and Mexican Americans. Both battled against the formidable obstacles of racism, disfranchisement, segregation, and discrimination, but they fought alone. Certainly the development of Jim Crow segregation, the racial geography of the state, the use of divergent tactics, and differences in leadership structures helped divide African Americans and Mexican Americans during the civil rights era. Racism generated considerable friction between blacks and browns and dealt cooperation and coalition building a most devastating blow. Both groups tended to see the battle for civil rights as a zero-sum game. The Mexican American strategy of demanding "inclusion as white" demonstrated an insensitivity to the history of black people. Brownness as a strategy emerged only when whiteness failed and did not encourage blacks to join with browns. Similarly, the single-minded focus of African Americans on their own history and movement ignored Mexican Americans as another oppressed group. The Chicano movement and Black Power did not lessen the divide. Indeed the attitudes that accompanied Black Power/Brown Power reified black-brown identity and strengthened racial separation. Ultimately, neither group successfully developed a multiracial, inclusive strategy, which explains why there were two separate civil rights movements in Texas.

Notes

1. Manuel [Avila] to Ed [Idar], February 7, 1956, Dr. Hector P. García Papers, Bell Library, Texas A&M University, Corpus Christi (TAMU-CC).

2. "Houston's Latin American Leaders Back Varied Views," *Houston Chronicle*, December 8, 1958; "Everett Split with Mexican-Americans,"

Houston Forward Times, September 19, 1970. For information on Tijerina and his views, see Thomas H. Kreneck, *Mexican American Odyssey: Felix Tijerina, Entrepreneur and Civic Leader, 1905–1965* (College Station: Texas A&M University Press, 2001).

3. See, for example, Brian D. Behnken, *Fighting Their Own Battles: Mexican Americans, African Americans, and the Struggle for Civil Rights in Texas* (Chapel Hill: University of North Carolina Press, 2011); Ramona Allaniz Houston, "African Americans, Mexican Americans, and Anglo Americans and the Desegregation of Texas, 1946–1957" (PhD diss., University of Texas, 2000); Brian D. Behnken, "On Parallel Tracks: A Comparison of the African-American and Latino Civil Rights Movements in Houston" (Master's thesis, University of Houston, 2001); Mark Brilliant, "Color Lines: Civil Rights Struggles on America's 'Racial Frontier,' 1945–1975" (PhD diss., Stanford University, 2002); Lauren Araiza, "For Freedom of Other Men: Civil Rights, Black Power, and the United Farm Workers, 1965–1973" (PhD diss., University of California, Berkeley, 2006); Gordon Mantler, "Black, Brown, and Poor: Martin Luther King Jr., the Poor People's Campaign, and Its Legacies" (PhD diss., Duke University, 2008).

4. Se, Steven H. Wilson, "*Brown* over 'Other White': Mexican Americans' Legal Arguments and Litigation Strategy in School Desegregation Lawsuits," *Law and History Review* 21, no. 1 (2003); Montejano, *Anglos and Mexicans in the Making of Texas*; Robin Duff Ladino, *Desegregating Texas Schools: Eisenhower, Shivers, and the Crisis at Mansfield High* (Austin: University of Texas Press, 1996); William Henry Kellar, *Make Haste Slowly: Moderates, Conservatives, and School Desegregation in Houston* (College Station: Texas A&M University Press, 1999); Glenn M. Linden, *Desegregating Schools in Dallas: Four Decades in the Federal Courts* (Dallas: Three Forks Press, 1995); Amilcar Shabazz, *Advancing Democracy: African Americans and the Struggle for Access and Equity in Higher Education in Texas* (Chapel Hill: University of North Carolina Press, 2004); Alwyn Barr, *Black Texans: A History of African Americans in Texas, 1528–1995* (Norman: University of Oklahoma Press, 1996); Guadalupe San Miguel, "*Let All of Them Take Heed*": Mexican-Americans and the Campaign for Educational Equality in Texas, 1910–1981* (Austin: University of Texas Press, 1987); Guadalupe San Miguel, *Brown, Not White: School Integration and the Chicano Movement in Houston* (College Station: Texas A&M University Press, 2001); Guadalupe San Miguel, *Contested Policy: The Rise and Fall of Federal Bilingual Education in the United States, 1960–2001* (Denton: University of North Texas Press, 2004); Carlos Kevin

Blanton, *The Strange Career of Bilingual Education in Texas, 1836–1981* (College Station: Texas A&M University Press, 2004).

5. See LULAC organizational history online, http://www.lulac.org/about/history/history.html (accessed January 22, 2009); Clare Sheridan, "'Another White Race': Mexican Americans and the Paradox of Whiteness in Jury Selection," *Law and History Review* 21, no. 1 (2003): 29; J. C. Machuca, speech given at LULAC's 26th anniversary celebration, William Flores Collection, Benson Latin American Collection (BLAC), Univeristy of Texas at Austin, 1; Arnoldo De León, *Ethnicity in the Sunbelt: A History of Mexican-Americans in Houston* (College Station: Texas A&M University Press, 2001), 47.

6. Cary D. Wintz, "Blacks," in *The Ethnic Groups of Houston*, ed. Fred R. von der Mehden (Houston TX: Rice University Studies, 1984), 20; "Notes and Diary," Jan De Hartog Collection, Courtesy of Special Collections and Archives, University of Houston Libraries.

7. Darwin Payne, *Big D: Triumphs and Troubles of an American Supercity in the 20th Century* (Dallas TX: Three Forks, 2000), 5, 81–84; Kenneth Mason, *African Americans and Race Relations in San Antonio, Texas, 1867–1937* (New York: Garland, 1998), 23–25, 36–38, 179–81; Robert A. Goldberg, "Racial Change on the Southern Periphery: The Case of San Antonio, Texas 1960–1965," *The Journal of Southern History* 49, no. 3 (1983): 349–52; Richard L. Schott, research project director, "Ethnic and Race Relations in Austin: A Report by the Policy Research Project on Ethnic and Race Relations in Austin," Austin History Center (Austin Public Library, 2000) (hereinafter cited as AHC), 5–8.

8. See Jacquelyn Dowd Hall, *Revolt Against Chivalry: Jessie Daniel Ames and the Women's Campaign Against Lynching* (New York: Columbia University Press, 1979); Norman D. Brown, *Hood, Bonnet, and Little Brown Jug: Texas Politics, 1921–1928* (College Station: Texas A&M University Press, 1984); Patricia Bernstein, *The First Waco Horror: The Lynching of Jesse Washington and the Rise of the* NAACP (College Station: Texas A&M University Press, 2006); William D. Carrigan, *The Making of a Lynching Culture: Violence and Vigilantism in Central Texas, 1836–1916* (Chicago: University of Illinois Press, 2006).

9. William D. Carrigan and Clive Webb, "The Lynching of Persons of Mexican Origin or Descent in the United States, 1848 to 1928," *Journal of Social History* 37, no. 2 (2003): 414. See also Carrigan and Webb, "Muerto por Unos Desconocidos (Killed by Persons Unknown): Mob Violence against Blacks and Mexicans," in *Beyond Black and White: Race,*

Ethnicity, and Gender in the U.S. South and Southwest, ed. Stephanie Cole, Alison M. Parker, and Laura F. Edwards (College Station: Texas A&M University Press, 2003), 35–74; San Miguel, *"Let All of Them Take Heed,"* 68–69.

10. Jonathan Kozol, *Savage Inequalities: Children in America's Schools* (New York: Harper Perennial, 1992), 206–33; San Miguel, *"Let All of Them Take Heed,"* 83–86. See also Paul A. Sracic, *San Antonio v. Rodriguez and the Pursuit of Equal Education* (Lawrence: University of Kansas Press, 2006).

11. "Bold Sit-ins In Marshall," *Texas Observer*, April 1, 1960; Donald Seals, "The Wiley-Bishop Student Movement: A Case Study of the 1960 Civil Rights Sit-ins" (Master's thesis, Baylor University, 2001), 73–84.

12. "Intensive Report on Marshall Sit-ins," *Texas Observer*, April 8, 1960; "From Chapel to Dousings," *Texas Observer*, April 8, 1960; "Dogs, Tear Gas," *Texas Observer*, April 8, 1960; "Marshall Becomes Tense, Suspicious City," *Texas Observer*, April 8, 1960; "Sit-in Demonstrators to Tell 'Marshall Story," *Dallas Express*, April 30, 1968; "Marshall Students Tell Dramatic Story of 'Sit-ins," *Dallas Express*, May 7, 1968; Seals, "The Wiley-Bishop Student Movement," 85–90.

13. Seals, "The Wiley-Bishop Student Movement," 110–17.

14. See http://www.texasalmanac.com/population/population-city -history.pdf (accessed July 28, 2008).

15. "Café Serves Negroes, White Sit-ins Are Jailed in Huntsville," *Houston Post*, July 26, 1965 (quotation); "Huntsville Businesses Told Negroes May Try Boycott," *Houston Chronicle*, July 26, 1965; "King Aide Is New Leader of Huntsville Racial Protests," *Houston Chronicle*, July 27, 1965; "'Hey-You' in Huntsville," *Texas Observer*, August 9, 1965; Martin Kuhlman, "Booker T. Bonner: Texas Civil Rights Activist," part of Bonner's ITC interview, 9–10.

16. "Los Cinco Candidatos," *Texas Observer*, April 18, 1963; "PASO Plans Drive from Crystal City," *San Antonio Express*, March 23, 1963; "Crystal City Vote to Get PASO Action," *San Antonio Express*, March 23, 1963; Navarro, *The Cristal Experiment*, 27–29.

17. "Crystal City: Confusion, Sorrow, Hate," *San Antonio Express and News*, April 14, 1963.

18. On LeRoy, see Moses LeRoy to Greetings, November 12, 1948, LeRoy Collection, HMRC; Henry B. Gonzalez, "Moses LeRoy: A Touch of Greatness," *Congressional Record*, Appendix, December 8, 1967, A6055; "Moses LeRoy Says He Believes Brotherhood to Come—Some Day," *Houston Chronicle*, August 29, 1971.

19. "The March into Corpus Christi," *Texas Observer*, August 5, 1966; Walter Katz to Dear Mose, December 2, 1967, Moses LeRoy Collection, Houston Metropolitan Resource Center (HMRC).

20. Emilio Zamora, *The World of the Mexican Worker in Texas* (College Station: Texas A&M University Press, 1993), 18–19; Montejano, *Anglos and Mexicans in the Making of Texas*, 167–68; Barr, *Black Texans*, 147–56; Neil Foley, *The White Scourge: Mexicans, Blacks, and Poor Whites in Texas Cotton Culture* (Los Angeles: University of California Press, 1999), 9–11, 32–39; Arnoldo De León, *Mexican Americans in Texas: A Brief History* (Wheeling: Harland Davidson, Inc., 1999), 51–59, 79–89.

21. Foley, *The White Scourge*, 5–8.

22. See David L. Chappell, *A Stone of Hope: Prophetic Religion and the Death of Jim Crow* (Chapel Hill: University of North Carolina Press, 2004).

23. Brian D. Behnken, "'Count on Me': Reverend M. L. Price of Texas, a Case Study in Civil Rights Leadership," *Journal of American Ethnic History* 25, no. 1 (2005): 63–65.

24. See Timothy Matovina, *Guadalupe and Her Faithful: Latino Catholics in San Antonio, from Colonial Origins to the Present* (Baltimore: Johns Hopkins University Press, 2005); Richard Edward Martinez, PADRES: *The National Chicano Priest Movement* (Austin: University of Texas Press, 2005); Roberto R. Treviño, *The Church in the Barrio: Mexican American Ethno-Catholicism in Houston* (Chapel Hill: University of North Carolina Press, 2006).

25. On Vatican II and Liberation Theology, see Giuseppe Alberigo, translated by Matthew Sherry, *A Brief History of Vatican II* (Maryknoll NY: Orbis, 2006); Matthew L. Lamb and Matthew Levering, eds., *Vatican II: Renewal Within Tradition* (New York: Oxford University Press, 2008); Gustavo Gutiérrez, *A Theology of Liberation: History, Politics and Salvation* (Maryknoll NY: Orbis, 1988); Gastón Espinosa, Virgilio Elizondo, and Jesse Miranda, eds., *Latino Religions and Civic Activism in the United States* (New York: Oxford University Press, 2005).

26. Behnken, "Fighting Their Own Battles," 187–88; Treviño, *The Church in the Barrio*, chap. 7; Martinez, PADRES, 81–82.

27. "Latin Leader Urges Negroes to be Patient," *Houston Chronicle*, May 13, 1960; Signed letter opposing sit-ins, ca. May 1960, Felix Tijerina Collection, HMRC; "Café Issue Splits Race Committee," *Houston Chronicle*, May 10, 1960; "Mayor's Bi-Racial Group to Disband," *Houston Post*, June 10, 1960. For comments from a black leader, see, Dr. David Williams interview with Cheri Wolfe, Institute of Texan Cultures (ITC), October 21, 1993, 10–13.

28. Cheri Wolfe interview with Harry V. Burns, ITC, August 9, 1994, 14–15.

29. Oral History Interview with Lauro Cruz, 1998, by José Angel Gutiérrez. CMAS No. 67, Special Collections, University of Texas at Arlington Libraries.

30. Signed letter opposing sit-ins, ca. May 1960, Felix Tijerina Collection, HMRC.

31. "President's Message," LULAC News (August 1963); "LULAC Leader Assails Public Demonstrations," August 29, 1963, (probably Houston Chronicle) clippings files, LULAC Council #60 Collection, HMRC.

32. Dr. David Williams interview with Cheri Wolfe, ITC, October 21, 1993, 5.

33. Marion Butts interview with Gary Houston, ITC, December 22, 1993, 34.

34. Ada Anderson interview with Cheri Wolfe, ITC, November 17, 1993, 22.

35. For the Mexican American response to neglect from blacks, see "Browns and Blacks Meet to Discuss Education," Papel Chicano, July 29, 1971.

36. For perhaps the most important recent addition to the scholarship on Mexican American labor activism, see Zaragosa Vargas, Labor Rights Are Civil Rights: Mexican American Workers in Twentieth-Century America (Princeton: Princeton University Press, 2004).

37. See, Tomás Almaguer, Racial Fault Lines: The Historical Origins of White Supremacy in California (Berkeley: University of California Press, 1994); Neil Foley, "Becoming Hispanic: Mexican Americans and the Faustian Bargain with Whiteness," Reflexiones (1997); Neil Foley, "Straddling the Color Line: The Legal Construction of Hispanic Identity in Texas," in Nancy Foner and George Frederickson, eds., Not Just Black and White: Historical and Contemporary Perspectives on Immigration, Race, and Ethnicity in the United States (New York: Russell Sage, 2005); Neil Foley, "Partly Colored or Other White: Mexican Americans and Their Problems with the Color Line," in Beyond Black and White: Race, Ethnicity, and Gender in the U.S. South and Southwest, ed. Stephanie Cole, Allison Parker, and Laura F. Edwards (College Station: Texas A&M University Press, 2003); Wilson, "Brown Over 'Other White'"; Clare Sheridan, "'Another White Race'"; Thomas A. Guglielmo, "Fighting for Caucasian Rights: Mexicans, Mexican Americans, and the Transnational Struggle for Civil Rights in World War II Texas," Journal of American History 92, no. 4

(2006); Michael Phillips, *White Metropolis: Race, Ethnicity, and Religion in Dallas, 1841–2001* (Austin: University of Texas Press, 2006).

38. San Miguel, *Brown, Not White*, 40.

39. Karen Mary Davalos, Eric R. Avila, Rafael Pérez-torres, et al., "Roundtable on the State of Chicana/o Studies," *Aztlán* 27, no. 2 (2002): 144–45; Martha Menchaca, *Recovering History, Constructing Race: The Indian, Black, and White Roots of Mexican Americans* (Austin: University of Texas Press, 2002), 1.

40. *Del Rio ISD v. Salvatierra*, 33 SW 2d 790 (1930); Guadalupe San Miguel, *"Let All of Them Take Heed,"* 78–80; Steven W. Prewitt, "'We Didn't Ask to Come to this Party': Self Determination Collides with the Federal Government in the Public Schools of Del Rio, Texas, 1890–1971" (PhD diss., University of Houston, 2000).

41. Clifford Forster (ACLU) to George I. Sánchez, May 19, 1947, George I. Sánchez Collection, BLAC.

42. See Behnken, "Fighting Their Own Battles," 45–48, 55, 57–58, 196–98, 346–47.

43. Rev. C. Anderson Davis interview with Cheri Wolfe, December 15, 1993, ITC, San Antonio, 32.

44. Dr. David Williams interview with Cheri Wolfe, ITC, October 21, 1993, 12.

45. Phil Montalbo to Felix Tijerina, May 27, 1957, LULAC Council #60 Collection, HMRC.

46. A. G. Ramirez to LULAC Council #2, May 30, 1957, v Council #60 Collection, HMRC.

47. "Pongase Listo a Todo lo que Sucede" [Get ready for anything that can happen], *Dallas Americano*, May 21, 1958; a few weeks later Ochoa encouraged Mexican Americans to "vote conservative" because the other candidates, most probably Henry B. Gonzalez, were attempting to unite black and Latino workers. See "Vote Conservativo; Use Pol Tax," *Dallas Americano*, July 16, 1958.

48. Advertisement, *Dallas Americano*, July 23, 1958, 5.

49. See "Negro-Latin Talk Demand Renewed," *Dallas Times Herald*, October 28, 1970; *The Black/Mexican-American Project Report*, a report of the Houston Council on Human Relations (July 1972); "Black San Antonio V: Political Inroads," *San Antonio Express*, February 17, 1972; "Chicanos," n.d., Salazar Papers, HMRC.

50. San Miguel, *Brown, Not White*.

51. San Miguel, *Brown, Not White*, 207–8.

52. George A. Martínez, "African-Americans, Latinos, and the Construction of Race: Toward an Epistemic Coalition," *Chicano-Latino Law Review* 19 (1998): 213–22.

53. "Senators Kazen, Gonzalez Set Filibuster Record," *Dallas Express*, May 11, 1957.

54. "The Segregation Filibuster of 1957," *Texas Observer*, May 7, 1957.

55. "State's Liberals Join in Coalition," *Dallas Morning News*, June 14, 1963; "A Four-Group Coalition," *Texas Observer*, August 9, 1963.

56. "Black and Brown Coalition Flyer," by Tomas García, circa May 4, 1972, Huelga Schools Collection, HMRC. The BBC attempted to push the University of Houston to adopt black and Chicano studies programs in 1972. See also "The Introduction of Appropriate Black and Chicano Content into a Social Work Curriculum," by the BBC, January 31, 1972, Leonel J. Castillo Papers, HMRC; Raul de Anda to Leonel J. Castillo, February 8, 1972, Leonel J. Castillo Papers, HMRC; Raul de Anda to Leonel J. Castillo, February 20, 1972, Leonel J. Castillo Papers, HMRC.

THREE

Complicating the Beloved Community

The Student Nonviolent Coordinating Committee and the National Farm Workers Association

LAUREN ARAIZA

Elizabeth Sutherland Martínez had chosen her dress just for the occasion—it was red and black to match the flag of the National Farm Workers Association (NFWA). Martínez had traveled from New York City to California's central valley to show support for the union of primarily Mexican American farm workers. Led by Cesar Chavez, the farm workers were marching 250 miles from Delano to Sacramento to draw attention to their struggles against Delano grape growers. That evening, as the marchers rested, ate, and visited in a community center in a small, dusty town along the route, Martínez was asked to give a speech as a representative of the Student Nonviolent Coordinating Committee (SNCC). She hurried to the ladies room where she scribbled a short address on a steno pad, changed into her specially selected dress, and ran back to the hall. In Spanish, Martínez spoke for SNCC when she proclaimed, "we are with you and we are proud of your march and your victory because it is a victory for all the poor of the world."[1]

SNCC's relationship with the farm workers illuminates previously hidden dimensions of the organization that expand our understanding of its philosophy, priorities, and mission.

Although far from SNCC's centers of organizing in the Deep South, the support that SNCC demonstrated for the NFWA was characteristic of the organization. In addition to combating racial inequality, SNCC challenged America's caste system, which it saw as antithetical to a democratic society. The intent to challenge not only American racial mores and the political system, but also the economic and class structure of the nation, set SNCC apart from other civil rights organizations. SNCC's commitment to economic issues led to an appreciation of multiracial equality that escaped many of the other civil rights organizations of the era. This dimension, which complicates the traditional understanding of SNCC as solely concerned with the plight of African Americans, was most explicitly demonstrated in its relationship with the NFWA, founded in 1962 by Cesar Chavez. Beginning in January 1965, SNCC provided the farm workers with physical, monetary, and tactical support. An examination of the relationship between SNCC and the NFWA reveals important aspects of black-Chicano relations during the civil rights era by demonstrating that coalitions between the two groups were only successful if they were based on more than one point of solidarity, not just a sense of camaraderie as racial minorities. Members of SNCC pioneered an alliance with the NFWA because they were acutely aware of the economic basis of oppression and understood its connection to racial discrimination. This caused SNCC activists to recognize that African Americans and Mexican Americans were victim to the same oppressive forces and led them to see the potential in an alliance between the civil rights movement and Mexican American farm workers. As Martínez told the marchers, "it is necessary that blacks and Mexicans see that there is only one cause—justice."[2]

The alliance between the two organizations came about at a time of transition for SNCC. After the tumultuous Freedom Summer of 1964, SNCC's central office called for members to present position papers at a staff meeting in Waveland, Mississippi in November 1964. In the wake of beatings, murders, voter intimidation, and the failure of the Mississippi Freedom Democratic Party (MFDP), SNCC experienced a period of disunity and disillusionment. Mike Miller, a white staff member who headed the San Francisco SNCC office, saw the meeting at Waveland as an opportunity to expand the mission of SNCC to confront the issue of economic inequality. In response to a questionnaire distributed to SNCC offices nationwide, Miller wrote: "[T]hat the question 'what should be SNCC's position on African affairs?' is raised and the question, for example, 'what is SNCC's position on the labor movement?' is not raised seems to me to ignore what we have to do here and now. . . . The day-to-day world in which we live is such that UAW affairs are probably more relevant to MFDP, COFO, and SNCC than African affairs." Many SNCC members were inspired by recent African liberation struggles and were thus motivated to form connections with countries freed from colonial rule. In fact, a SNCC delegation toured the continent and met with some of the leaders of the newly independent countries in September 1964. But Miller questioned the relevance of Africa's anticolonial struggles and instead wanted to see SNCC aligned with the farm labor movement.[3]

Miller's interest in the plight of workers long predated his involvement in SNCC. He recalled, "when I was little, I was on my father's shoulders on picket lines." Miller's father, James Miller, wrote for the newspaper of the International Fishermen and Allied Workers of America, which was expelled from the Congress of Industrial Organizations (CIO) in 1950 for being "communist dominated." As an undergraduate at the University of California, Berkeley, Miller organized rallies and food and clothing drives on behalf of the United Packinghouse Workers, who were striking against cantaloupe growers in the Imperial Valley of California. In 1960 Miller organized the Student Committee for Agricultural Labor, which conducted grassroots organizing among farm workers. His experience could have led directly to a career working on behalf of agricultural workers. However, SNCC was in need of his considerable organizing skills. At the request of SNCC chairman Charles McDew, Miller became the SNCC representative in the Bay Area in 1962. Miller joined the SNCC staff full-time the following winter.[4]

After a stint working with SNCC in Mississippi in 1963, Miller returned to expand SNCC's activities in the Bay Area. Along with fellow activist Terry Cannon, Miller established the Freedom House, which organized against the redevelopment of the Fillmore District, a historically African American neighborhood in San Francisco. Cannon shared Miller's sympathy for agricultural workers; his mother had reported on sharecroppers during the Great Depression. When Miller set up a Friends of SNCC office in San Francisco, part of a network of volunteers who worked to support SNCC's activities in the South, he asked Cannon to edit the organization's newsletter. That newsletter quickly transformed into *The Movement* newspaper. The San Francisco Friends of SNCC soon became a bona fide SNCC chapter, one of nine "northern offices" outside of the Deep South.[5]

Miller firmly believed that SNCC's organizing techniques could—and should—be applied to farm workers in California. In December 1964 he wrote a letter to the national SNCC staff outlining a proposal to organize farm workers in California. Miller explained: "[S]ome of you have heard me talk about the California Valley. It is our Delta. It is a land of immense richness and the deepest of poverty." SNCC had recently begun conducting voter registration among migrant farm workers on the East Coast. Even though these farm workers were primarily African American, Miller persuaded SNCC to explore the idea of voter registration among California's Mexican American farm workers. Immediately after SNCC approved his program, Miller contacted the NFWA in January 1965 through his friend Coleman Blease, a Sacramento lawyer who had worked with NFWA organizer Dolores Huerta, to discuss voter registration.[6]

The meeting requested by Blease, which occurred in late January 1965, established the first formal connection between SNCC and the NFWA. This connection proved invaluable for the farm workers a few months after the initial meeting. In July 1965 the NFWA and the California Migrant Ministry, an interdenominational group that both ministered to farm workers and assisted them in their fight for justice and self-determination, organized a rent strike against the Tulare County Housing Authority. The housing authority had doubled the rent at the Woodville and Linnell labor camps, despite no increase in pay and no improvement of the unsanitary, Depression-era tin huts. Finding themselves ill-prepared for a rent strike, the California Migrant Ministry's Gilbert Padilla and Reverend Jim Drake called on the San Francisco SNCC office to send organizers. Padilla greatly appreciated the SNCC members who helped with the rent strike and valued their experience: "[T]hose young men, or these young people I should say, were guys who had been in Mississippi and stuff. So they were already trained in marches and how to deal. They came with the perspective."[7]

The SNCC newspaper, *The Movement*, diligently reported on the Tulare County rent strike. According to Cannon, the newspaper's staff "saw early just simply the need to publicize what was going on." Although San Francisco SNCC published the newspaper, it was disseminated to SNCC and Friends of SNCC offices nationwide. Through *The Movement*, many in SNCC first learned of racial and social problems outside of the South. For example, to illustrate the similarities between farm workers on the East and West Coasts, the front page of the August 1965 issue of *The Movement* placed an article on the Tulare County strike next to an article on the Tennessee Freedom Labor Union. Subsequent issues of *The Movement* included additional pieces on farm workers and reprinted articles from *El Malcriado*, the newspaper of the NFWA.[8]

The Movement's staff focused attention on the NFWA because they shared an interest and background in the labor movement. For example, one of *The Movement*'s most prolific photographers and writers was George Ballis. Following a short stint as a factory worker in Chicago, Ballis moved to Fresno, California in January 1953 to edit the *Valley Labor Citizen*, a weekly AFL-CIO newspaper. He soon became interested in farm workers and began photographing them. In 1964 Ballis volunteered for SNCC as a photographer. When Miller established the SNCC office in San Francisco, Ballis joined the staff. Ballis's decades-long interest in agricultural workers provided *The Movement* with a significant degree of knowledge and sophistication about the plight of the farm workers. Hardy Frye, another early staff member of *The Movement*, helped establish the Sacramento Friends of SNCC while a student at Sacramento City College. In this capacity, Frye worked closely with Father Keith Kenney, parish priest of Our Lady of Guadalupe Church in Sacramento, who ministered to farm workers in the area and strongly supported the NFWA. In September 1965, Frye and other Sacramento activists met with Ballis and expressed interest in working with farm workers in San Joaquin County.[9]

Thus by September 1965 the NFWA had formed relationships with a group of SNCC activists who, in addition to being experienced civil rights organizers, had previous connections to the labor movement. Moreover, these organizers had a profound understanding of the relationship between racial discrimination and economic oppression and were thus sympathetic to the struggles of Mexican American farm workers. These qualities proved essential to the NFWA as it embarked on the most pivotal moment of its history. On September 16, 1965, Mexican Independence Day, the NFWA voted to join the Agricultural Workers Organizing Committee (AWOC), a union of Filipino farm workers, in their strike of grape growers in the Delano area. As soon as the NFWA joined the strike, the growers, police, and townspeople became increasingly hostile and violent toward the farm workers. Chavez had studied Gandhi and was determined that the strike be nonviolent. Therefore, he personally asked the San Francisco SNCC office to send skilled organizers to Delano to teach courses on nonviolent resistance to the farm workers.[10]

The NFWA welcomed the civil rights activists who came to their aid with open arms. Farm worker Eliseo Medina appreciated the skills that SNCC workers brought to the strike. Medina recalled, "I think SNCC people were the only ones that really had any kind of concept about what to do. Particularly in things like marches and demonstrations and all those tools of the Civil Rights Movement, hell, we didn't have a clue." NFWA organizer Wendy Goepel Brooks acknowledged that at the beginning of the strike very few farm workers had a practical knowledge of protesting, which resulted in "the blind leading the blind." Brooks believed that SNCC's greatest contribution was teaching the "not particularly nonviolent" farm workers about the importance of nonviolence. She recalled that SNCC organizers who joined the strike "came up with new ideas about non-violent methods to use to convey our message about the strike in Delano . . . , [they] preached non-violence and supported Cesar's contention that the strike had to remain non-violent or we would all be losers." Indeed, NFWA meeting minutes reveal that the farm workers warmly received SNCC's lessons in nonviolent resistance. At one meeting, picket captain Julio Hernandez thanked volunteers from SNCC "for classes in non-violence which they have conducted for other staff members."[11]

The relationship between SNCC and the farm workers was facilitated by the fact that the NFWA had positioned itself as a movement rather than as a labor union. As such, the farm workers felt a kinship with civil rights activists and took inspiration from the milestones of the civil rights movement. A flier advertising a march and rally for the Tulare County rent strike dubbed the region "California's Selma." The NFWA newspaper *El Malcriado* editorialized about the situation in Tulare

County: "In the rent strike once again the farm worker is showing what he learned from the Negro movement. . . . Each day the working people are proving their courage more and more as the Negroes do in their movement. The day in which we the farm workers apply this lesson with the same courage which has been shown in Alabama and Mississippi, this will be the day in which the misfortune of the farm workers will end." When the NFWA joined AWOC in its strike against Delano grape growers, *El Malcriado* likened the strike to the 1955 Montgomery bus boycott. *El Malcriado* elaborated: "[T]his is how a movement begins. This is why the farm workers association is a 'movement' more than a 'union.' Once a movement begins it is impossible to stop. It will sweep through California and it will not be over until the farm worker has the equality of a living wage and decent treatment." The members of SNCC also related to the NFWA as a movement. Unlike the Southern Christian Leadership Conference (SCLC), which had worked closely with the AFL-CIO, SNCC frequently had a contentious relationship with some of the leaders of the other major unions. Those in SNCC who did not approve of an alliance with organized labor nonetheless eagerly supported the NFWA on the basis of the farm workers' pursuit of racial equality. As Terry Cannon explained, "the core of the connection [between SNCC and the NFWA] was the similarity in treatment of blacks in the South and Latinos in the West and Southwest." The fact that the union combated both economic and racial discrimination enabled its alliance with SNCC.[12]

With the approval of the national SNCC office, overall SNCC participation in the strike accelerated. The group organized to supply the NFWA with two-way radios, which were vital to the effectiveness of the strike. The total area of the strike was one thousand square miles, which made it difficult for the NFWA to monitor farm owners' use of scab labor. With the radios, scouts could quickly inform the NFWA office when scabs entered the fields. The union could then send pickets to the fields being worked by scabs. Moreover, as SNCC was well aware, two-way radios could be life-saving apparatus in the face of violence by growers and police. SNCC not only supplied the radios, but also obtained a business band license for the NFWA to use.[13]

Although SNCC's assistance was substantial, Miller worked to ensure that this support not only continued, but increased. At Miller's invitation, Chavez and James Forman, SNCC's executive secretary, spoke at the statewide meeting of California SNCC and Friends of SNCC groups in November 1965. Later that month, Miller and Marshall Ganz, a native of Bakersfield, California who had joined SNCC after volunteering for Freedom Summer, attended the national SNCC staff meeting and gave a presentation on the Delano strike as part of a panel on migrant labor organizing. As a result of their presentation, the SNCC staff voted to give full support to the NFWA and to allow Ganz to represent SNCC on the NFWA staff while still paying him as a SNCC staff member. Additionally, the national SNCC office also agreed to provide the farm workers with extra manpower. In December 1965 a small delegation from SNCC including Stokely Carmichael, Cleveland Sellers, and Ralph Featherstone visited Chavez at the NFWA office in Delano to discuss how SNCC could further help the union. After the meeting, the group adjourned to the local hangout, People's Bar, to drink beer and play pool. Ganz recalled, "Cesar was quite a pool player and so was Stokely and I think they surprised each other." As a result of this meeting, SNCC sent Dickie Flowers, a staff member from Greenwood, Mississippi, to work with Ganz. Flowers also organized farm workers in Bakersfield, a farming town in south-central California with more African American farm workers than in other parts of the central valley.[14]

That same month Chavez asked Miller to coordinate a national boycott of Schenley Industries, a liquor company that owned one of the largest of the ranches being struck by the NFWA. This boycott had been the idea of Jim Drake, who took

5. Cesar Chavez consults with Marshall Ganz, UFW executive board member and former SNCC organizer, at a UFW rally, 1971. Walter P. Reuther Library, Wayne State University.

his cue from the civil rights movement: "Blacks used to boycott stores that wouldn't hire them. So we decided to try it." The decision to boycott came about after Chavez asked SNCC volunteers to research the connections of the Delano growers. The SNCC volunteers discovered that Schenley distributed well-known whiskeys such as Cutty Sark, as well as wine made with Delano grapes. Miller, Drake, Chavez, and others recognized that Schenley products would be effective boycott targets because Americans could easily identify the company's brands. Although Miller was not an NFWA organizer, his position in SNCC made him an appropriate choice because not only did he have experience with boycotts, but he also could tap into SNCC's network of activists and supporters to ensure the effectiveness of the boycott. Shortly before the NFWA announced the Schenley boycott, SNCC began weekly picket lines in front of Schenley's San Francisco offices. Upon discovering the pickets, Schenley executives wrongly assumed that SNCC wanted the company to hire more African Americans. They quickly informed various civil rights organizations that they had a "Negro Vice-President." *The Movement* reported, "on learning that the issue was not their treatment of Negroes, but their treatment of Mexican-Americans, they had nothing to say."[15]

The New York City SNCC office was also instrumental to the Schenley boycott. San Francisco SNCC and the NFWA sought their help because Schenley's national headquarters were in New York and the local SNCC office could effectively pressure the company. In early December, Wendy Goepel Brooks visited New York SNCC and suggested that both SNCC and the local Congress of Racial Equality (CORE) chapter could coordinate picket lines at New York and New Jersey grocery stores and schedule a meeting with Schenley executives to urge negotiations with the union. New York SNCC and CORE went into action immediately, organizing a letter writing campaign and holding meetings on boycott action. They also conducted visits to liquor stores where delegations asked managers to remove Schenley products from their shelves and to display posters acknowledging their support of the strike. If managers did not comply, picket lines appeared outside the stores to inform consumers about the boycott. Twenty liquor stores in Brooklyn complied with the boycott within three weeks. SNCC and CORE were even more successful in Harlem, where all forty-nine stores visited by the activists agreed to cooperate with the boycott. SNCC and CORE's stunning success on behalf of the NFWA in majority African American areas reveals that the organizations' actions educated their constituencies on the connections between African Americans and Mexican Americans.[16]

SNCC offices in other areas also assisted the boycott in ways that reflected an understanding of the similarities between African Americans and Mexican Americans. The final issue of *The Student Voice*, SNCC's national newsletter, urged readers to boycott Schenley products. Cynthia Washington in the Atlanta office sent a memo to all Friends of SNCC chapters informing them of the strike details and instructing all to support the strike and the boycott. Washington also linked the struggles of SNCC and the NFWA when she explained, "the workers have been harassed by strikebreaking tactics reminiscent of the 1930s and with police oppression typical of Birmingham's Bull Connor and Selma's Jim Clark.[17]

SNCC members became most useful to the NFWA when the union chose to utilize the march, a long-favored tactic of the civil rights movement. During an NFWA staff retreat, someone suggested marching from California to Schenley headquarters in New York, likening it to the Selma to Montgomery march of 1965. Realizing that New York was too far, someone else suggested they march to the Schenley offices in San Francisco. But Chavez questioned whether Schenley would respond, so he suggested marching to Sacramento to put pressure on Governor Edmund "Pat" Brown to intervene. He further argued that since the season of Lent neared, this protest should not be a march at all. Rather, the protest should be a pilgrimage in the tradition of a Mexican *peregrinación* that would coincide with Easter Sunday. Chavez requested that Ganz coordinate the march while Cannon would serve press secretary. With Miller, Ganz, and Cannon in charge of the boycott and march, SNCC activists became the nerve center of the NFWA protest.[18]

The march began on March 17, 1966 with sixty-eight farm workers and NFWA staff members, and included Flowers of SNCC. Although the farm workers were the heart and soul of the march, the collective organizing experience of the SNCC volunteers proved essential to the success of the march. Cannon issued press releases and handled press relations to promote the march and boycott, but despite his efforts the march initially received little attention. "When we started, I couldn't get anyone. Nobody was interested. Nobody cared," Cannon recalled. SNCC was one of the few organizations that supported the march from the beginning. In addition to the work of Ganz, Miller, and Cannon, SNCC and Friends of SNCC groups lent assistance to the march by raising money and donating supplies. For example, the Marin Friends of SNCC raised two hundred dollars for the NFWA, which the union used to purchase shoes and sleeping bags for the marchers. Other SNCC chapters collected food and clothing for the marchers, while members of various California Friends of SNCC groups marched themselves. At the conclusion of the march, Frye gave a speech on the capitol steps that explicitly connected the NFWA to SNCC and the civil rights movement by comparing Governor Brown's refusal to meet with the marchers to Alabama Governor George Wallace's refusal to meet with those who marched from Selma to Montgomery in 1965.[19]

While SNCC was intimately involved in the Schenley boycott and Delano to Sacramento march, none of the other major civil rights organizations participated in the protests. The Portland branch of the NAACP attempted to issue a resolution in support of the NFWA, but the NAACP national headquarters prevented this. NAACP executive director Roy Wilkins enjoyed a close relationship with Schenley Industries and he consequently refused to allow NAACP branches to support the NFWA. Additionally, Schenley attempted to curry favor with the black community by donating large amounts of money to black-owned banks and businesses. When the NFWA ended its boycott of Schenley products in April 1966, Wilkins issued a press release drafted by the corporation congratulating Schenley for resolving the strike. At no point did Wilkins congratulate Chavez and the NFWA.[20]

Schenley Industries also used its connections in the black community in an attempt to hinder any potential support for the NFWA from the Southern Christian Leadership Conference. Two days before the NFWA began the Delano to Sacramento march, Martin Luther King Jr. received a telegram from Jackie Robinson asking him to meet with his brother-in-law Charles T. Williams, an executive at Schenley, regarding the boycott. Robinson wrote, "I think there are some facts you would like to know which shows both sides of the situation." It is unknown if King ever met with Williams, but King did not issue a statement in support of the march and did not urge SCLC members to boycott Schenley products, despite his pro-labor stance and productive relationships with other labor unions.[21]

The failure of SCLC and the NAACP to come to the aid of the NFWA did not surprise the SNCC activists involved in the strike and boycott. In contrast to these older, more middle class civil rights organizations, SNCC activists clearly understood class inequality. While many SNCC staff members came from middle class backgrounds, they had rejected middle class values by dropping out of school and leaving lucrative career paths to work for the organization full-time. SNCC field secretaries earned less than ten dollars per week and supplemented their meager earnings by living communally or in the homes of local residents. By living and working in small towns in the rural Deep South, SNCC staff members witnessed firsthand the crippling poverty experienced by those they were attempting to organize. They quickly drew a direct connection between gaining the vote, racial equality, and economic betterment. For example, SNCC organizer Lawrence Guyot explained that when African Americans in Greenwood, Mississippi, attempted to register to vote, "[T]he county decided that what it would do was it would cut off all welfare supplies. So it did just that. All food was cut off." Ivanhoe Donaldson, who organized for SNCC in the Mississippi Delta town of Clarksdale, elaborated that when plantation workers tried to register to vote or organize others to do so, "plantation owners were not only being hostile in terms of pushing people off the plantation, but were economically isolating people from credit at stores or from banks." Farm owners in California also frequently fired or evicted farm workers for seeking union representation. Therefore, SNCC recognized the connection between racial and economic oppression, which enabled SNCC members to appreciate the similarities between African Americans in the Deep South and Mexican Americans in California's Central Valley.[22]

Thanks in large part to the involvement of SNCC, the NFWA's march from Delano to Sacramento in the spring of 1966 was a tremendous success. Not only did Schenley Industries agree to recognize the union shortly before the conclusion of the march, but the spectacle of the march itself gained national attention for the farm workers. With the increased media coverage, organizations representing a variety of progressive causes called on the NFWA to offer their support and manpower. Following SNCC's example, the various facets of the civil rights movement also began to recognize the similarities between their own struggle and that of the farm workers. Many groups also came to see the wisdom of forming multiracial coalitions. The NFWA needed these new sources of support because the Delano to Sacramento march, while it attracted national attention and hastened the end of the boycott of Schenley products, did not end the grape strike in the Delano region. It did, however, prove to the farm workers that success through nonviolent means was indeed possible.

The NFWA put those nonviolent tactics to the test once more when they did battle with the DiGiorgio Corporation, the largest grape grower in the Delano area. The NFWA began pickets at DiGiorgio's Sierra Vista Ranch on April 14, only four days after the conclusion of the Delano to Sacramento march, because the company attempted to restrict the farm workers' rights to union representation and collective bargaining. Using the experience gained during the Schenley strike, the NFWA chose to boycott S&W Fine Food and Treesweet Juices, DiGiorgio's most popular brands, rather than attempt to boycott DiGiorgio grapes. The NFWA's strike and boycott of DiGiorgio had an immediate effect and the union began meeting with the corporation to negotiate the terms of an election for union representation of its workers. However, in attempt to circumvent the NFWA, DiGiorgio began meeting with the International Brotherhood of Teamsters regarding union representation of the Mexican American farm workers. DiGiorgio welcomed the intervention of the Teamsters, an overwhelmingly white union that did not truly represent the farm workers and had no qualms about agreeing to no-strike clauses in their contracts. The company therefore agreed to an election for union representation on the condition that the Teamsters be on the ballot and then attempted to rig the election by restricting organizing on its ranches solely to the Teamsters. In response to the fraudulent election, the NFWA established picket lines around the Sierra Vista Ranch, shouting "No voten viernes" ("Do not vote Friday").[23]

SNCC staff members organized most of the protest activities against DiGiorgio. For example, Ganz and Flowers recruited African Americans from Bakersfield to join a vigil outside the home of Reverend R. B. Moore, the African American minister of St. Paul's Baptist Church in Delano who was to observe the DiGiorgio election and had spoken out against the NFWA by arguing that farm workers did not suffer discrimination. Ganz, along with farm worker Medina, also conducted house meetings to educate farm workers on the issues of the election. SNCC also sponsored the NFWA Student Summer Project. Based on SNCC's Mississippi Freedom Summer Project of 1964, the Student Summer Project brought together eighty students from activist groups such as the National Student Association, Students for a Democratic Society, and Young Christian Students to work for the NFWA from June through August 1966. This provided the union with additional manpower that proved invaluable to the DiGiorgio strike and boycott. Friends of SNCC chapters also continued to support the NFWA by organizing food caravans and hosting fundraisers. Due in large part to the union's support from progressive groups like SNCC, DiGiorgio agreed to conduct elections for union representation of its workers supervised by the American Arbitration Association and with rules agreed upon by the NFWA. In turn, the NFWA ceased picketing at DiGiorgio ranches and called off the boycott of DiGiorgio products.[24]

Despite the momentum generated by another SNCC-supported NFWA victory, the decision of the NFWA to officially merge with Agricultural Workers Organizing Committee to form the United Farm Workers Organizing Committee, AFL-CIO (UFWOC) in August 1966 threatened this productive alliance. Months before the merger, farm workers and activists worried that the bureaucracy of the AFL-CIO would kill the farm workers' movement. One NFWA staff member asked, "if the AFL is so damn great, why couldn't they organize the workers?" Nevertheless, the NFWA needed the AFL-CIO because it required additional sources of money and power. After the long battles against Schenley and DiGiorgio, the NFWA was cash-strapped and had only one foreseeable option—to join AWOC and the AFL-CIO. This did not sit well with SNCC and others on the left because it appeared that the AFL-CIO had co-opted the independent NFWA. In an analysis of the merger, *The Movement* declared that despite misgivings about the AFL-CIO, SNCC should still support the UFWOC because of "the justice of the cause itself."[25]

When the UFWOC began a new strike against A. Perelli-Minetti and Sons and resumed its boycott against DiGiorgio, which refused to allow elections for union representation at its Arvin Ranch, SNCC spearheaded support for the new union. SNCC staff members traveled to DiGiorgio's San Francisco headquarters and protested the company by unfurling a sixty-two foot banner from the roof that stated: "DiGiorgio—One Man One Vote—Workers Demand Elections." Police arrested Cannon along with seven UFWOC and AFL-CIO officials for entering the DiGiorgio offices and refusing to leave until they were granted a meeting with the president of the corporation. San Francisco stations broadcast the news of the arrests of Cannon and the labor leaders that evening. Rather than risk additional bad press, DiGiorgio agreed to an election at Arvin Ranch, which the UFWOC easily won. During the battle with Perelli-Minetti, Ganz participated on behalf of the UFWOC in their negotiations with the grower. The UFWOC boycott of Perelli-Minetti products became so damaging that Perelli-Minetti sought a quick resolution of the dispute and signed a contract with the UFWOC in July 1967.[26]

Even though SNCC members were at the forefront of the DiGiorgio and Perelli-Minetti campaigns, outside support proved crucial to UFWOC's success as inner turmoil began to plague SNCC. Tensions within the organization began to surface during the Mississippi Freedom Summer Project of 1964, when hundreds of primarily northern white college students came to Mississippi to conduct voter registration among blacks in rural areas. Disagreements over the purpose of the project, the impact of white volunteers on local black leadership, and interracial relationships caused deep divisions within SNCC. Continued violence directed against African Americans and SNCC volunteers compounded these tensions. Many in SNCC began to question the value of their work, the wisdom of depending on white allies and, in some cases, of working with whites at all. As a result, many black SNCC staff members began to consider dismissing white SNCC workers. Distance had shielded San Francisco SNCC from these conflicts and had allowed SNCC members in California to focus on issues of economic inequality, rather than be distracted by the debate over black separatism that began disrupting SNCC's organizing in the South. However, distance could not shield the San Francisco office from SNCC's decision in 1966 to restrict whites to organizing in white communities and to deny white workers the right to vote within the organization. Although the meaning of this decision was—and still is—debated, many white staff members felt that they had been expelled from the organization and therefore left SNCC.[27]

One of the whites to leave SNCC immediately following the December 1966 staff meeting was Miller, who had recently accepted an offer to work as an organizer for Saul Alinsky. Miller's departure spelled the end of San Francisco SNCC. Cannon remained editor of *The Movement*, but in December 1966 the newspaper informed its readers that it was no longer published by SNCC and would incorporate as The Movement Press. Ganz transitioned from serving as a SNCC staff member working with the UFWOC to being a full-fledged UFWOC staff member. Since Ganz had worked almost entirely with the UFWOC and came to be relied upon for his organizing skills, it seemed only natural that he would come to work for the union full-time. SNCC never officially dismissed Ganz. Instead, after not being in contact with the Atlanta SNCC office, he eventually stopped receiving paychecks from SNCC.[28]

The expulsion of white activists from SNCC did not bode well for the UFWOC in more than one way. First, by dismissing white workers like Miller, SNCC deprived the UFWOC of some of the union's most important organizers. Second, SNCC included non-black racial minorities in its expulsion of whites. This meant that two Mexican American women, María Varela and Elizabeth Sutherland Martínez, who had been on the SNCC staff since the early 1960s, were also forced out of the organization. Never having identified as white, Varela and Martínez were shocked to learn that blacks wanted them out of SNCC. The expulsion of Varela and Martínez indicates that SNCC no longer recognized the connections between African Americans and Mexican Americans, which undermined the basis of its relationship with the UFWOC. Furthermore, if SNCC believed that Mexican Americans were white, then the organization could no longer work with the farm workers.[29]

This about-face in SNCC's perception of Mexican Americans resulted in the end of its once productive relationship with the UFWOC. In February 1967 a donation to the UFWOC by the East Bay Friends of SNCC was the last time that SNCC supported the union financially. Chavez was dismayed that SNCC no longer supported the farm workers. For him it represented a larger pattern of early UFWOC supporters moving on to other causes. In an April 1967 interview, Chavez complained, "[T]he labor movement is by and large our biggest help. And we've been able to keep the church help. But we're getting very little help from the student groups or the civil rights groups—well, some, but not anywhere what we were getting before. Even our correspondence with our contacts in these groups is almost nil." Although SNCC had criticized the UFWOC for coming under the fold of the AFL-CIO, this alliance proved even more important and necessary once SNCC ended its support of the farm workers.[30]

When SNCC initially pursued its alliance with the UFWOC, it became the first major civil rights organization of the era to explicitly connect the fight against racial discrimination with economic oppression. This created one of the first coalitions between the black civil rights and Chicano movements.

Furthermore, the relationship between SNCC and the UFWOC not only led to important victories for the union, but it also expanded SNCC's mission in beneficial ways by forcing its members to consider and confront multiple levels of oppression. In the process, SNCC became the vanguard of civil rights activity and showed other organizations the wisdom in forming multiracial coalitions. But when SNCC adopted the position of black separatism and dismissed all whites, it abandoned the struggle against economic oppression and thereby destroyed the possibility of forming alliances with Mexican Americans. No longer were discrimination, poverty, police brutality, and the lack of political power common denominators for African Americans and Mexican Americans. Without the recognition of shared economic oppression and class unity, multiracial solidarity was no longer possible for SNCC. Race became the sole unifying factor for the remaining members of SNCC who, after challenging the American caste system, decided that Mexican Americans were white and that they therefore no longer shared a common struggle. This led directly to the end of SNCC's relationship with the UFWOC. While the once-productive alliance between SNCC and the farm workers dissolved, it provided a model for black/Chicano solidarity and paved the way for the union to build successful multiracial coalitions with other civil rights organizations, such as the Black Panther Party.[31]

Although a minority of Mexican Americans joined the UFWOC and an even smaller percentage of African Americans joined SNCC, the relationship between the two organizations illuminates important aspects of black/Chicano relations and multiracial coalition building during the civil rights era. The emphasis of most civil rights organizations was on the attainment of racial equality, often achieved through cooperation with other groups and movements. Although some of these alliances were multiracial, these coalitions could not be sustained solely by a sense of commonality and solidarity based on race. Due to the unrelenting internal and external pressures on organizations of the era (such as violence and harassment from their enemies, tension and dissent within their ranks, and frequent defeat), coalitions needed more than one dimension of solidarity in order to survive. In the case of SNCC and the UFWOC, a recognition that both African Americans and Mexican Americans were discriminated against because of their race was supported by an understanding that both groups' oppression was compounded by economic forces. Therefore, racial discrimination and economic oppression combined to sustain a productive coalition between the two organizations. However, when SNCC abandoned the issue of economic inequality, its belief in multiracial solidarity disintegrated, which resulted in the end of its once-productive coalition with the UFWOC. The history of the alliance between these organizations shows that African Americans and Chicanos could and did come together during this tumultuous era, but were only successful in doing so when the foundation of their alliance was multidimensional.

Notes

1. Elizabeth Sutherland Martínez, Notes on the Delano to Sacramento March, March 17–April 10, 1966, The Student Nonviolent Coordinating Committee Papers, 1959–72 (hereinafter cited as SNCC Papers), Sanford NC: Microfilming Corp. of America, 1982, Reel 21.

2. Wesley Hogan, *Many Minds, One Heart: SNCC's Dream for a New America* (Chapel Hill: University of North Carolina Press, 2007), 160; Martínez, Notes on the Delano to Sacramento March.

3. Hogan, *Many Minds, One Heart*, 198; Memo from Mike Miller to SNCC National Staff, October 23, 1964, Charles M. Sherrod Papers, Wisconsin Historical Society Archives (quotation); Clayborne Carson, *In Struggle: SNCC and the Black Awakening of the 1960s* (Cambridge MA: Harvard University Press, 1995), 134–36.

4. Mike Miller, interview by author, San Francisco CA, February 19, 2004; Geoff Mann, "Class Consciousness and Common Property: The International Fishermen and Allied Workers of America," *International Labor and Working Class History* 61 (2002): 141–60; Mike Miller, telephone

interview by author, December 20, 2003; "SLATE Newsletter," SLATE Archives Digital Collection, http://archive.slatearchives.org/gs/HASH01ff/c76e3241.dir/ncse320.pdf (accessed May 19, 2009).

5. Letter from Terry Cannon to author, September 8, 2004; Terry Cannon, telephone interview by author, December 11, 2003.

6. Letter from Mike Miller to SNCC staff, December 21, 1964, SNCC Records, Wisconsin Historical Society (quotation); Miller interview by author, February 19, 2004; Miller interview by author, December 20, 2003; Letter from Coleman Blease to Dolores Huerta, January 20, 1965, National Farm Workers Association Collection, Box 1, Folder 3, Archives of Labor and Urban Affairs, Wayne State University (hereinafter cited as NFWA Collection).

7. "Viva! Tulare County Rent Strike, March," *The Movement* (August 1965); Ronald B. Taylor, *Chavez and the Farm Workers* (Boston: Beacon, 1975), 108; Flier, "Why We Are Picketing," July 1965, Box 12, Folder 9, NFWA Collection; Gilbert Padilla, interview by author, Berkeley CA, May 18, 2004.

8. Terry Cannon, interview by author, December 11, 2003; "Viva! Tulare County Rent Strike, March," *The Movement* (August 1965): 1; "Tennessee Freedom Labor Union: Poorest County Organizes," *The Movement* (August 1965): 1.

9. George Ballis, interview by author, Oakland CA, November 19, 2003; Hardy Frye, interview by author, Berkeley CA, November 18, 2003; Wendy Goepel Brooks, "The Story of Wendy Goepel Brooks, Cesar Chavez and La Huelga," December 2003, Farmworker Movement Documentation Project, www.farmworkermovement.org/essays/essays/007Brooks_Wendy.pdf (accessed May 19, 2009); Letter from Terry Cannon to Cesar Chavez, September 8, 1965, Box 13, Folder 22, NFWA Collection.

10. Goepel Brooks, "The Story of Wendy Goepel Brooks"; Memo, "Dateline: Delano, Tuesday," September 1965, Box 12, Folder 5, NFWA Collection.

11. Eliseo Medina, telephone interview by author, August 12, 2004 (first quotation); Wendy Goepel Brooks, telephone interview by author, September 13, 2004; Wendy Goepel Brooks, "The Story of Wendy Goepel Brooks, Cesar Chavez and La Huelga"; Memo, "Dateline: Delano," October 1, 1965, Box 12, Folder 5, NFWA Collection.

12. Flier, "Tulare County—California's Selma," July 1965, Box 12, Folder 9, NFWA Collection; "Editoral: Iqual Que Los Negritos," *El Malcriado*, July 1965, 2, translated and reprinted as "The Voice of the Farm

Workers Same as the Negroes," *The Movement* (August 1965): 1 (first quotation); "Editorial: Enough People With One Idea," *El Malcriado* (September 1965): 2 (second quotation); Cannon interview by author, December 11, 2003 (third quotation).

13. "SNCC Radios Go to CORE, Delano Strike," *The Movement* (October 1965); Letter from Joe Schulman to Richard Haley, November 5, 1965, Box 1, Folder 5, NFWA Collection; Letter from Joe Schulman to Cesar Chavez, n.d., United Farm Workers Organizing Committee Collection, Box 2, Folder 2, Archives of Labor and Urban Affairs, Wayne State University (hereinafter cited as UFWOC Collection).

14. Student Nonviolent Coordinating Committee, Tentative Agenda, Third Staff Meeting for 1965, November 24–28, 1965, SNCC Papers, Reel 3; Miller, interview by author, February 19, 2004; Marshall Ganz, telephone interview by author, May 4, 2004; Marshall Ganz, interview by author, November 25, 2003.

15. Miller, interview by author, February 19, 2004; Letter from Mike Miller to Wayne C. Hartmire, December 5, 1965, SNCC Papers, Reel 9; Fred Ross Sr., "History of the Farm Worker Movement," October 1974, Fred Ross Papers, Box 13, Folder 1, Department of Special Collections, Stanford University Libraries, Stanford University (hereinafter cited as Ross Papers); Marshall Ganz, *Five Smooth Stones: Strategic Capacity in the Unionization of California Agriculture* (Ann Arbor MI: University Microfilms, 2000), 323–24; "Schenley (Roma Wine) Offices in SF Picketed," *The Movement* (November 1965); "Farm Labor Pickets in S.F.," *San Francisco Chronicle*, October 13, 1965.

16. Minutes, Report on Delano Farm Workers Strike given by Wendy Goepel, New York SNCC office, December 6, 1965, SNCC Papers, Reel 21; George Wiley and Elizabeth Sutherland, "Boycott Schenley!" December 24, 1965, SNCC Papers, Reel 21; "National Delano Boycott Report," *The Movement* (January 1966): 3.

17. Washington SNCC Staff Meeting, December 13, 1965, SNCC Papers, Reel 34; "News Notes, California," *The Student Voice*, December 20, 1965: 3; Memo from Cyn [Cynthia Washington] to Friends of SNCC, SNCC Papers, Reel 59.

18. Ganz, *Five Smooth Stones*, 333–34; Letter from Terence Cannon to Members of the Press and Media, SNCC Papers, Reel 21; Terence Cannon, Press Release, "Striking Farm Workers Begin 300 Mile March," March 16, 1966, SNCC Papers, Reel 21.

19. "The history of the pilgrimage," *El Malcriado*, April 10, 1966; "List

of honor," *El Malcriado*, April 10, 1966; Cannon, interview by author, December 11, 2003 (quotation); Cesar Chavez to Marin Friends of SNCC, April 16, 1966, Box 14, Folder 6, NFWA Collection; Letter from Mike Miller to Karen Whitman, April 13, 1966, SNCC Papers, Reel 33.

20. Lorna Marple, Report of the Political Action Chairman to Portland Branch NAACP, March 20, 1966, Records of the National Association for the Advancement of Colored People, West Coast Region, Box 19, The Bancroft Library, University of California, Berkeley (hereinafter cited as West Coast NAACP Records); Letter from Harry C. Ward to Roy Wilkins, March 22, 1966, West Coast NAACP Records, Box 19; Letter from Roy Wilkins to Harry C. Ward, April 12, 1966, The Papers of the NAACP, Part 28A: Special Subject Files, 1966–1970, Reel 18 (hereinafter cited as NAACP Papers); Letter from Robert O. Powell to Roy Wilkins, April 21, 1966, NAACP Papers, Reel 17; Roy Wilkins, Statement, NAACP Papers, Reel 17.

21. Telegram from Jackie Robinson to Martin Luther King Jr., March 15, 1966, Martin Luther King Jr. Papers, Box 20, Folder 24, Martin Luther King Jr., Center for Nonviolent Social Change, Atlanta GA.

22. Carson, *In Struggle*, 71; Howell Raines, *My Soul is Rested: The Story of the Civil Rights Movement in the Deep South* (New York: Penguin, 1983), 242, 256.

23. Chronology, United Farm Workers Office of the President, Part 2: Cesar Chavez Collection Papers, 1947–1990, Box 23, Folder 26, Archives of Labor and Urban Affairs, Wayne State University (hereinafter cited as Chavez Collection); "History of the Delano Grape Strike and the DiGiorgio 'Elections,'" Box 33, Folder 10, Chavez Collection; "The DiGiorgio Struggle, *The Movement* (June 1966): 5; "The National Farm Workers Association Asks You: Please Don't Buy Tree-Sweet Fruit Juices, S & W Fine Foods," *The Movement* (June 1966): 5; "United Farm Workers: Chronological History," Box 9, Folder 11, Ross Papers; "The DiGiorgio Struggle," *The Movement* (June 1966): 5; "Field Workers Boycott Di Giorgio Rigged Election," *The Movement* (July 1966): 1.

24. "Field Workers Boycott DiGiorgio Rigged Election," *The Movement* (July 1966): 1; Chronology, Box 23, Folder 26, Chavez Collection; Flier, "The Student Summer Project of the National Farm Workers Association, June 19 through August 1966," United Farm Workers Organizing Committee Collection Box 7, Folder 18, Archives of Labor and Urban Affairs, Wayne State University (hereinafter cited as UFWOC Collection); Ganz, *Five Smooth Stones*, 388; Flier, "Urgent Lack of Food Right Now: United Labor 'Food for Delano' Committee," Box 7, Folder 18, UFWOC Collection; "Film Benefit for Delano Strikers," *Sun-Reporter*, September

24, 1966; "Behind the August 30 Di Giorgio Election," *The Movement* (August 1966): 6, 8.

25. "After the Pilgrimage—A Burst of Organizing," *The Movement* (June 1966): 8; "NFWA and AFL-CIO Merge: A Movement Analysis," *The Movement* (September 1966): 8.

26. "Is Arvin Next?" *El Malcriado*, September 9, 1966, 3; Terence Cannon, "Arvin Workers Win Right to DiGiorgio Election: Farm Workers, Labor Officials, SNCC Editor Arrested," *The Movement* (November 1966): 1, 10; Dick Meister, "Arrests of DiGiorgio Pickets Here," *San Francisco Chronicle*, October 21, 1966, 1, 18; Brooks Penny, "Arvin Farm Workers Vote UFWOC," *The Movement* (December 1966): 4; "United Farm Workers: Chronological History," Box 9, Folder 11, Ross Papers.

27. Charles M. Payne, *I've Got the Light of Freedom: The Organizing Tradition and the Mississippi Freedom Struggle* (Berkeley: University of California Press, 1995), 368; Carson, *In Struggle*; Elizabeth Sutherland Martínez, interview by author, San Francisco CA, October 30, 2000; Miller, interview by author, December 20, 2003.

28. Miller, interview by author, February 19, 2004; "To Our Readers," *The Movement* (December 1966): 2; Cannon, interview by author, December 11, 2003; Ganz, interview by author, May 4, 2004; Ganz, interview by author, November 25, 2003.

29. María Varela, "My Sixties Was Not Drugs, Sex, and Rock and Roll," in *Hands on the Freedom Plow: The Untold Story of Women in SNCC*, ed. Faith Holsaert, et al. (Urbana: University of Illinois Press, 2010); Elizabeth Sutherland Martínez, "Black, White and Tan," June 1967, SNCC Papers, Reel 47; Martínez, telephone interview by author, October 30, 2000; María Varela, interview by author, November 11, 2000; Frye, interview by author, November 18, 2003.

30. Letter from Cesar Chavez to Denise F. Reeves, February 15, 1967, Box 4, Folder 22, UFWOC Collection; "Cesar Chavez: 'Nothing Has Changed,'" *The Movement* (April 1967): 6.

31. Lauren Araiza, "'In Common Struggle Against a Common Oppression': The United Farm Workers and the Black Panther Party, 1968–1973," *Journal of African American History* 94, no. 2 (2009).

FOUR

The Neighborhood Adult Participation Project

Black-Brown Strife in the War on Poverty in Los Angeles

ROBERT BAUMAN

On a warm September afternoon in 1966, a crowd of nearly fifty Mexican Americans carrying picket signs marched along 42nd Avenue and Avalon in South Central Los Angeles outside of the old Wrigley Field ballpark. The marchers targeted the offices of the Neighborhood Adult Participation Project (NAPP), an antipoverty program, and in particular the program's director, Opal Jones. One marcher, NAPP employee Bob Ramirez, told a reporter, "[U]ntil now it was the Negroes who used these tactics. Now we're picketing. And we're going to keep picketing until our problems are recognized." Another march participant and NAPP employee, Irene Tovar, later summed up some of the anger of the demonstrators: "[W]hat's good for Watts and the civil rights movement is not necessarily good for the Mexican-American community."[1]

In the 1960s, relationships between African Americans and Mexican Americans in Los Angeles in the War on Poverty proved volatile, at times explosive, and seldom fruitful. In particular, this chapter examines black-brown relations through the NAPP, a program of the Los Angeles city/county-controlled Community Action Agency (CAA) of the Economic and Youth

Opportunities Agency (EYOA). NAPP was the only EYOA program that emphasized citizen participation and it became embroiled in significant controversies, most centered on racial divisions and tensions between blacks and Mexican Americans. From the creation of NAPP, Mexican Americans questioned its racial configuration in terms of the location of most of the neighborhood centers, the numbers of Mexican American versus black employees, and the actions of NAPP's African American director Opal Jones. This interracial turmoil took place amidst burgeoning black power and Chicano movements in Los Angeles, both of which focused on community cultural and economic empowerment rather than interracial cooperation. Thus, many blacks and Chicanos involved in EYOA and NAPP saw each other as competitors rather than allies. NAPP, then, serves as a useful prism through which to view black-brown relations in Los Angeles during the War on Poverty in the 1960s.

Mexican Americans and African Americans in Los Angeles shared similar histories. Most of the forty-four founders of the Spanish pueblo of Los Angeles in 1781 were of African or Mexican origin, or both. Both black and Mexican communities eventually experienced segregation from the expanding white population, especially in the late nineteenth and early twentieth centuries. For members of both communities, jobs, housing, and education were restricted. For instance, the suburb of Glendale boasted in the 1920s that "no Negro ever sleeps overnight in our city." Indeed, a combination of racially restrictive covenants and real estate practices circumscribed blacks to the Central Avenue District and Watts, a residential area seven miles south of downtown Los Angeles, and Mexican Americans to East Los Angeles. Segregation in Los Angeles serves as a reminder that Jim Crow was a national phenomenon, not solely a southern issue.[2]

While both groups shared similar experiences of segregation and discrimination, African Americans and Mexican Americans also had a checkered past which vacillated between periods of tension interrupted by occasional attempts at interracial solidarity. Much of that distrust and tension came as a result of competition for jobs that began during World War II and continued through much of the remainder of the twentieth century. African Americans and Mexican Americans made several attempts at interracial coalitions through civil rights organizations, like the Southeast Interracial Council, the Council for Civic Unity, and the County Committee for Interracial Progress. Each of those organizations was short-lived, all failing due to anticommunist purges or strategic-political divisions between and within Mexican American and African American groups and members. Black activists in the early 1960s made another attempt at interracial cooperation with the formation of the Democratic Minority Conference. This effort also failed due to strategic and political differences between black and Mexican American leaders. When Mexican American city councilman Ed Roybal, who had served on the council since 1949, left after his election to Congress in 1962, he was replaced by Gilbert Lindsay, an African American. The replacement of the only Mexican American council member with an African American angered some Mexican Americans and added to growing distrust between the two groups.[3]

Recognizing the probable failure of interracial coalitions, African Americans refused to include Mexican Americans as members when they formed the all-black United Civil Rights Committee in 1963. This only added to tensions between the two groups. Responding to the conflict, the prominent Mexican American Congressman Ed Roybal and Leon Washington, African American newspaper publisher of the *Los Angeles Sentinel*, initiated a meeting of black and Mexican American leaders in November 1963. Both Washington and Roybal believed "it would be tragic if tension and conflict" escalated between blacks and Mexican Americans. Unfortunately for Roybal and

Washington, the meeting resulted in no agreement. In May 1965 the County Human Relations Commission reported significant tension between African Americans and Mexican Americans. Another study from that same period noted that only 16% of Mexican Americans supported a black-Chicano coalition. Those tensions and a sense of growing competition carried over from these civil rights organizations into the War on Poverty.[4]

It was in this period of racial flux and dynamism that the War on Poverty and NAPP materialized. President Lyndon Baines Johnson called for a "national war on poverty" in March 1964. In August of that year he signed the Economic Opportunity Act, which provided a number of programs to attack poverty in local communities throughout the nation. One of the key aspects of the legislation was the creation of Community Action Agencies (CAAs). These agencies, once established, could select the antipoverty programs they wanted to implement in their local communities. The EYOA, after a long, tumultuous battle, became the official CAA for the city and county of Los Angeles in August 1965.[5]

The city and county antipoverty efforts in Los Angeles actually predated the development of the EYOA. In 1963, a year prior to LBJ's declaration of a War on Poverty, Los Angeles City and County governments had joined together to form the Youth Opportunities Board (YOB). The YOB reflected a national movement, encouraged by the Kennedy administration and Congress that focused on the prevention of juvenile delinquency. YOB staff initially proposed NAPP to the OEO in November 1964 as an employment and on-the-job training program, while various groups in Los Angeles continued to battle over the creation of EYOA. YOB staff recruited Jones to head NAPP, which opened on April 1, 1965, in an office at Wrigley Field. NAPP became one of the few War on Poverty programs begun in Los Angeles prior to the creation of the War on Poverty and the revolt in Watts.[6]

The choice of Jones to head the new agency was both logical

and curious. Jones had worked as a social worker and headed the Avalon Community Center in South Central Los Angeles for several years prior to her selection to lead NAPP. She was intricately connected to the network of social service agencies in Los Angeles and actively participated in the Los Angeles Welfare Planning Council and the Los Angeles Area Federation of Settlements and Neighborhood Centers (LAAFSNC). Yet, Jones had adamantly opposed the creation of EYOA as the CAA for Los Angeles, fearing that Mayor Sam Yorty would control the agency and not allow significant participant of African Americans and other representatives of the poor in Los Angeles. Indeed, she held a meeting of social workers, civil rights activists, and others opposed to EYOA in her home in 1964. That group formed their own organization, the Economic Opportunity Federation (EOF), as a direct challenge to EYOA. Despite Jones's initial opposition to EYOA, however, YOB pursued her because of her years of experience. Jones signed on, in large part, because YOB promised her that community organizing would be central to the mission of NAPP.[7]

NAPP, as constructed by Jones and her staff, consisted of thirteen outposts, or offices. Each outpost served one of thirteen areas identified by the Los Angeles Welfare Planning Council as needing antipoverty programs and assistance. Each of the offices employed approximately thirty aides. NAPP aides were poor and unemployed residents who lived in the community in which they worked. Jones considered the employment of local residents a crucial part of the program, arguing that the direction of a community action program like NAPP had "to be done from the bottom up . . . rather than from the top down. . . . It [had] to come from the grass roots." Jones referred to NAPP aides as "change agents," because they would not only be employed by public or private agencies, but would also change the agency's traditional methods. Jones admitted that the notion of change agents was "frightening to the agencies," but, as she explained, NAPP was "only trying to bring them in closer touch with the grass roots." Some of those change agents served in schools as teacher aides and registered children for Head Start; others served as liaisons between the public and various government agencies; and three employees at each outpost worked as information aides. These employees went door to door in each neighborhood asking families about their needs, what changes they would like in their neighborhood, and how the community could work together to accomplish those changes. NAPP workers also provided adult education classes, conducted voter registration drives, and aided the unemployed in finding jobs.[8]

Jones's and NAPP's focus on community participation and organization stirred significant controversy and turmoil in early 1966. Indeed, EYOA director Joe Maldonado, who disagreed with Jones's focus on community activism, fired Jones in April. However, following objections from African American leaders like councilman Tom Bradley, Maldonado rehired her shortly thereafter. Jones had become well-acquainted with Bradley from her days at the Avalon Center and from various protests in which both had participated. Jones survived her controversial firing only to be surrounded by another controversy later that same year. This one revolved around interracial tensions and antagonisms within NAPP and in Los Angeles as a whole.[9]

While the controversy over citizen participation led to Jones's temporary firing and created significant turmoil within EYOA and NAPP, the issue of racial tension within the organization became the most important and volatile issue for Jones and NAPP. NAPP faced serious questions from Mexican Americans from its inception. Those initial concerns surrounded the racial configuration of NAPP's thirteen outposts. NAPP had located only three outposts in predominantly Mexican American neighborhoods and only these three were headed by Mexican American directors. Some Mexican Americans, then, questioned what they saw as underrepresentation of Mexican American communities among NAPP outposts.[10]

Mexican American leaders initially responded to the creation of the War on Poverty the way African Americans had; strategizing on how to bring much-needed resources to the communities they represented. After the Watts revolt in 1965, Mexican Americans became more determined to compete with African Americans for governmental programs and funds. Although Mexican American efforts to bring the programs of the War on Poverty to East Los Angeles should not be seen as, and were not, merely a reaction to black efforts, Mexican American groups clearly stepped up their attempts after Watts and the concomitant increase of federal money to black organizations. Leaders of traditional Mexican American civil rights organizations, like the League of United Latin American Citizens (LULAC), the American G.I. Forum, and the Mexican American Political Association (MAPA) hesitated to align with African Americans because they wanted to ensure that Mexican Americans received their share of War on Poverty programs. Some Mexican American leaders believed that African Americans were receiving more than their share of War on Poverty funds following the Watts revolt; that they obtained War on Poverty programs and funds because they rioted, not because they were deserving. On the other hand, Mexican Americans had not rioted and had received little from the federal government. As a result, LULAC president Alfred Hernandez argued that perhaps Mexican Americans "should resort to marches, sit-ins, and demonstrations." Roybal, who previously had attempted to create a black-brown coalition, complained to the OEO that they had a policy of "Negroes first," and that perhaps Mexican Americans would "have to riot to get attention." He also predicted racial violence in Los Angeles "unless something is done to indicate that the Mexican-American group is getting a good deal." Rudy Ramos, the lead attorney for the American G.I. Forum, complained that Mexican Americans in Los Angeles had lower incomes than blacks in Watts, yet Mexican Americans had received little War on Poverty funding. In September 1965 a group of Mexican American civil rights leaders sent a telegram to Sargent Shriver, the OEO director, asking him to investigate the distribution of War on Poverty programs in Los Angeles. One of the purposes of the investigation, they argued, would be "to bring a halt to the rising bitter feelings of the Mexican-American in the streets that antipoverty funds and job opportunities are going principally to Negroes."[11]

While established Mexican American civil rights leaders and organizations argued for a more equitable distribution of War on Poverty resources, Mexican American youths began to organize around themes of self-determination and community control. In 1966, inspired by the War on Poverty's focus on community action, a group of young Mexican Americans led by Vickie Castro formed Young Citizens for Community Action, which later became Young Chicanos for Community Action (YCCA). Two years later YCCA became the Brown Berets, an organization emphasizing group empowerment and cultural nationalism. They represented the beginnings of the nascent Chicano movement in Los Angeles. Focused on community control and self-definition, most Chicano nationalist organizations looked to strengthen their neighborhoods and communities economically, politically, and culturally. Because of racially segregated housing, those neighborhoods and communities were overwhelmingly Mexican American. Focusing on community control, then, almost necessarily meant a focus on a separate Chicano economic, political, and cultural power. The segregated realities of their existence and the separatist economic and cultural ideology of the Chicano movement, then, led groups such as the Brown Berets away from working across racial lines with African Americans.[12]

These interracial conflicts spilled over into NAPP and became a central issue for Jones. Already-existing concerns from Mexican Americans about NAPP escalated to widespread antagonism in September 1966 when Jones fired Gabriel Yánez, the Mexican American director of the NAPP outpost in the historically Mexican American community of Boyle Heights. Jones informed Yánez that she was terminating him for "failure to give cooperation in the project and to follow the leadership and accept the supervision of the Project Director" and because he had been "a very negative element" in NAPP. Jones argued that Yánez had instructed his aides not to attend meetings called by her and had discouraged residents in Boyle Heights from involvement in NAPP because it favored African Americans. More important, according to Jones, Yánez had contributed to, and exacerbated, divisions between Mexican Americans and African Americans both within NAPP and in Los Angeles as a whole. In essence, Jones fired Yánez for insubordination, for refusing to follow some of her directives, and for creating or increasing tensions between blacks and Mexican Americans within NAPP. Ironically, Jones's firing of Yánez intensified black-brown tensions and triggered the protest outside NAPP headquarters mentioned at the beginning of this chapter. That protest clearly pitted blacks and Mexicans Americans against each other, as competitors within NAPP specifically and in the greater Los Angeles area more generally.[13]

Jones initially defended her firing of Yánez and responded to the picket signs and protests by arguing that she had received a number of complaints about Yánez's hostile and condescending attitude towards NAPP workers, particularly African Americans. Indeed, Jones wrote a memo to Isobel Clark, the African American executive director of the LAAFSNC, which the EYOA had designated to oversee NAPP. In her memo to Clark, Jones argued that the "*real* issues" were "being obscured in a wave of emotionalism which focuses on the Negro-Mexican-American relationship question and the allocation of War on Poverty funds between the two communities." She informed Clark that she fired Yánez because he "was actively pushing for a widening of the schism between the Mexican-American and Negro poverty communities." Indeed, Jones had written a scathing rebuke to Yánez three months earlier in June, castigating him for his "attitude of hostility and non-cooperation" toward herself and others in NAPP. She also reminded Clark and informed her Mexican American critics that she had organized the NAPP outposts based on a Welfare Planning Council study of the pockets of poverty in Los Angeles. In other words, the reason black neighborhoods had received more outposts was a result of that study, not any prejudice of hers against Mexican Americans. As a result of the protests by Mexican Americans, Jones offered to divide NAPP outposts more equally between black and Latino neighborhoods. Ironically, this move to calm tensions angered black NAPP staff members, who already felt threatened by challenges from Mexican Americans. She closed her memo to Clark arguing that "despite the fact that there are those who claim that the program discriminates against others in favor of the Negro community, an objective analysis of the facts will prove this is not true."[14]

Jones's memo to Clark was not effective. Due to continued protests by Mexican Americans and at the insistence of Clark and the Federation of Settlements board of directors, Jones rehired Yánez a few days after her memo to Clark. This was not enough to quell the anger of some Mexican Americans. Irene Tovar resigned in protest over Yánez's firing, stating that she could "no longer work within the framework of NAPP." Despite Yánez's rehiring, Tovar refused to return to NAPP and expressed the sentiments of many Mexican Americans in Los Angeles when she commented that what benefited blacks did "not necessarily" help Mexican Americans. In other words, Tovar not only believed that different strategies and antipoverty programs would redress the wrongs Mexican Americans experienced; she also saw blacks and Mexican Americans as competitors more than potential allies. In addition, Yánez's reinstatement angered some African American NAPP aides who agreed with Opal Jones and believed that Yánez harbored prejudice against blacks. The Jones-Yánez controversy had become a black versus Mexican American conflict. Resulting tensions continued to create turmoil within NAPP long after Yánez was rehired.[15]

The issue of Mexican American representation in NAPP dominated the correspondence, meeting minutes, and agendas of NAPP, the Federation of Settlements, and EYOA from late 1966 through 1967. Mexican Americans consistently complained to Clark that NAPP needed to be more representative. In her bimonthly report for September-October 1966, Clark noted that "crucial issues, relative to ethnic group participation and representation in federally funded programs continue to create problems primarily among the Mexican-American constituents of NAPP, Teen Post and Head Start projects." The board of directors of the Federation of Settlements and Neighborhood Centers described NAPP as having "grave problems" related to tensions between blacks and Mexican Americans. At the December meeting of the EYOA-NAPP Project Committee, Jones raised concerns about a "major confrontation with the Mexican-American community and the Negro community" over the issue of representation within NAPP. The following month, the Federation of Settlements board of directors again expressed concern with the "implementation of the number of Mexican Americans participating in NAPP" and offered "assistance to [the] Project director in funding and hiring Mexican Americans."[16]

Another incident in the spring of 1967 recalled the Yánez firing and controversy and demonstrated that interracial conflicts continued to haunt NAPP and Jones. In May 1967 Jones fired Mrs. Hernandez, a NAPP aide, for being "bigoted against Negroes."[17] Once again, Mexican Americans within NAPP protested, and as with Gabriel Yánez, Jones reinstated Hernandez, which again led to disgruntled African American employees. Clearly, African Americans and Mexican Americans in NAPP tended to see each other as competitors, not colleagues. Chicano NAPP employees did not trust Jones. As a black woman heading an interracial organization in the late 1960s, Jones could not please her Chicano employees. On-the-job conflicts and personnel issues, whether initially racial in nature or not, became racially charged at NAPP. Anytime Jones fired a Mexican American employee, Chicanos protested and claimed racial discrimination, and if she relented, as in both the Yánez and Hernandez cases, black employees objected. In May and June, Jones and other NAPP staffers met with representatives of the Mexican American United Council of Community Organizations (UCCO) to discuss the "imbalance" of representation of Mexican Americans as NAPP aides. Jones committed NAPP to hiring more Mexican American aides, but she reported in June that the relatively low number of Mexican Americans in NAPP remained "a continual problem" for the agency. She also noted that she was attending "many meetings and conferences . . . to involve more Mexican Americans" in NAPP.[18]

Congressman Roybal became directly involved in the effort to increase Mexican American interest and numbers in NAPP and in the War on Poverty as a whole. In a note to a Mexican American NAPP employee, Roybal wrote that the situation surrounding the Gabriel Yánez firing was "unfortunate," but stated "[i]t did . . . bring to the forefront a troublesome problem of longstanding, as well as highlight the many inequities which should have been resolved long ago." Roybal was disturbed both by the ongoing and escalating tensions between African Americans and Mexican Americans in Los Angeles and also by the small number of outposts in Mexican American neighborhoods. He wrote to NAPP employee Paul Ramirez, indicating that he hoped "to correct" the lack of NAPP outposts in Mexican American neighborhoods, and that he hoped "through the cooperation of all concerned, the Mexican-American community will eventually receive the attention due them in the anti-poverty war."[19]

Roybal actively pursued a dual strategy of ensuring the creation of NAPP outposts in Mexican American neighborhoods and efforts at interracial cooperation. In October 1966 he met with African American U.S. Representative George Brown, Isobel Clark, and Opal Jones to discuss Mexican American complaints and to work toward interracial cooperation in NAPP. In October 1967 Roybal and Congressmen Hawkins and Brown, along with Bert Corona, president of the MAPA, met with Jones to plan the implementation of increased Mexican American representation in NAPP. The following year Roybal and Corona visited Jones at NAPP headquarters. Jones later wrote Roybal, "[I]t was like our old association back at the Avalon Center. . . . I am glad that we were able to be together again after our years of absence." She also expressed her recognition of "the importance of our teamwork and cooperation together, for that will be the only way that we will make it." Jones, Roybal, and others continued to work at increasing Mexican American involvement in NAPP and at trying to make interracialism work. But, in the late 1960s in Los Angeles, clearly any efforts at interracial cooperation through civil rights or War on Poverty organizations faced significant challenges.[20]

Indeed, the EYOA itself was continually in turmoil due to interracial tensions between African Americans and Mexican Americans, primarily over hiring practices. In 1968 only 37 of EYOA's 260 staff members were Mexican American, while 100 were black. Mexican Americans consistently protested what they saw as EYOA's unfair hiring practices. In October 1971, 50 Latino employees walked off the job, accusing EYOA of bias. Congressman Roybal continued his efforts, writing a letter to the EYOA board of directors and claiming that the "walkout of Mexican American workers has raised serious legal and moral issues dealing with racial equity at EYOA." He also warned OEO acting director Phil Sánchez that waiting to do anything "would be a dangerous mistake, and an act of negligence." He further urged Sánchez "to intervene so that racial equity can be obtained and a most serious confrontation between these two groups [blacks and Latinos] prevented." Roybal's efforts at the time failed—EYOA fired the employees in November. After months of protests, however, EYOA rehired the employees in April 1972.[21]

The growing Chicano movement significantly influenced efforts to increase Mexican American representation in EYOA, NAPP, and all War on Poverty programs. In 1971 representatives from the Congress of Mexican American Unity and the Chicano Caucus, reflecting the community-control ideology of the Chicano movement, wrote to OEO demanding direct funding to Chicano organizations that served the poor. They argued that the EYOA had "seriously shortchanged the Chicano poor in its allocation of resources." They also charged that "without a total rearrangement of the EYOA power relationships, something which would cause great friction and conflict between the Chicano and the Black communities and is therefore not a worthwhile effort, we cannot get equity in funding, in attention, or in treatment." Arguing that they were "stung by the repeated and continuing insensitivity of . . . EYOA to the special needs of the Mexican-American poor," these Chicano activists lobbied for the creation of Chicano War on Poverty organizations and increased funding to already existing Chicano antipoverty agencies.[22]

At the same time, African Americans organized to meet any challenges from Mexican Americans involving War on Poverty programs. Congressman Gus Hawkins called a meeting of black leaders "to consider the best strategy for coping with the many attacks being made by Mexican Americans against agencies led by blacks." The idea for the meeting came from Hawkins's assistant Charles Knox, who wrote Hawkins that "unless black leaders confront brown leaders with our understanding of what they are doing and its ill effects the problem will mushroom beyond repair. . . . Obviously [Ed Roybal] is having difficulty in rationally handling the pressure by the radical elements in his community." This group of African American leaders, including Jones, met twice in 1972, with interracial strife at EYOA being the focal point of their lengthy discussions. So, while Jones steadily worked toward interracial cooperation in NAPP, she was also part of a group that wanted to make sure that any Mexican American gains did not result in African American losses.[23]

Later in 1972 the OEO reorganized EYOA into the Greater Los Angeles Community Action Agency (GLACAA), but the reorganization did not decrease racial tensions within the organization. In 1974 the Chicano Coalition, directed by Irene Tovar, the former NAPP aide who had resigned in the Gabriel Yánez controversy, charged GLACAA with being "as ineffective as was EYOA" in terms of hiring Mexican Americans. Indeed, only 25 percent of GLACAA employees were Mexican American, while 44 percent were black. In addition, the Chicano Coalition initiated a lawsuit against GLACAA for its failure to fund projects in Mexican American neighborhoods. The lawsuit alleged that GLACAA was "not only incapable of equitably administering social service programs, as they affect the Chicano community, but also seriously discriminates in its hiring and promotional patterns." In 1975 GLACAA and the Chicano Coalition settled the lawsuit with GLACAA agreeing to a 35 percent Latino workforce by 1977.[24]

Despite the settlement, interracial disputes continued to burden GLACAA until its demise in 1978. With the death of GLACAA, the official government-agency-controlled War on Poverty in Los Angeles ended. In reality, though, African Americans and Mexican Americans had already shifted their focus to the development of community-controlled antipoverty organizations based in their own neighborhoods. These organizations, like the Watts Labor Community Action Committee (WLCAC), the East Los Angeles Community Union (TELACU), and the Chicana Service Action Center (CSAC) were formed in black and brown neighborhoods by African American and Chicano/a activists who sought to use the framework of the War on Poverty to expand the opportunities of African Americans and Chicanos/as in Los Angeles. Important, they were community-controlled and racially/ethnically exclusive. They were African American or Chicano antipoverty organizations and the racial/ethnic identity proved to be an important part of how those organizations defined themselves. Those organizations all remained active into the twenty-first century, long after the demise of EYOA/GLACAA.[25]

The failure of EYOA/GLACAA and the creation and endurance of the community-controlled organizations reflected the divisions between African Americans and Chicanos in Los Angeles. African Americans tended to view the War on Poverty, especially its community-action aspect, as a logical extension of the democratization of American society initiated by the black civil rights movement. In addition, as the ideology of Black Power became more influential in the second half of the 1960s, African Americans demonstrated an unwillingness to align themselves with any other racial or ethnic group. At the same time, Mexican-origin people comprised a larger percentage of the population in Los Angeles, and many believed they should have an increased share of War on Poverty programs. Their growing population and burgeoning cultural and political activism led some Chicanos to demand more programs and services from the local War on Poverty. In addition, the increasingly active Chicano movement in Los Angeles led Mexican Americans to seek antipoverty programs they could control in their communities.

This interracial animosity and emphasis on racial/ethnic separatism was most clearly expressed in the War on Poverty in Los Angeles, primarily through EYOA and NAPP. The only EYOA program that incorporated multiethnic poor residents, NAPP, struggled throughout its existence with racial divisiveness. Whether it was over the number and location of NAPP outposts or the number and ethnicity of NAPP aides, NAPP and EYOA became the chief battlegrounds between African Americans informed by Black Power and Mexican Americans influenced by the emerging Chicano movement. Although some African American and Mexican American leaders attempted to cross that racial divide and create interracial alliances using the framework established by the War on Poverty, those attempts were limited and largely fell short of their goals. Instead, both African Americans and Chicanos proceeded separately, going outside the EYOA to use the ideals of the War on Poverty to advance the cause of the black and Chicano freedom struggles. Indeed, the failure of interracialism through EYOA, GLACAA, and NAPP led to the creation of independent, ethnically nationalist antipoverty agencies in African American and Mexican American neighborhoods in Los Angeles. In the 1960s and 1970s in Los Angeles, many African Americans and Chicanos chose economic and cultural nationalism over interracialism in the War on Poverty.

Attempts at interracialism and conflicts between blacks and Latinos achieved prominent attention again in Los Angeles in the first decade of the twenty-first century. In 2001 Antonio Villaraigosa failed in his attempt to become the city's first Latino mayor in well over a century. He lost in large part because of his poor showing among black voters, who gave 80 percent of their votes to Villaraigosa's opponent, James Hahn, the son of Kenneth Hahn who had championed black causes on the Los Angeles County Board of Supervisors for decades. In addition to supporting Hahn because of his family legacy, many blacks voted against Villaraigosa due to their fear and suspicion of Latinos. Key black politicians, like representative Maxine Waters, feared that a Villaraigosa victory would cost blacks political power.[26]

Four years later the story had a different ending, indicating some of the possibilities of interracial cooperation and coalition. In 2005 Villaraigosa was elected mayor, this time with significant support from certain sectors of the black community (including endorsements from representative Waters and city councilman

Bernard Parks, who were angry with Hahn for his ousting of Parks from the office of chief of police). Indeed, Villaraigosa doubled his portion of the black vote from 20 to 40 percent. At the same time many blacks opposed Villaraigosa's election, with a majority still voting for Hahn, and Villaraigosa's campaign at times exacerbated tensions between blacks and Latinos.[27]

That same year, black and Latino students at Jefferson High School in South Central Los Angeles battled during lunch-time, and interracial fights erupted at other Los Angeles-area high schools in the days afterward. The fight at Jefferson High School seems to have been related to changing racial and geo-graphic boundaries. In the 1960s Jefferson High was a predom-inantly black high school; by 2005 it was 92 percent Latino. As the racial, demographic, and geographic landscapes shift again in Los Angeles in the early twenty-first century, the region will continue to experience episodes of both interracial conflict and cooperation, much as it did in the 1960s and 1970s when black and Chicano residents challenged and changed racial definitions and boundaries.

Notes

1. Art Berman, "Latin-American Quits Antipoverty Job in a Row," *Los Angeles Times* (hereafter LAT), September 16, 1966, I-32. For an extended discussion of NAPP and the controversies surrounding it, see Robert Bau-man, *Race and the War on Poverty: From Watts to East L.A.* (Norman: University of Oklahoma Press, 2008), especially chap. 3.

2. On segregation of African Americans and Mexican Americans in Los Angeles, see Leonard and Dale Pitt, *Los Angeles A to Z: An Encyclopedia of the City and County* (Berkeley: University of California Press, 1997), 263; and Lawrence B. De Graaf, "The City of Black Angels: Emergence of the Los Angeles Ghetto, 1890–1930," *Pacific Historical Review* 39, no. 3 (1970): 328. Racial segregation of African Americans and Mexican Americans per-meated the American West. See, for example, Quintard Taylor, *In Search of the Racial Frontier: African Americans in the American West, 1528–1990* (New York: Norton, 1998); and Robert Bauman, "Jim Crow in the Tri-Cit-ies, 1943–1950," *Pacific Northwest Quarterly* 96, no. 3 (2005): 124–30.

3. Edward Banfield, *Big City Politics* (New York: Random House, 1965), 87–90; Benjamin Marquez, LULAC: *The Evolution of a Mexican American Political Organization* (Austin: University of Texas Press, 1993), 7.

4. John A. Buggs to Alex Garcia, September 1963, Ed Roybal Papers, Box 19, Folder 24–"Discrimination, Human Relations," California State University, Los Angeles, Special Collections Library (hereafter CSLA). See also Gerald Horne, *Fire This Time: The Watts Uprising and the 1960s* (Charlottesville: University of Virginia Press, 2005), 102, 260–61; Josh Sides, "Rethinking Black Migration: A Perspective from the West," in *Moving Stories: Migration and the American West 1850–2000*, ed. Scott E. Caspar and Lucinda M. Long (Reno: Nevada Humanities Commission, 2001), 204–8; Kevin Allen Leonard, *The Battle for Los Angeles: Racial Ideology and World War II* (Albuquerque: University of New Mexico Press, 2006), 311, 326–27; Charles P. Henry, "Black-Chicano Coalitions: Possibilities and Problems," *Western Journal of Black Studies* 4, no. 4 (1980): 222–32; and Juan Gómez-Quiñones, *Chicano Politics: Reality and Promise, 1940–1990* (Albuquerque: University of New Mexico Press, 1990), 95.

5. Lyndon Baines Johnson, *Public Papers of the Presidents, Lyndon B. Johnson*, Vol. 1 (Washington DC: Government Printing Office, 1963–64), 125. For more on the battle over EYOA, see Bauman, *Race and the War on Poverty*, especially chaps. 1 and 2.

6. For more on anti-juvenile delinquency efforts during the Kennedy administration, see Bauman, *Race and the War on Poverty*, chap. 1. See also, NAPP Progress Report, August 1, 1965, NAPP Records, Box 3, California Social Welfare Archives, Specialized Libraries and Archival Collections, University of Southern California (hereafter USC); and "NAPP Now: An Explanation of the Neighborhood Adult Participation Project," NAPP Records, Box 1, USC.

7. "NAPP Now," NAPP Records, Box 1, USC.

8. NAPP Progress Report, August 1, 1965, NAPP Records, Box 3, USC; NAPP Annual Report, 1966, LAAFSNC Records, Box 2, USC; "NAPP Now," NAPP Records, Box 1, USC; Jack Jones, "Opal Jones Mellows as Poverty Project Grows," *LAT*, March 30, 1967; "NAPP Fights Poverty with Total Grass-Roots Approach," *Los Angeles Sentinel* (hereafter LAS), June 10, 1965, 10A.

9. For more on Jones's firing, see Bauman, *Race and the War on Poverty*, 53–58.

10. Opal Jones, "The Mexican Americans in NAPP," n.d., NAPP Records, Box 3, USC.

11. Hernandez is quoted in Julie Leininger Pycior, *LBJ and Mexican Americans: The Paradox of Power* (Austin: University of Texas Press, 1997), 163. The Roybal quotes are from Andy Hilton to Sargent Shriver, October 14, 1965, Boutin Papers, Box 3, "FA California" Lyndon Baines Johnson Library (LBJL). The telegram is quoted in Jack Jones, "Irate Mexican-American Units Demand Poverty War Equality," *LAT*, September 25, 1966, A3. See also Rodolfo F. Acuña, *A Community Under Siege: A Chronicle of Chicanos East of the Los Angeles River, 1945–1975* (Los Angeles: Chicano Studies Research Center, University of California, Los Angeles, 1984), 132–33; Pycior, *LBJ and Mexican Americans*, 153–63, and Henry, "Black-Chicano Coalitions," 222–32.

12. Ernesto Chávez, *¡Mi Raza Primero!: Nationalism, Identity, and Insurgency in the Chicano Movement in Los Angeles, 1966–1978* (Berkeley: University of California Press, 2005), 43–47; and Ian F. Haney López, *Racism on Trial: The Chicano Fight for Justice* (Cambridge MA: Harvard University Press, 2003), 178–82.

13. Opal Jones to Gabriel Yánez, September 8, 1966, NAPP Records, Box 3, USC; and "Opal Jones Fires Aide for 'Ineffectiveness,'" *LAS*, September 6, 1966, A1, A3.

14. Opal Jones to Isobel C. Clark, September 26, 1966, and Opal Jones to Gabriel Yánez, June 10, 1966, both NAPP) Records, Box 3, USC; Art Berman, "Latin-American Quits Antipoverty Job in a Row," *LAT*, September 16, 1966, I-32.

15. Irene Tovar's career was just beginning. She was a member of the Chicano Moratorium Committee which organized to oppose the Vietnam War in 1970 and later served on the Los Angeles County Civil Service Commission and as Special Assistant to California Governor Jerry Brown. Jones, "Irate Mexican-American Units."

16. NAPP Project Committee minutes, October 19, 1966, NAPP Records, Box 3, USC; NAPP Project Committee minutes, December 7, 1966, EYOA Records, Box 1, USC; LAAFSNC, Executive Director's Report, September-October 1966, LAAFSNC Records, Box 2, USC; LAAFSNC Board of Directors Meeting Minutes, October 20, 1966, November 17, 1966, and January 19, 1967, all LAAFSNC Records, Box 2, USC.

17. Mrs. Hernandez's first name remains unclear.

18. LAAFSNC Board of Directors Meeting Minutes, May 18, 1967 and June 15, 1967, LAAFSNC Records, Box 1, USC; NAPP Quarterly Report, April-June 1967, NAPP Records, Box 1, USC.

19. Roybal to Paul Ramirez, October 5, 1966, Roybal Papers, Box 193, Folder 25, CSLA.

20. Roybal to Sarah Taylor, October 20, 1967, and Jones to Roybal, August 21, 1968, both Roybal Papers, Box 190, CSLA.

21. Roybal to EYOA Board of Directors, October 8, 1971, and Roybal to Phil Sánchez, October 8, 1971, both Roybal Papers, Box 192, CSLA; EYOA Board Minutes, June 1, 1969, Augustus F. Hawkins Papers, UCLA; Acuña, *A Community Under Siege*, 185, 219–20; Robert Kistler, "Chaos Follows Conference on 'Harmony' in EYOA program," *LAT*, April 29, 1972, II-1, 8.

22. Esteban Torres and Richard Martinez, Congress of Mexican-American Unity to OEO, January 15, 1971; David Lizarraga, Chicano Caucus to OEO, January 11, 1971; and David Lizarraga to Congressman Carl Perkins, February 16, 1971, all Roybal Papers, Box 191, CSLA.

23. Knox to Hawkins, November 17, 1971; Knox to Lorenzo Taylor, March 17, 1972; and Knox to Virna Canson, September 21, 1972, all Hawkins Papers, Box 96, UCLA.

24. Chicano Coalition Press Release, March 8, 1974; Chicano Coalition Meeting Minutes, May 30, 1974; John Serrano, Chair of Chicano Coalition to Supervisor Baxter Ward, June 7, 1974; and Chicano Coalition Press Release, October 29, 1974; all Roybal Papers, Box 37, CSLA; and "County Poverty Unit Settles Suit Charging Bias," *LAT*, June 2, 1975, I-30.

25. For more on these organizations, see Bauman, *Race and the War on Poverty*, especially chaps. 4–6.

26. Nicolás C. Vaca. *The Presumed Alliance: The Unspoken Conflict between Latinos and Blacks and What It Means for America* (New York: HarperCollins, 2004), 85–107.

27. "Progressive City leaders," *The Nation*, June 18, 2005, 18–19.

FIVE

"Mexican versus Negro Approaches" to the War on Poverty

Black-Brown Competition and the Office of Economic Opportunity in Texas

WILLIAM CLAYSON

As early as 1965, the Office of Economic Opportunity (OEO), the agency charged with fighting President Lyndon Johnson's War on Poverty, employed affirmative action to preempt criticism of racial bias or exclusion. Bill Crook, the head of the OEO's Southwest Regional Office in Austin, prioritized placing minorities in high-profile positions. Crook hired an African American, Herbert Tyson, as deputy director and a Mexican American, Tom Robles, as regional manager of the Community Action Program (CAP), the OEO's largest effort. Crook felt that hiring these two men "would fill our top three spots with an Anglo [himself], Negro, and Mexican American . . . while this wouldn't be the most popular thing [in Texas], it is something that I would like to do."[1] The OEO also required that each regional office submit a monthly "Minority Gap Report" to the agency's headquarters in Washington. The report detailed how many members of minority groups worked for each regional office. By November 1968 the Southwest Region employed fifty-six members of minority groups out of a total of 217 employees, including twenty-three African Americans, twenty-eight Mexican Americans, four American Indians, and one "Oriental-American."[2]

The use of affirmative action policies, long before they became a divisive political issue, illustrates the significance of race to the history of the War on Poverty. As the OEO groped for solutions to alleviate poverty, the agency also had to wrestle with the complex race politics of the 1960s. Both unrepentant racism and the reluctance of low-income whites to become involved in antipoverty programs created insurmountable political obstacles for the OEO. But competition over limited funding among nonwhites also hindered the War on Poverty.

Unexpected difficulties like race competition stymied the OEO, an agency already overwhelmed by the Great Society's lofty ambitions. Lyndon Johnson charged his antipoverty warriors with nothing less than ending poverty in the United States. Rather than a cure for poverty, however, the OEO primarily generated controversy, particularly in the agency's main local effort: the CAP. Conservatives viewed the OEO as, at best, another expensive layer of federal bureaucracy and, at worst, an attempt to extend the civil rights agenda into economic policy. The Johnson administration expected this, but failed to foresee the divide the War on Poverty created among liberals. Mayors and governors complained that the OEO, through local Community Action Agencies (CAAs), funded civil rights groups and radical community activists in battles against local political establishments, including those run by Democrats allied with LBJ. At the same time, the militant agenda shifted the ideological bent of the civil rights movement away from an emphasis on integration toward one of self-determination and cultural identity, leading both black and Mexican American groups to criticize the OEO's effort to make the War on Poverty a "colorblind" fight. Black and brown leaders demanded control of local OEO programs within their own communities and without interference from even well-intentioned outsiders. Competition for OEO funding, in short, pitted groups within the liberal coalition against one another, injuring the spirit of consensus that had ushered Johnson into the White House in 1964.[3]

Historical memory tends toward a romantic view of the sixties, when those left outside the affluent society joined together to fight the white establishment. The history of the War on Poverty suggests that racial identity trumped black-brown solidarity in regard to race politics in the era. An analysis of OEO programs in Texas reveals that tensions emerged between African Americans and Mexican Americans as legal barriers to racial equality collapsed in the 1960s. An increasing proportion of the Mexican American population concluded that their values and the practical needs of their communities often conflicted with those of blacks. Latino leaders also took exception with the assumption that they merely followed the lead of blacks in civil rights struggles. After all, *Delgado v. Bastrop ISD* came before *Brown v. Board of Education*. Similarly, as the Mexican American population poised to surpass African Americans as the nation's largest minority, many black leaders came to view Mexican Americans as a threat to their political agenda and the economic betterment of their communities. As OEO programs expanded in Texas, leaders from both groups vied for limited funds. Mexican American leaders complained that the Johnson administration had all but ignored the chronic poverty of the barrios due to the president's overarching concern with black poverty. Although the OEO made special efforts to include Mexican Americans, such feelings of neglect remained and continued to inform memory of the War on Poverty long after the OEO faded away. In major cities in the state, a similar pattern emerged in which the smaller minority, be it African Americans in San Antonio or Mexican Americans in Houston, complained of neglect from local CAAs which seemed focused on the concerns of the larger group.[4]

On the level of national policy, it is important to understand that OEO director Sargent Shriver and his staff made an intensive effort to disassociate the War on Poverty and the black civil rights movement, an effort that ultimately failed. A "colorblind" war on poverty was necessary both for political reasons and principle. Johnson and his antipoverty team recognized that any federal program that explicitly targeted minorities would be politically unacceptable, both South and North. The antipoverty warriors also insisted on the colorblind principle to keep faith with the egalitarian ideals of postwar liberalism. From their perspective, the Economic Opportunity Act (EOA), the War on Poverty's enabling legislation, would tear down economic barriers to equality as the Civil Rights Act tore down barriers based on race.[5]

Shriver and his staff went to great lengths to portray the OEO as colorblind. For example, in an address to the NAACP the director went so far as to emphasize that "80 percent of the poor people in America are white."[6] Although civil rights groups ranked among the strongest supporters of the EOA, Johnson and Shriver did not solicit input from such organizations in drafting the legislation. The experience of Adam Yarmolinsky, Shriver's assistant, helps illustrate the OEO effort to maintain its distance from the civil rights movement. In order to assure lawmakers and the public that the poverty program "was in no sense a help-the-blacks program," Yarmolinsky recalled weaving into speeches the slogan that "most poor people are not black, most black people are not poor." "Of all the people involved in the civil rights business," he explained, "none of them were involved in this business."[7] Ironically, however, Shriver removed Yarmolinsky as his assistant as part of the effort to disassociate civil rights from the antipoverty fight. A former Defense Department official, Yarmolinsky had a record as a defender of civil rights. While working for Secretary of Defense Robert McNamara, for example, Yarmolinksy had ordered segregated housing off-limits to troops stationed in the South. LBJ sent Yarmolinsky back to the Department of Defense, but his removal from the number two position in Shriver's office sent a clear message: the OEO was no place for civil rights activists.[8]

Despite the OEO's best efforts to present the War on Poverty as colorblind, both opponents and supporters continued to view it as a "help the blacks" program. Southern Democrats regarded the War on Poverty as an extension of the Civil Rights Act. When one of LBJ's spokesmen went to Representative Wilbur Mills of Arkansas to ask support for the Economic Opportunity Act, Mills threw the proposal across the room and said that "he was not going to be involved in any program to help a bunch of niggers."[9] In the OEO southerners foresaw, according to Taylor Branch, "integrated job training programs, newfangled Head Start classes, perhaps even federal grants to the NAACP."[10] Supporters also categorized the OEO as a program primarily directed at African Americans. Many liberals considered an emphasis on black poverty necessary to realize the goals of the civil rights movement. As economist Ben Seligman pointed out in 1968, "it would not be far off the mark to say that it was necessary to convert a civil rights movement into a War on Poverty."[11]

The association between the War on Poverty and black civil rights also persisted because of OEO policy. To address complaints of discrimination in local programs, in March 1965 Shriver created an Office of Civil Rights directed by Samuel Yette, a former *Ebony* magazine editor. According to Shriver, Yette's appointment came in response to "questions that have been raised in the press and elsewhere concerning equal employment in the OEO."[12] A year later, Shriver also appointed seven "civil rights coordinators" for each of the OEO regions. Gregorio Coronado, an attorney who served as the Equal Employment Opportunity Commission compliance officer in Lubbock, became the OEO civil rights coordinator for the Southwest Regional Office in Austin.[13] After Shriver appointed the regional coordinators, civil rights issues became central to OEO policy at the local level. Compliance with the Civil Rights Act and the inclusion of representatives of minority groups in proportion to each community's population had been a guideline for the OEO's CAPs from the beginning. By 1966, however, the regional civil rights coordinators, who were responsible only to Yette and Shriver, could deny the approval or continuation of CAP grants if local organizations failed a "civil rights clearance."[14] With such policies in place, Yarmolinsky later recalled, "by '65, '66, OEO was, if not a black, a very dark gray agency, and when we were putting it together it hadn't the faintest touch of gray tinge to it."[15]

More than anyone else, President Johnson himself created the association between the War on Poverty and the black civil rights movement. Johnson demonstrated a commitment to civil rights that few southern politicians shared. In the Senate, only Johnson and Tennesseans Estes Kefauver and Albert Gore Sr. refused to sign the Southern Manifesto in response to the *Brown* case.[16] As president, Johnson coordinated the passage of the two most important civil rights laws passed in the twentieth century: the Civil Rights Act of 1964 and the Voting Rights Act of 1965. The fact that Congress passed LBJ's Economic Opportunity Act of 1964 in the same legislative season created a natural association with the War on Poverty and federal civil rights initiatives, most of which were targeted at African Americans. Johnson further confirmed the connection between poverty and black civil rights in his highly publicized 1965 commencement address at Howard University:

> You do not take a person who, for years, has been hobbled by chains and liberate him, bring him up to the starting line of a race and then say, "You are free to compete with all the others," and still justly believe that you have been completely fair. Thus it is not enough just to open the gates of opportunity. All our citizens must have the ability to walk through those gates. This is the next and the more profound stage of the battle for civil rights. We seek not just legal equity but human ability, not just equality as a right and a theory, but equality as a fact and equality as a result.

The Howard address in the minds of many clearly linked the struggle for black equality and antipoverty efforts. As one scholar put it, "what seemed like a reasonable, fair, and even moderate statement would not be taken as such" by civil rights activists.[17] With the Howard address, according to historian Gareth Davies, Johnson publicly acknowledged for the first time "that blacks, as a group, confronted obstacles that precluded their advance as individuals."[18]

The OEO staff continued to fight against the perception of black bias throughout the decade. For example, the Job Corps publicized "The Ten Biggest Myths About the OEO" to dissociate the OEO from black civil rights. These myths included the belief that "Job Corps serves only Negroes," though 54 percent of Corpsmen were African American.[19] Because Americans in the 1960s associated the term "civil rights," as in the Office of Civil Rights, with blacks, Yette's assistant Harvey Friedman suggested changing the name of the Office of Civil Rights to dilute the association between the movement and the War on Poverty. Friedman stated that "due to the extreme hostility manifested in many southern communities by the words 'civil rights,' we [should] change the name of our office from civil rights to something less antagonistic, such as Division of Equal Opportunity."[20] Friedman's efforts notwithstanding, a bias toward African Americans remained a basic misconception of the OEO throughout its history.

One other reason why the OEO was often considered a "help the blacks" program involved the agency's focus on urban poverty.[21] Despite the fact that the EOA was drafted before the Watts riot, a common assumption among contemporaries was that the OEO targeted urban blacks in order to prevent riots. Jerome Vacek of Navarro County Community Action complained to Senator Ralph Yarborough that his program and other rural programs in South Texas had been cast aside because of the fear of riots. Vacek informed Yarborough that rural War on Poverty activists "resent the use of [OEO funds] to cool demonstration in the hot cities. . . . The big cities hog far more than their share of OEO funds."[22] In reality, big cities received more OEO funding because they had larger concentrations of poor people. Urban governments and organizations also had the staff and expertise to develop CAAs.[23] While rural antipoverty activists like Vacek resented the OEO's focus on the "hot cities," Mexican Americans complained that the black bias of the OEO excluded them from the War on Poverty altogether.

Mexican Americans faulted the administration's preoccupation with black poverty for the Great Society's general neglect of their community. When, in the wake of riots in 1965, Johnson held a White House Conference entitled "To Fulfill These Rights," the president extended no invitation to Mexican American groups. This "insult by omission" enraged Mexican American leaders.[24] In March of 1966, Mexican American leaders walked out of the Equal Employment Opportunity Commission (EEOC) meeting in Albuquerque, New Mexico to protest this neglect. EEOC chair Franklin Roosevelt Jr. had organized the meeting specifically to discuss the commission's focus on job discrimination of blacks, at the expense of Mexican Americans. When Roosevelt failed to attend the meeting, Bexar County Commissioner Albert Peña called for a boycott of the gathering. The meeting came to an abrupt end because almost all of the invited delegates answered Peña's call.[25] The leaders of the walkout, however, did not simply disappear. They picketed the meeting and sent a letter of protest to President Johnson. They accused the EEOC of "a total lack of interest and understanding of the problems facing six million Mexican Americans."[26]

The War on Poverty stood out as the Great Society effort that offered the least to Mexican Americans. Rudy Ramos, the attorney for the American G.I. Forum (an organization that had strongly supported Johnson), accused Shriver and the OEO staff of excluding Mexican Americans from administrative positions and of neglecting Mexican Americans in local programs. Ramos condemned the OEO for including "only one Mexican American in OEO DC headquarters; no Mexican Americans in policy making functions, no Mexican Americans in Migrant branch, no Mexican Americans in Shriver's office."[27] Ramos and other leaders not only felt the OEO concentrated too much on blacks, but also that the federal government seemed unconcerned with the plight of the Mexican American poor.

Even some of Johnson's closest Mexican American friends complained that the OEO neglected their communities. Dr. Hector P. García, a strong Johnson ally and the founder of the American G.I. Forum, complained to Shriver personally of a lack of Mexican American involvement in the CAA in García's hometown of Corpus Christi. Dr. García represented the "Community Committee on Youth Education and Job Opportunities," which had been formed to protest the lack of Mexican American representatives on the Corpus Christi CAA board and staff. García explained to Shriver that, while Mexican Americans comprised the vast majority of the poor population in Corpus Christi, Anglos heavily outnumbered Mexican Americans in CAA administrative positions and on the board of directors. Although "90 percent of people living in the target areas [were] Mexican Americans, most of whom [didn't] speak English," none of the administrative staff spoke Spanish. García implored the director, "Is this right in your opinion?"[28]

In response, CAA director Cecil Burney reported to Shriver that the board had difficulty finding Mexican American applicants with the experience and qualifications he sought. While Burney did not specify the qualifications he hoped for, he agreed that "preference should be given to residents of target areas which are predominately Mexican Americans."[29] He informed the OEO that he "violently" disagreed, however, with the practice of hiring "less qualified persons based on the color of their skin."[30] Shriver apparently agreed with García, forwarding his letter to the regional office with a handwritten note that said: "García does make sense here. Can't we get more Mexican Americans in jobs of high visibility and power in [Corpus Christi] CAP?"[31] García and other officials of the G.I. Forum continued throughout the decade to urge more Mexican American employment in the OEO.[32]

To compensate for such neglect, the OEO made an extra effort to include Mexican American civil rights organizations in antipoverty programs. These groups included the American G.I. Forum and the League of United Latin American Citizens (LULAC), both of which had been traditionally allied with LBJ and the Democratic Party. In the wake of the EEOC walkout in 1966, LULAC and the G.I. Forum became the only civil rights organizations in Texas to receive a direct grant from the OEO to run an antipoverty program. One such program, Project SER (Service, Employment, Redevelopment), which LULAC and G.I. Forum created two years earlier, received an OEO grant for $362,450 in the summer of 1966. SER offered job training, remedial education, English language classes, and a "skills bank" (a list of skilled Hispanic workers for employers) to help Mexican Americans find jobs.[33] LULAC and the G.I. Forum billed SER as a program "for those in the Southwest who face unique problems largely because of cultural differences."[34] In Texas, SER opened job centers in Houston, Corpus Christi, El Paso, and San Antonio. The design of the SER program drew widespread applause. Labor Secretary Willard Wirtz praised SER as a "unique" program that blazed "new trails to full employment and higher earning power."[35]

The OEO made further efforts to compensate for the neglect of Mexican Americans. In response to the G.I. Forum's criticism of the OEO, for example, Shriver informed Rudy Ramos that six Mexican Americans worked in the Washington office and thirty-four worked in the regional office, including the Western Regional Director Dan Luevano.[36] Bob Allen, the director of the

Texas OEO, proclaimed in 1967 that Texas Mexican Americans had "not been neglected in the over-all effort to fight poverty."[37] To support this statement, Allen listed nearly $12 million in programs that specifically benefited Mexican Americans in Texas. Yet, considering the prevalence of poverty among Mexican Americans in the state, $12 million out of $140 million the OEO spent in Texas by 1967 might have seemed neglectful.[38]

The OEO's efforts failed to convince Mexican American leaders, many of whom continued to argue that the OEO did not adequately address their needs. And an increasing number of voices began to argue that the primary cause of this neglect was the OEO's focus on black poverty. Young activists coming out of the Chicano youth movement complained forcefully that the OEO's emphasis on African Americans led to the neglect of Chicanos. "Chicanos had high hopes," Rodolfo Acuña explained in Occupied America; "in the end they fared badly: [OEO] planners knew little about Chicanos, fitting most programs to preconceived needs of blacks."[39] José Angel Gutiérrez, the founder of the Mexican American Youth Organization, also recalled in his autobiography that "the War on Poverty . . . was basically aimed at and geared toward blacks . . . the rhetoric from Washington was that the war was for all people."[40] Gutiérrez recognized an irony of the War on Poverty's neglect of Mexican Americans: as an educator in Cotulla before he entered politics, LBJ had gained firsthand knowledge of Mexican American poverty in South Texas. Despite this, Gutiérrez noted, Johnson "did little to incorporate our national community into his domestic policies."[41]

Similar accusations emerged at the local level, but the perception of bias seemed to depend on which group had the larger low-income population. Just as the national Mexican American community accused the OEO of bias toward African Americans, in cities where Mexican Americans formed the largest proportion of the poor, African Americans accused the local CAA of bias toward Mexican Americans. In San Antonio for instance, the African American community complained of neglect while a conflict between two agencies, the Equal Opportunity Development Corporation (EODC), the city's main CAA, and the San Antonio Neighborhood Youth Organization (SANYO), a local delegate of the Neighborhood Youth Corps, hindered the progress of antipoverty efforts in the city.[42] SANYO was founded by Father John Yanta, a local Roman Catholic Priest, before EODC opened for business. SANYO, which ranked among the state's largest and most well-respected War on Poverty programs, operated for the most part in the barrios of the city's West Side, among the poorest urban neighborhoods in the nation. As it expanded, SANYO became highly politicized through its "federation of neighborhood councils," which challenged the EODC and city government for control of OEO funding coming into the city. In the late sixties, a conflict also developed within SANYO because activists influenced by the Chicano youth movement battled with local liberal leaders, including Father Yanta and Congressman Henry B. Gonzalez, over the direction and purpose of the agency.[43] While SANYO fought with EODC and the Chicanos fought with the liberals, the leaders of the city's African American community felt left out of the War on Poverty altogether.

In early 1967 leaders from San Antonio's African American community successfully lobbied the EODC, the city's main CAA, for the establishment of Project FREE (Family, Rehabilitation, Education, Employment), a family service agency for San Antonio's predominately black East Side. FREE functioned in a similar way to SANYO, but FREE activities placed greater emphasis on African American culture and the specific needs of blacks. Although SANYO had operated on the East Side of the city, African American leaders deemed a separate organization necessary because they sought to control antipoverty funding for their own neighborhoods and since SANYO was headquartered on the opposite side of town.[44] According to Project FREE

director Reverend Claude W. Black, a well respected local leader and pastor of Mt. Zion Baptist Church, blacks needed a separate agency to serve, as "a protector of the Negro community
in a city where the Mexican-American population was, by many
standards, poorer but better organized and closer to the power structure."[45]

Reverend Black accused Father Yanta of neglecting the needs
of the African American East Side.[46] Yanta, who had organized
SANYO neighborhood centers on the East Side and who had cooperated with other black leaders, responded by criticizing the
EODC chairman, Pepe Lucero, for "[throwing] in his lot with
Rev. Black and his black brothers" because FREE cost SANYO
about $150,000 a year in funding from the OEO.[47] Although
FREE never developed the political pull that characterized SAN-
YO, an OEO inspection report indicated that competing "Mexican versus Negro approaches" to poverty debilitated the over-
all War on Poverty in San Antonio.[48] The rivalry came to an end
in 1969 when OEO discontinued funding for Project FREE. Julian
Rodriguez recalled that some tension remained between SANYO
and African American leaders, but SANYO "worked well on the
East Side."[49]

A similar pattern emerged in El Paso. That city's main CAA,
called Project BRAVO (Building Resources and Vocational Opportunities), focused on lowering dropout rates and youth crime
in the barrios of the city's south end.[50] Through its "Barrio Program," Project BRAVO ran a Head Start preschool, various job
training, and remedial literacy courses. The history of the War
on Poverty in El Paso has much in common with that of San
Antonio. Like the struggle between EODC and SANYO, competition emerged between Project BRAVO, a service-oriented agency,
and a more politically motivated community action group called
MACHOS (Mexican American Committee on Honor Opportunity and Service).[51] As in San Antonio, El Paso's small black minority protested the neglect of their concerns from both agencies.

In March of 1968, three African Americans, all of whom had either been fired or were refused employment by Project BRAVO, accused the CAA staff of discrimination. Executive Director Fred Smith reported the case to the OEO in Austin. The regional office sent CAP inspectors to El Paso to investigate the accusations. While the inspectors found no hard evidence of discrimination, they reported to OEO that "there is *at least* covert discrimination against Negro employees."[52]

Black El Paso residents involved in the program argued that discrimination in Project BRAVO was obvious. One African American who worked for Project BRAVO as a barrio worker reported to the inspectors that "wherever possible, Negroes are excluded from employment and only enough Negroes [are] employed to keep the Negro community['s] mouth closed."[53] Robin Robinson, a black retired Army officer, accused the Project BRAVO staff of "systematic exclusion" of African Americans, not only in employment but in CAP services.[54] Robinson argued that Project BRAVO only began to involve African Americans in the program, either as employees or as clients, when black leaders confronted the CAA in the local media. In all, ten African Americans who had been involved with Project BRAVO agreed that the CAA discriminated against the black community.

Many blacks believed that the CAA had not "taken the initiative" to involve African Americans in the program.[55] Reverend Albert Pitts, a prominent black community leader in El Paso, concluded that Project BRAVO was "designed to deal with Latin-Americans, with their special cultural differences and language barriers, who comprise most of the El Paso poor."[56] While the task would be more difficult because the African American population was scattered throughout the city, Pitts urged the agency to employ more black "barrio" leaders to reach out to African Americans.[57]

The patterns that emerged in San Antonio and El Paso also emerged in Houston, with, as might be expected, the roles reversed between the city's minority residents. Activists identifying with the Black Power movement challenged the Harris County Community Action Agency (HCCAA) for its failures to include black leaders in the distribution of OEO funds. Further, the HCCAA drew national attention when opponents accused employees of the agency of participating in a near riot on the campus of Texas Southern University, a historically black college in the city.[58] While controversies involving the city's black community hindered the HCCAAs programs, Mexican American leaders in Houston accused the HCCAA of neglect due to the agency's emphasis on black poverty. Although they represented a smaller minority with less political pull, Mexican American leaders demanded separate control of War on Poverty funds for their community.

Among civil rights organizations in Houston, none strove more diligently to gain a fair share of War on Poverty for Mexican Americans than the United Organizations Information Center (UOIC). The UOIC had been formed to provide a "united front" for thirty-seven different Mexican American organizations in Houston. The War on Poverty ranked among the highest priorities of the UOIC. As Arnoldo De León explained, the organization led drives to improve employment and education but, "most importantly," strove "to secure a share of the poverty program funds for the Mexican American neighborhoods."[59] The UOIC accused the HCCAA specifically of ignoring the needs of the barrios. A. D. Azios, a spokesperson for the group, complained in 1968 to Walter Richter that the HCCAA developed "no tangible program" in Mexican American neighborhoods with high rates of unemployment. Azios concluded that Mexican Americans received only a "token program which is totally inadequate, unequal in its application, and completely discriminatory."[60]

Hector del Castillo, president of the Sembradores de Amistad (Sowers of Friendship), also accused the HCCAA of the unfair transfer of funds away from programs benefiting Mexican Americans.[61] The Sembradores de Amistad focused on providing educational financial aid to poor Mexican Americans in Houston.[62] Like many other such organizations in the state, the Sembradores considered the OEO a vital ally in struggles with local power structures. "We know that you have the interest of the Mexican American at heart," del Castillo reported to Richter, "[but] we also know that your wishes are not being carried out in Harris County."[63] Del Castillo informed Richter that the HCCAA made an "arbitrary and capricious" transfer of $305,000 from a program for an impoverished barrio for "programs not related to the Mexican American community."[64] As in other communities, the focus on one ethnic group over another exacerbated tensions, but even more problematically the transfer of funds clearly irked leaders like del Castillo and increased ethnic tension.

The Houston story also illustrates a grassroots effort by the Republican Party to gain support from Mexican Americans. Republican congressman George H. W. Bush used these feelings of neglect to gain political favor with Mexican Americans in his Houston-area district. In a proposal for his congressional platform entitled "For the Mexican American Texans—A Future of Fairplay and Progress," Bush concluded that "at the federal level less attention has been paid to Mexican Americans than to Negroes."[65] The congressman argued that most of his Mexican American constituents felt neglected by the OEO's focus on black poverty: "[B]ecause of the demonstrations and threats of violence, Negroes are 'bought off' with federal jobs while the quieter law abiding citizens get nothing but promises."[66] Bush specifically cited Project Go, a program operated by the HCCAA, as an example of a program that benefited "troublemakers."[67] The HCCAA had introduced Project Go to involve black youth from the city's ghettoes in the program. Two of Go's community organizers had been indicted for involvement in the near riot at TSU in 1967. Such accusations led to a strong protest from the OEO. In a letter to Bush, Sargent Shriver stated flatly that he and his staff had "since the inception of the poverty program, tried to make it abundantly clear that ours is not an anti-riot agency."[68]

Congressman Bush's efforts to lure Mexican American voters by contrasting their concerns with those of blacks reflected a new national trend in Republican strategy. Republican strategists recognized a potential ally in the Latino population due to their patriarchal family values and strong Catholic ties, in contrast to the Democratic Party's association with new liberal causes like feminism and reproductive rights. Throughout the Southwest, leading Republicans like Texas Senator John Tower, Arizona Senator Barry Goldwater, and California Governor Ronald Reagan had worked diligently to attract Mexican American voters. When Richard Nixon entered the White House, he appealed to Latinos by supporting bilingual education, an issue that had just begun to emerge in the late 1960s. Historian Gareth Davies has estimated that Nixon's support from Latinos expanded to one-third by 1972, more than double what he had received in 1968.[69]

The Republicans did not stand alone in their efforts to lure Mexican Americans away from the Democrats. In 1968 George Wallace's American Party also created an organization in Texas to draw Mexican American votes. The so-called "Viva Wallace" campaign in the 1968 election hoped to tap into the sense among Mexican Americans that the Democratic Party had "too long taken minority groups for granted." Tony Sanchez, cochair of the Viva Wallace effort, argued that Wallace offered Mexican Americans "a 'choice' while there is little difference between Democrat Hubert Humphrey and Republican Richard Nixon."[70] Although Humphrey carried the state in 1968, thanks primarily to Mexican American voters, the fact that the Wallace campaign went to the trouble of launching an organization to draw Mexican American votes suggests that the politician who

made his career defending "segregation now, segregation forever" recognized the wide disparity of political opinion among
Mexican Americans. [71]

Historian Nicholás Vaca refers to the sixties as a time when
idealistic Americans viewed black-brown relations through
"rose-colored lenses." The "Latinos and Blacks united against
the 'white oppressor' perspective," Vaca concludes, "expressly
swept any differences between the minorities under the rug."[72]
A spirit of unity between the nation's two largest minority
groups continues to characterize historical memory of the decade. As the history of the OEO indicates, however, tensions between the two groups were never far below the surface. In the
end, the financial and political limitations of the War on Poverty
compelled Mexican Americans and African Americans in Texas
to work toward the immediate interests of their communities,
rather than working together to alleviate poverty as a whole.

The black-brown conflict over OEO funds in Texas exemplifies how the ascendency of race identity in the sixties worked
at cross purposes with the goals of American liberalism in the
postwar era. Lyndon Johnson's domestic initiatives were not
simply populist proposals designed to gain favor with voters.
Rather, they epitomized what the agenda of American liberalism had become by 1965. For LBJ, the primary goal of progressive policy was not entitlement but equality of opportunity.[73]
Nothing obstructed equality in mid-twentieth-century America
more than racial discrimination and intergenerational poverty.
The Johnson administration, in turn, created legislation to tear
down these barriers—the Civil Rights and Economic Opportunity Acts of 1964. Neither of these initiatives was designed to
give special consideration to one race or group at the expense
of another. Indeed, the Civil Rights Act was meant to nullify
race in American public life. The EOA targeted an economically defined group—the poor. Yet, the story of black-brown conflict within OEO programs suggests that Mexican Americans and

African Americans prioritized the interests of their group and defined their own poverty along racial and economic lines.

The lack of interracial cooperation evident in the War on Poverty in Texas bolsters the argument, put forth best by Jill Quadango in *The Color of Welfare*, that the association between racial minorities and "welfare" created opposition to government antipoverty policy among whites.[74] The history of OEO programs in Texas indicates that many nonwhites came to associate poverty with race. Mexican American and African Americans in Texas well knew that poverty pervaded their communities to a greater extent than among whites, and they also knew why that was the case. Poverty prevailed in the barrios and ghettoes due to centuries of legally enforced white supremacy. The administration's insistence on a "colorblind" poverty fight was tantamount to acknowledging that low income whites faced the same barriers to equality as poor blacks or Chicanos. Black and brown groups in Texas, already organized along racial lines for the freedom struggle, competed over the limited resources of the OEO because they viewed the War on Poverty as more than just a fight to end the paradox of poverty amidst affluence, but as long overdue recompense for centuries of discrimination and abuse inflicted on their separate communities.

Notes

1. Bill Crook to Hayes Redmon, Memorandum RE Personnel for Southwest Regional Office, August 18, 1965, White House Central File, Confidential File (hereafter WHCF-CF), Lyndon Baines Johnson Library, Austin, Texas (hereafter LBJL).

2. "Minority Gap Report," OEO Records, Group 381, Records of the Director, Reference Correspondence, National Archive, College Park MD (hereafter NA). The term Mexican American will be used in this chapter, as the Latino population in Texas was almost entirely of Mexican descent. The term Chicano will be used to refer to those associated with the Chicano youth movement of the period.

3. Alan Matusow, *The Unraveling of America: A History of Liberalism in the 1960s* (New York: Harper, 1984), 243–71.

4. Houston, San Antonio, and El Paso provide the most fruitful source material on local War on Poverty programs in the state. Due to the conservative political culture of the Dallas–Fort Worth area, the Metroplex started after most of the controversial features of the CAP had been eliminated by both the OEO bureaucracy and the congress.

5. Gareth Davies, *From Opportunity to Entitlement: The Rise and Decline of Great Society Liberalism* (Lawrence: University of Kansas Press, 1996), 45.

6. Davies, *From Opportunity to Entitlement*.

7. Dona Cooper Hamilton and Charles V. Hamilton, *The Dual Agenda: Race and Social Welfare Polices of Civil Rights Organizations* (New York: Columbia University Press, 1997), 157.

8. Taylor Branch, *Pillar of Fire: America in the King Years, 1963–1965* (New York: Touchstone, 1998), 445.

9. Robert Dallek, *Flawed Giant: Lyndon Johnson and His Times* (New York: Oxford University Press, 1998), 108.

10. Branch, *Pillar of Fire*, 444.

11. Ben Seligman, *Permanent Poverty: An American Syndrome* (Chicago: Quadrangle, 1968), 165.

12. Sargent Shriver to A. Philip Randolph, March 10, 1965, OEO Records, Group 381, Office of Civil Rights, Director's Alphabetical File, NA.

13. OEO Press Release, February 16, 1966, OEO Records, Group 381, Office of Civil Rights, Director's Alphabetical Files, NA.

14. "Civil Rights Clearance Screen for Community Action Programs," March 14, 1965, completed form for San Angel Independent School District, OEO Records, Group 381, Office of Civil Rights, Records Relating to Civil Rights in the Regions, Box 30, NA.

15. Hamilton and Hamilton, *The Dual Agenda*, 157–58.

16. Dallek, *Lone Star Rising*, 486.

17. Hamilton and Hamilton, *The Dual Agenda*, 134–35.

18. Davies, *From Opportunity to Entitlement*, 72.

19. Deborah Wagner, "The Ten Biggest Myths About the OEO," *Communities in Action* 2, no. 3 (1967): 22–23.

20. Harvey Friedman to Samuel Yette, August 3, 1966, OEO Records, Group 381, Office of Civil Rights, Director's Alphabetical Files, 1964–69, NA.

21. James Patterson, *America's Struggle Against Poverty, 1900–1994* (Cambridge MA: Harvard University Press, 1994), 150.

22. Jerome Vacek to Ralph Yarborough, May 19, 1967, Ralph Yarborough Papers, Senate Records, Legislative Files, Box 3w294, CAH, UT.

23. William Clayson, "Texas Poverty and Liberal Politics: The Office of Economic Opportunity and the War on Poverty in Texas" (PhD diss., Texas Tech University, 2001), 143.

24. Carl Allsup, *The American G.I. Forum: Origins and Evolution* (Austin: Center for Mexican American Studies, University of Texas, 1986), 137.

25. Julie Leininger Pycior, *LBJ and Mexican Americans: The Paradox of Power* (Austin: University of Texas Press, 1997), 166.

26. "Bias, Indifference Charged: Mexican American Walkout Mars U.S. Job Conference," *Los Angeles Times*, March 29, 1966, clipping found in OEO Records, Group 381, Office of Civil Rights, Director's Alphabetical Files, 1964–69, NA.

27. Harman Bookbinder to David North (head of LBJ's task force on Mexican Americans), October 25, 1966, OEO Records, Group 381, Office of Civil Rights, Director's Alphabetical Files, 1964–69, NA.

28. Hector García to Sargent Shriver, July 7, 1966, OEO Records, Group 381, Office of Civil Rights, Director's Alphabetical Files, 1964–69, NA.

29. *Corpus Christi Caller*, September 29, 1966, n.p., clipping found in OEO Records, Group 381, Office of Civil Rights, Director's Alphabetical Files, 1964–69, NA.

30. *Corpus Christi Caller*, September 29, 1966.

31. *Corpus Christi Caller*, September 29, 1966 handwritten note dated July 11, 1966.

32. OEO, Press Release, "The American G.I. Forum of Texas Supports War on Poverty," July 10, 1967, OEO Records (microfilm), reel 8, LBJL.

33. OEO, Press Release, "Project SER to Benefit Spanish Americans," June 10, 1966, League of United Latin American Citizens Records, William Flores Papers, Benson Latin American Collection, University of Texas at Austin (hereafter BLAC, UT).

34. OEO, Press Release, "Project SER to Benefit Spanish Americans," June 10, 1966.

35. Quoted by Senator Ralph Yarborough, Congressional Record, 90th Congress, 1st Session, Joint Resolution 128, "Request to the President to Authorize LULAC Week, February 11–17, 1968," December 12, 1967, vol. 113, 196. Ultimately, OEO budget constraints disappointed SER supporters in LULAC and the G.I. Forum. The G.I. Forum passed a resolution in 1967 to withdraw support from SER because few "tangible efforts" had been made to implement the program. Nevertheless, SER expanded to become a national program and continues to function today. See Pycior, *LBJ and Mexican Americans*, 190; Cynthia Orozco, "SER Jobs for Progress,"

Handbook of Texas Online (http://www.tshaonline.org/handbook/online/articles/SS/oas1.html).

36. Harman Bookbinder to David North (head of LBJ's task force on Mexican Americans), October 25, 1966, OEO Records, Group 381, Office of Civil Rights, Director's Alphabetical Files, 1964–69, NA.

37. Bob Allen to John Connally, March 31, 1967, John Connally Papers, Box 25, Series 38, LBJL.

38. Allen to Connally, March 31, 1967.

39. Rodolfo Acuña, *Occupied America: A History of Chicanos,* 3rd ed. (New York: Harper Collins, 1988), 309.

40. Jose Angel Gutiérrez, *The Making of a Chicano Militant: Lessons from Cristal* (Madison: University of Wisconsin Press, 1998), 112.

41. Gutiérrez, *The Making of a Chicano Militant,* 112.

42. The NYC, like Headstart or other OEO programs, was administered by the CAAs on the local level. This was required by the so-called Green Amendment of 1966. Devised by Oregon Congressmen Edith Green, the amendments to the EOA required that each municipality could have only one CAA to avoid competition but also to prevent the paradox of the federal government financing protests on city governments through OEO programs.

43. William Clayson, "'The Barrios and the Ghettoes Have Organized!' Community Action, Political Acrimony, and the War on Poverty in San Antonio," *Journal of Urban History* 28, no. 2 (2002): 158–83.

44. Julian Rodriguez, interview with author, September 5, 2000, San Antonio TX.

45. Price to May, Report of Inspection of San Antonio EODC, July 18, 1968.

46. Price to May, Report of Inspection of San Antonio.; Don Politico, "Deal Splits Local NAACP," *San Antonio Light,* September 28, 1968, 8.

47. John Yanta to Archbishop Robert E. Lucey, December 15, 1967, Archbishop Robert E. Lucey Papers, SANYO file, Catholic Archives of San Antonio (hereafter CASA).

48. Paulette A. Washington, "EODC and the Neighborhood Corporations" (Master's thesis, Trinity University, 1971), 35. The quote within the chapter title is drawn from this reference.

49. Rodriguez, interview with author.

50. "BRAVO Starts Formal Operation," *El Paso Times,* May 24, 1965, 1A.

51. "Poverty Director to be named," *El Paso Times,* June 4, 1965, 1A.

52. Morgan Groves to Jim Duck, March 20, 1968, OEO Records, Group 381, City Economic Opportunity Boards Files, El Paso File, National Archives Southwest Region, Fort Worth, Texas (hereafter NASWR).

53. Charles W. Pankey to Jim Duck, March 25, 1968, OEO Records, Group 381, City Economic Opportunity Boards Files, El Paso File, NASWR.

54. Pankey to Jim Duck.

55. Pankey to Jim Duck.

56. "Poverty Meeting Held," *El Paso Herald Post*, May 6, 1965, 3.

57. "Poverty Meeting Held," *El Paso Herald Post*.

58. William Clayson, "The War on Poverty and the Fear of Urban Violence in Houston, 1965–1968," *Gulf South Historical Review* 18, no. 2 (2003): 38–59.

59. Arnoldo De León, *Ethnicity in the Sunbelt: Mexican Americans in Houston* (Houston: University of Houston Center for Mexican American Studies, 1989), 181–82.

60. A. D. Azios to Walter Richter, January 23, 1968, OEO Records, Group 381, Southwest Regional Office Records, Director's Records, Correspondence Files, NASWR.

61. Hector del Castillo to Walter Richter, February 2, 1968, OEO Records, Group 381, Southwest Regional Office Records, Director's Records, Correspondence Files, NASWR.

62. De León, *Ethnicity in the Sunbelt*, 152.

63. Del Castillo to Richter, February 2, 1968.

64. Del Castillo to Richter, February 2, 1968.

65. George Bush to Flores, February 3, 1968, LULAC Records, Flores Papers, box 1, folder G, BLAC, UT.

66. Bush to Flores, February 3, 1968.

67. Bush to Flores, February 3, 1968.

68. Davies, *From Opportunity to Entitlement*, 196.

69. Gareth Davies, "The Great Society After Johnson: The Case of Bilingual Education," *Journal of American History* 88, no. 4 (2002): 1410–12.

70. Jon Ford, "Viva Wallace Drive Launched in Texas," *San Antonio Express News*, September 21, 1968, 9A.

71. Pycior, *LBJ and Mexican Americans*, 232.

72. Nicolas Váca, *The Presumed Alliance: The Unspoken Conflict Between Latinos and Blacks and What it Means for America* (New York: Rayo, 2004), ix, 62–84.

73. Davies, *From Opportunity to Entitlement*, 6–7.

74. Jill Quadango, *The Color of Welfare: How Racism Undermined the War on Poverty* (New York: Oxford University Press, 1996), 196–98.

SIX

Cesar and Martin, March '68

JORGE MARISCAL

In early 1968 the philosophy of nonviolence was sinking beneath a tidal wave of bloodshed and death. The previous summer, rioting had erupted in major urban centers across the United States. In Detroit, where the worst violence took place, forty-three people died. The Tet Offensive cut a path through the month of February and ended with 2,259 U.S. servicemen and thousands more Vietnamese dead. Since late February, U.S. Marines at Khe Sanh had been under seige from North Vietnamese regulars in what would become the longest battle of the U.S. war in Southeast Asia.

In the California grape fields, the two-and-a-half-year-old-strike by Filipino, Mexican, and Mexican American workers was under attack from corporate growers and their allies. The violence directed against the picket lines had generated talk among the strikers about retaliation. In order to recommit his organization to the philosophy of nonviolence, on February 15 the forty-year-old farm worker organizer Cesar Chavez began what would become a twenty-five-day fast. Reflecting on his philosophy a few years later, Chavez told an interviewer: "Some great nonviolent successes have been achieved in history. . . .

6. Cesar Chavez in his office, 1968. Photo by Arthur Schatz. Used by permission of Time & Life Pictures.

The most recent example is Gandhi. To me that's the most beautiful one. . . . It's fantastic how he got so many people to do things, which is the whole essence of nonviolent action."[1]

Where the Mississippi river leaves Tennessee, sanitation workers organized by the American Federation of State, County, and Municipal Employees (AFSCME) Local 1733 walked off the job in Memphis on February 12 when supervisors used inclement weather as an excuse to send African American workers home without pay but kept nonblack employees working at full pay. The following day and again two weeks later, police attacked peaceful marches in support of the strikers. Union members adopted the slogan "I Am a Man" and the Memphis-based Reverend James Lawson, who had trained in India in the nonviolent philosophy of Gandhi, became chairman of the strike committee. He asked his longtime friend, thirty-nine-year-old Reverend Martin Luther King Jr., to come to Memphis to support the strike.[2]

Moving through the eye of this violent storm in March of 1968 were two men who today are recognized as the most famous American practitioners of Gandhian nonviolence. Both struggled to adhere to the philosophy of nonviolent civil disobedience within the turbulence of cresting mass mobilizations deeply rooted in the particular histories and traditions of two distinct communities. Cesar Chavez and Martin Luther King never met and probably never communicated except by telegram. In hindsight, their coming together would appear to have been the ultimate black-brown alliance. But in March of '68, conditions on the ground did not allow for such clarity.

My purpose in this chapter is less to imagine what might have been than to describe the extremely hostile conditions through which both men moved. In this way, we can begin to sharpen our understanding of the philosophy and organizing practices of two key black and brown social movements and how they overlapped at a critical juncture in the revolutionary sixties. In order to unpack the many reasons why a King-Chavez alliance never took place, we need to disabuse ourselves of over forty years of hagiography and cooptation. In other words, the contemporary stature of both men as the object of holidays and postage stamps ought not be inserted back in time if we are to avoid distorting the historical record. In 1968 both men were known but not yet beatified. More important, each was fully immersed in a complex social movement at a perilous moment in that movement's development; each was aware of the other's actions but the complex series of contacts and maneuvers that more than likely would have led them to collaborate had only just begun.

On February 23, President Lyndon Johnson issued a statement in response to the recommendations just released by the Inter-Agency Committee on Mexican American Affairs. He concluded by stating, "With this report of progress and action, we have begun the journey toward full opportunity for the Mexican-Americans, Puerto Ricans, and other Spanish-speaking people of our land."[3] Less than one week later on March 1, the National Advisory Commission on Civil Disorders, known as the

Kerner Commission, issued its report. Johnson had charged the commission to analyze the social causes of the urban riots that had taken place in the summer of '67 and that had led to a total of eighty-four deaths. Among the report's conclusions was the statement: "It is time now to turn with all the purpose at our command to the major unfinished business of this nation. It is time to adopt strategies for action that will produce quick and visible progress. It is time to make good the promises of American democracy to all citizens—urban and rural, white and black, Spanish-surname, American Indian, and every minority group."[4]

Dr. King called the Kerner Report "a physician's warning of approaching death, with a prescription for life," and added, "the duty of every American is to administer the remedy without regard for the cost and without delay."[5] In contrast to his rhetoric earlier in the civil rights struggle, King's language now was becoming increasingly apocalyptic. In a telegram sent to Kerner Commission member Roy Wilkins, he wrote: "My only hope is that white America and our national government will heed your warnings and implement your recommendations. By ignoring them we will sink inevitably into a nightmarish racial doomsday. God grant that your excellent report will educate the nation and lead to action before it is too late."[6] Although the report sold almost three-quarter of a million copies in the first week of March and created an uneasy wave of optimism among activists, the election of Richard Nixon in November and the continuation of the war in Southeast Asia meant that there would be minimal follow up to any of its policy recommendations. Race relations in the United States seemed to be headed off a cliff and so did the U.S. military adventure in Vietnam. While King speculated about the potential for racial conflict, on February 27 the most authoritative voice in the U.S. media, Walter Cronkite of CBS News, delivered an editorial predicting that a military victory in Vietnam would never come.[7] One of the war's primary architects, Robert McNamara, had expressed his doubts to President Johnson as early as October of the previous year. On March 1, he relinquished his post to a new secretary of defense.

A few days after the release of the Kerner Report, Mexican American high school students, frustrated by their school board's refusal to address their demands regarding conditions in the schools, streamed out of several high schools in East Los Angeles. The first phase of the "blowouts" or walkouts lasted from March 5 to 8 and marked the acceleration of youth militancy in Mexican American communities across the Southwest. During the next few months, African American students joined with Chicano/a students to engage in nonviolent protest designed to call attention to the dilapidated condition of their schools, racist teachers, Eurocentric curricula, and tracking that channeled them toward vocational training and the military and away from higher education.[8] Inspired by the ongoing actions of Chavez and the United Farm Workers (UFW), many of the student activists went on to participate in antiwar and electoral politics. Some joined the farm workers, while others met with Robert Kennedy during a March campaign caravan organized by activist Bert Corona of the Mexican American Political Association (MAPA). Kennedy's motorcade moved slowly across a long section of Los Angeles county stretching from Long Beach to Compton, through East L.A., and ending at the heart of Mexican L.A.—La Placita on Olvera Street—where enthusiastic supporters mobbed him.

On March 5, Martin Luther King sent a telegram addressed to "Cesar Chaves [sic], United Farm Workers, P.O. Box 120, Delano, Calif." "I am deeply moved by your courage in fasting as your personal sacrifice for justice through nonviolence," King wrote:

> Your past and present commitment is eloquent testimony to the constructive power of nonviolent action and the destructive impotence of violent reprisal. You stand today as a living

7. Bobby Kennedy at Olvera Street in downtown Los Angeles, March 24, 1968. Photo by William Reagh. Security Pacific National Bank Collection, Los Angeles Public Library.

example of the Gandhian tradition with its great force for social progress and its healing spiritual powers. My colleagues and I commend you for your bravery, salute you for your indefatigable work against poverty and injustice, and pray for your health and your continuing service as one of the outstanding men of America. The plight of your people and ours is so grave that we all desperately need the inspiring example and effective leadership you have given.

Ten years later, Chavez recalled, "I was profoundly moved that someone facing such a tremendous struggle himself would take the time to worry about a struggle taking place on the other side of the continent."[9]

Looking back, King's message would seem to be a discreet follow-up to an invitation to Chavez to take part in the Poor People's Campaign scheduled for summer. Andrew Young, one of King's closest aides, had visited Chavez in Delano in

February to deliver the personal request from Dr. King. According to Young, "We were happily surprised at the positive response from Cesar Chavez and the California Farm Workers." Although Chavez never participated directly in the Campaign, a UFW representative was present at the March 14 planning meeting at King's Atlanta office.[10] Chavez later told an interviewer that at one point he had spoken with King by telephone but the timing of the call remains unclear and those closest to Chavez wonder why, if in fact Chavez had received a call from King, he never mentioned it.[11] LeRoy Chatfield, for example, when asked about the call responded, "Had you asked me straight out, I would have said 'no,' they never talked. I have no reason to contradict Cesar about this, but I would offer the opinion that such a conversation had to be in the nature of a 'courtesy' call because Cesar, to my knowledge, never made it a topic of conversation or the subject of a meeting."[12]

On Sunday, March 10, Chavez ended his fast at an open air Mass held at Delano Memorial Park. The fast had begun on February 15 when Chavez left Filipino Hall and walked the three miles to the old adobe gas station at Forty Acres. In the third year of the Delano Grape strike, an elevated sense of violence permeated the California fields. Some strikers had been shot at or physically threatened and there were rumblings about some of them burning sheds and throwing stones at strikebreakers. Chavez hoped to use the fast as an opportunity to reflect on the true meaning of nonviolence and the ethical values of the farm workers' movement. In an announcement to union members, he noted that because the nation was experiencing a period of great violence it was important to show that violence was morally wrong and counterproductive. He emphasized that what he wanted to do was not a hunger strike because a strike would be a form of coercion and therefore not truly nonviolent. UFW attorney Jerry Cohen would later say that at that point in the grape strike, when internal divisions had begun to surface, the fast was "the glue that held the union together." Other volunteers were less sanguine. Former Catholic priest John Duggan, for example, even in later years referred to the fast as "religious spectacle engineered by propagandists (however well intentioned)."[13]

At the mass celebrating the end of the fast, Father Mark Day presided over clergy from several different faiths and denominations. Three hundred loaves of bread were distributed to over four thousand people (eight thousand according to some participants). The bread was *pan de semita*, the round anise-flavored bread said to be based on the recipe for matzo used by crypto-Jewish Spaniards in the seventeenth century. Jim Drake of the California Migrant Ministry read a statement prepared for Chavez by Drake and Chris Hartmire. The statement included the sentence, "We are poor, but we have something the rich do not own—our bodies and our spirits and the justice of our cause."[14]

Throughout the fast Robert Kennedy had stayed in contact with union members and at one point wrote to Chavez urging him to monitor his health carefully. As the fast came to an end, an invitation was extended for Kennedy to attend the mass. One of the senator's advisors pointed out that his support of Chavez in 1966 had caused a wave of red baiting messages and that meeting with Chavez now might cost Kennedy much needed votes in the California primary should he decide to enter the presidential race. "I know," Kennedy replied, "but I like Cesar."[15] Kennedy had met Chavez for the first time in 1959 in Los Angeles where Chavez was organizing voter registration drives. They met again on March 16, 1966, in the first year of the Grape Strike, when Kennedy accompanied Chavez, Dolores Huerta, and others to the Delano vineyards, the picket lines, and Filipino Hall where the senator spoke to union members. Kennedy then joined Senators Harrison Williams of New Jersey and George Murphy of California at the local high school to conduct hearings on migrant farm labor. At an earlier session of these hearings, Chavez ended his testimony with an oblique reference to the Watts riots of the previous summer, saying "I am hoping we don't have to go as far as the Negro revolution and its resulting bloodshed to prove that farm workers are tired of occupational discrimination and that we are ready for our freedom." Kennedy and Chavez would meet again briefly in late 1967 at a fundraiser in Marin County, California.[16]

Senator Kennedy decided to attend and flew from an appearance in Des Moines, Iowa, to California. Cohen and Drake met Kennedy at the airport and drove him and his aide from Bakersfield to Delano. Cohen recalls that the senator looked nervous and later in the day Kennedy told Dolores Huerta and Mack Lyons that he had seen a man in the crowd carrying a gun. Union members surrounded Kennedy in a protective circle as he left the rally.[17] Kennedy's official statement released to reporters read:

> This is a historic occasion. We have come here out of respect for one of the heroic figures of our time—Cesar Chavez. But I also come here to congratulate all of you, you who are locked with Cesar in the struggle for justice for the farm worker, and the struggle for justice for the Spanish-speaking American. . . . The world must know that the migrant farm worker, the Mexican American, is coming into his own right. . . . And when your children and grandchildren take their place in America—going to high school, and college, and taking good jobs at good pay—when you look at them, you will say, "I did this. I was there, at the point of difficulty and danger." And though you may be old and bent from many years of labor, no man will stand taller than you when you say, "I marched with Cesar."

As he was about to leave, Kennedy suddenly climbed on top of his car and began to speak to the farm workers in a Spanish so badly mangled that many of those cheering had no idea what he was saying. According to Chavez, Kennedy looked over at him and said "I'm murdering the language, Cesar, is that right?" Chavez smiled and answered, "Yes." Kennedy departed a short time later.[18]

The Kennedy visit provided the farm workers' movement with the kind of national exposure it had hoped for but never anticipated. One thing that might have added to the media frenzy was the presence of Martin Luther King. Although some observers have raised the issue of whether or not King was invited to attend the rally and Mass, Chavez confidante Chatfield said, "I am not aware that we gave any consideration to inviting Martin Luther King Jr. to Delano to celebrate the end of the fast. At that point in time, I'm not sure we saw Dr. King as a future national holiday figure but rather as one leader, competing, and cooperating, with many others to advance the cause of blacks."[19] It should not surprise us that Chavez and his associates, so focused on the mechanics of a prolonged strike that in March '68 seemed very far from victory, were not particularly concerned with extending invitations to civil rights leaders engaged in their own separate albeit related struggles.

According to one of his closest advisors, Cesar had adopted a "cautious, wary, and detached" stance toward King, primarily because of King's strong public denunciation of Johnson administration policy in Vietnam. Although Chavez and the rest of the UFW leadership opposed the war, their allies in the AFL-CIO, Seafarers, and other unions supported the war policy of the Democratic president. As late as 1970, construction unions paid workers in New York City to stage pro-war rallies and attack antiwar demonstrators. George Meany, the head of the AFL-CIO was particularly hawkish, and in 1972 refused to support the antiwar candidate George McGovern. However, when the Teamsters and the United Auto Workers pulled out of the AFL-CIO in mid-1969, large sectors of organized labor slowly began to voice opposition to the war.[20]

In March '68, Chavez could not risk a dramatic break over the issue of Vietnam with the large unions that supported him. At the same time, many of the UFW rank and file considered it unpatriotic to oppose a war in which many of its young men were fighting. In a 1970 interview Chavez explained, "They thought it was being disloyal to be—I think they didn't want the war, but it was a question of if they speak out, 'I'm being disloyal,' and this is very pronounced with the Mexicans, you know." As volunteers from college campuses mixed with the farm workers, tensions and misunderstandings related to the war and military service increased. Chavez told an interviewer that "some of the volunteers were for ending the Vietnam war above all else, and that shocked the workers because they thought that was unpatriotic."[21] Given the complex nature of his coalition, Chavez in 1968 would take a much less public profile against the war than King.

On the morning of March 14 at the Paschal's Motor Lodge in Atlanta, King convened a meeting of some eighty "non-black" organizers and organization leaders. Billed as the "Minority Group Conference," the leaders began the preliminary planning for the Poor People's Campaign. Despite opposition from within his own inner circle with regard to the idea of a broad-based coalition, King was about to attempt on the national level what Chavez was slowly building in Delano in a local context. Several years earlier, Chavez had articulated plans for a broad mobilization of the poor with its origins in the "militant particularity" of California agricultural workers. "Our goals have to be broader than the traditional goals of unions," he had stated, "It is more than a union as we know it today that we have to build. It is a movement. It is a movement of the poor." For King, the multiracial alliance he attempted to create would mark "the day when the bones get back together," as in the biblical story of Ezekiel.[22]

The Minority Group Conference revealed that the depth

of knowledge each group had of one another was superficial at best. King's twenty-eight-year-old aide, Bernard Lafayette, struggled to explain to him the cultural differences between Chicanos and Puerto Ricans. Bert Corona, however, recalled that King "always exhibited a sensitivity to the needs of *mexicanos* . . . [h]e was very sympathetic and supportive." King also made a particularly strong impression on Baldemar Velásquez, the leader of a farm labor organization in Ohio.[23] Representatives from Mexican American and Native Americans groups and poor white coal miners listened as King described his ideas for the actions planned for that summer in Washington DC. According to Reies López Tijerina, King was pressed about the need to foreground the rights of Native Americans. Tijerina lectured black leaders on the complexities of the 1848 Treaty of Guadalupe Hidalgo and the land grant issue. Although they had met briefly at the New Politics conference in Chicago the year before, King did not know a great deal about Tijerina. More important, King's advisors had to deal with the fact that Tijerina's resume included an armed clash with New Mexico state authorities; a 1967 "mutual defense treaty" signed with Native American and radical Black militants representing SNCC, the Black Panthers, and Ron Karenga's Us organization, among others; and a fiery speech in February at UCLA in which Tijerina vowed to aggressively challenge the federal government.[24]

The dialogue among diverse constituencies and their principal leaders lost its primary interlocutor when King left to give a scheduled speech in Michigan that evening. Speaking at the high school in Grosse Pointe near Detroit, King told the audience: "Somewhere we must come to see that human progress never rolls in on the wheels of inevitability, it comes through the tireless efforts and the persistent work of dedicated individuals who are willing to be co-workers with God and without this hard work time itself becomes an ally of the primitive forces of social stagnation. And so we must always help time and realize that the time is always right to do right."[25] A heckler in the audience shouted "traitor" while outside the auditorium members of a right-wing militia called the Breakthrough carried signs that read "Beware—King Snake" and "Antichrist Must Go." According to those who drove him to his hotel, King was visibly shaken.

The potential for violence was now palpable inside the immediate circle of both Chavez and King. Not long after his fast, Chavez related to Dolores Huerta his attitude regarding the constant threats against his life. "I've just made up my mind that I know it's going to happen sooner or later," he said, "there's nothing I can do."[26] King's associates were no less concerned that their leader was resigned to the dangers that surrounded him. During an impromptu vacation to Mexico with Ralph Abernathy and a small group of advisors, King seemed distracted and morbid. Many of King's associates sensed that something or someone was stalking the civil rights leader. We now know that their fears were well founded. White supremacists and paid hit men were not the only ones tracking King and Chavez. On March 6, Director of the FBI J. Edgar Hoover had created a special unit to shadow, and if necessary sabotage, all potential participants in the Poor People's Campaign.[27]

King was now fully immersed in a whirlwind cross-country tour to promote the Poor People's Campaign and to speak out against the widening war in Vietnam. On March 16, he spoke in Anaheim, California, to the California Democratic Council convention. At the unlikely location of the Disneyland Hotel, he stated, "the government is emotionally hostile to the needs of the poor" and called for the Democratic Party to withdraw its support from President Johnson.[28] Well aware that Bobby Kennedy had visited Delano the week before, King vowed that in the near future he would conduct a fact-finding tour of migrant labor camps. We can only suppose that a meeting with Chavez would have been the high point of that tour.

Two other decisive events occurred on March 16. In the

caucus room of the Old Senate Office Building, Kennedy announced that he would seek the nomination of the Democratic Party. "I am announcing today my candidacy for the presidency of the United States . . . [in order to] close the gaps that now exist between black and white, between rich and poor, between young and old," he said. Thousands of miles away, a U.S. Army platoon executed between two hundred and five hundred unarmed civilians at My Lai 4, a cluster of hamlets in northern South Vietnam. The legalized and indiscriminate violence—the foundation of all wars—played itself out in all of its contradictions with some U.S. soldiers committing mass murder and others trying to stop it. This was precisely the kind of senseless violence that Chavez and King had committed their lives to stopping.

The two leaders that today are most identified as leaders of "race-based" social movements were also deeply implicated in the labor struggles of their time. In 1968 the issue of worker's rights melded seamlessly into the struggle for equal rights for communities of color. Increasingly, the category of race was morphing into the intellectual category and organizing principle of racialized class. Despite the relative racial and ethnic homogeneity of the communities for which they spoke, King and Chavez did not practice a narrow "identity politics," as that term came to be defined at a later moment. By March '68 especially, their agendas were tightly focused on the economic conditions of their constituents as well as their racialized status.

The plight of exploited labor had always been Chavez's focus, and he considered himself first and foremost a community organizer. It was not until the early 1970s that he recognized the ways in which the UFW had influenced and contributed to the broader mobilization of Mexican American communities across a wide range of issues ranging from educational reform to the war in Southeast Asia. The Chicano movement in all of its variations was at its base an ethnic pride or ethnic "nationalist" movement insofar as it attempted to mobilize a racialized and politically disenfranchised Mexican American community. While in the late 1960s Chavez was still wary of the "Brown Power" activists, the growth of Chicano militancy was unthinkable without the example of the farm workers struggle.[29]

By 1968, Dr. King had moved increasingly toward an economic analysis of the situation confronting African Americans. On February 18, King had told his parishioners at Ebenezer Baptist Church, "Until mankind rises above race and class and nations, we will destroy ourselves by the misuse of our own power and instruments." In his book, *Where Do We Go From Here: Chaos or Community?* published the year before, he had written: "The displaced are flowing into proliferating service occupations. These enterprises are traditionally unorganized and provide low wage scales with longer hours. The Negroes pressed into these services need union protection, and the union movement needs their membership to maintain its relative strength in the whole society. . . . To play our role fully as Negroes we will have to strive for enhanced representation and influence in the labor movement. Our young people need to think of union careers as earnestly as they do of business careers and professions." In contrast to the suspicion King had displayed around unions early in his career, especially those unions that promoted racist practices, King now embraced unions as key allies in the struggle.[30]

The decision to make repeated forays into the charged environment surrounding the Memphis sanitation workers was the kind of gamble King had to make if he wanted to transform the African American civil rights movement into a pan-ethnic coalition of workers and the poor. In *Where Do We Go From Here*, he had argued: "In a multi-racial society no group can make it alone. It is a myth to believe that the Irish, Italians, and the Jews. . . . [R]ose to power through separatism. . . . Their group unity was always enlarged by joining in alliances with other groups such as political machines and trade unions." The sanitation workers' strike melded issues of race and class in ways so stark that they perhaps were not seen quite so clearly again until the aftermath of Hurricane Katrina in 2005.

On March 18, King traveled to Memphis to speak to a rally of some twenty thousand (the FBI estimate between nine and twelve thousand) at the Bishop Charles Mason Temple. "You are demanding that this city will respect the dignity of labor," he stated. "[S]o often we overlook the work and the significance of those who are not in professional jobs, of those who are not in the so-called big jobs. But let me say to you tonight that whenever you are engaged in work that serves humanity and is for the building of humanity, it has dignity and it has worth."[31] This same message could just have easily applied to the farm workers. This language resonated with what Chavez had said since at least the beginning of the Grape Strike in 1965 and what he would articulate most succinctly one year after his fast in a letter to a corporate grower who opposed the union. In that letter, Chavez wrote, "[W]e are men and women who have suffered and endured much, and not only because of our abject poverty but because we have been kept poor. The color of our skin, the language of our cultural and native origins, the lack of formal education, the exclusion from the democratic process, the numbers of our men slain in recent wars—all these burdens generation after generation have sought to demoralize us, to break our human spirit. But God knows that we are not beasts of burden, agricultural implements, or rented slaves; we are men."[32]

In Memphis, the flyer announcing a "March for Justice and Jobs" reflected the philosophy of Gandhian nonviolence that marked the careers of both King and Chavez. "This will be a march of dignity," King stated, adding, "the only force we will use is soul-force which is peaceful, loving, courageous, yet militant."[33] On March 28, King marched with the sanitation workers and their supporters. Provocateurs began to break windows

8. Martin Luther King Jr. and Ralph Abernathy in Memphis, April 3, 1968. Photo by Sam Melhorn. Used by permission of Memphis Publishing Company, the *Commercial Appeal*.

and police moved into the crowd with nightsticks, mace, tear gas, and gunfire. Police arrested two hundred and eighty people and sixty were injured. Police shot sixteen-year-old Larry Payne to death. As supporters whisked King away from the mayhem, he must have wondered how a mass mobilization in Washington DC could possibly succeed if he could not avoid violence in Memphis. He considered starting a fast as Gandhi and Cesar Chavez had done.[34]

On March 31, Cesar Chavez celebrated his forty-first birthday in California. Dr. King, speaking at the National Cathedral in Washington DC, reiterated his opposition to the war in Vietnam and announced the final plans for the Poor People's Campaign. "We are coming to ask America to be true to the huge promissory note that it signed years ago. And we are coming to engage in dramatic nonviolent action, to call attention to the gulf between promise and fulfillment; to make the invisible visible," he stated during the speech. In Vietnam, the month ended with 1,764 U.S. and thousands of Vietnamese fatalities. At the conclusion of a nationally televised address on the war, President Johnson made the unexpected announcement that he would withdraw from the presidential race, stating: "There is division in the American house now. There is divisiveness among us all tonight. And holding the trust that is mine, as President of all the people, I cannot disregard the peril to the progress of the American people. . . . So, I would ask all Americans, whatever their personal interests or concern, to guard against divisiveness and all its ugly consequences."[35]

Thus March '68 ended with Chavez weakened by his prolonged fast, King increasingly overtaxed and exhausted, continuing violence in Southeast Asia, and the downfall of a president. The potential for a powerful coalition led by Cesar and Martin, the preeminent representatives of their respective communities, was never realized. We can only imagine what they might have accomplished together. What is clear is that in March '68 both men were navigating the same treacherous waters of race and class, poverty and war, and multiracial coalitions and narrow ethnic nationalisms in the fragile vessel of militant nonviolence. Forty years later, how can we best understand the Chavez-King relationship?

As we totalize the complex moment of March '68 in order to better understand its conditions of possibility, it becomes clear that this month was not composed of linear structures in which one leader passively followed the example of the other, but rather that both men independently selected specific tactics that would be potentially useful to their cause. Chavez had been struck by the use of the boycott by civil rights activists in the Montgomery Bus Boycott. But as one of Chavez's closest advisors explained in an interview, "The last thing that Cesar wanted was to be considered a farm worker version of a Martin Luther King Jr."[36] As the two telegrams sent by King to Chavez suggest, King recognized the logical affinities between the two movements although he had only a superficial knowledge of the conditions faced by California farm workers. In short, the militant and nonviolent tactics of both leaders resulted from a shared historical context and mutual influences, not because one leader copied the other.

The misconception among some historians that Chavez's actions simply imitated those of Dr. King, especially with regard to the religious practices and iconography that framed Chavez's actions, betrays an ignorance of the genealogy of Mexican and Mexican American insurgencies. In particular, the use of the fast, the pilgrimage, and the Catholic mass as tools for mobilizing communities is relatively commonplace in the history of Latin American social movements. Moreover, as Dr. King's second message noted, Chavez operated fully within a second tradition—the militant pacifism inspired by Gandhi—from which King too had found inspiration. In effect, both men were linked through agendas that reflected corresponding social critiques and practical goals within a context of analogous conditions, especially racialized communities, second-class citizenship, and the exploitation of labor.

The farm worker and the Memphis sanitation worker mobilizations foregrounded labor struggles even as they negated U.S. capitalism's denial of the worker's basic humanity. The "I Am a Man" slogan captured the essence of not only the struggle for racial equality but also for humane working conditions. As Andrew Young remarked years later, "The civil rights movement up until 1968 anyway, was really a middle-class movement. . . . Cesar Chavez and George Wiley had poor people's movements."[37] The farm worker campaign mobilized workers around the demand for decent working conditions and an implicit rejection of anti-Mexican racism in the Southwest; the Memphis strike opposed both the exploitation of labor and racism in the South. In both cases, it was the paradoxical combination of militant pacifism and the violent reaction of state authorities that led to aggrieved and racialized groups in local contexts becoming part of a serial chain of disparate social movements today known as the sixties.

On that stormy evening of April 3, the night before he died, Dr. King had told a standing-room only crowd in Memphis: "The question is not, 'If I stop to help this man in need, what will happen to me?' . . . 'If I do not stop to help the sanitation workers, what will happen to them?' That's the question." As the speech that would become known as the "I've been to the mountaintop" address rose to a crescendo, he warned, "[T]he nation is sick. Trouble is in the land. Confusion all around. . . . It is no longer a choice between violence and nonviolence in this world; it's nonviolence or nonexistence." The next day, King spent the morning in meetings with his staff and a group of young black activists who questioned the effectiveness of nonviolence, placed a call to his mother, phoned in the title of his upcoming sermon to his staff in Atlanta, took a short nap, and around six o'clock stepped out on the balcony of his motel on his way to have dinner with friends. Towards the end of the CBS evening news broadcast, Walter Cronkite announced that King had been murdered. In California, Chavez was scheduled to speak at Our Lady of Guadalupe Church in Sacramento. Chavez later told an interviewer, "Martin Luther King definitely influenced me, and much more after his death. The spirit doesn't die, the ideas remain." The title of Dr. King's undelivered sermon was "Why America May Go to Hell."[38]

It is not at all clear what a King-Chavez alliance might have produced. It would be utopian to believe that a SCLC-UFW coalition, assuming it had survived government disruption of the Poor People's Campaign, could have swelled the ranks of a nationwide mobilization led by two charismatic followers of Gandhian nonviolence. After all, black and Chicano youth were beginning to move toward a confrontational form of ethnic nationalism more associated with the early Malcolm X. As Stokely Carmichael famously said after the murder of Dr. King, "White America just killed nonviolence."[39] In March of 1969, Mexican American youth from across the Southwest met in Denver to declare the principles of the new Chicano movement while the Puerto Rican Young Lords and the Black Panther Party slowly increased their membership rolls. Add to this shift away from what was perceived as ineffectual pacifism, the intensification of law enforcement operations aimed at disrupting progressive groups, and the election of Richard Nixon on a "law and order" platform and one begins to sense that a King-Chavez partnership would have been lost in a storm of centrifugal interests and organizations. By the mid-1970s, as we are just now learning, serious internal dissension produced by changes in Chavez's leadership style would weaken the United Farm Workers.[40] The dream of a unified black-brown liberation movement spanning the entire nation and launching a strong critique of the economic order was (is?) probably always only a dream.

President Johnson had spent April 4, 1968, at St. Patrick's Cathedral in New York City with his daughter Luci and the five thousand people who had gathered for the installation of Terence Cooke as archbishop of New York. Later that evening in the White House, he learned of King's murder and hurriedly prepared an address to the nation. "America is shocked and saddened by the brutal slaying tonight of Dr. Martin Luther King," he said. "I ask every citizen to reject the blind violence that has struck Dr. King, who lived by nonviolence." The following day in a meeting with civil rights leaders, Johnson said, "If I were a kid in Harlem, I know what I'd be thinking right now: I'd be thinking that the whites have declared open season on my people, and they're going to pick us off one by one unless I get a gun and pick them off first."[41]

In Indianapolis on the campaign trail, Bobby Kennedy announced King's death and told the mostly African American audience, "We can do well in this country. We will have difficult times; we've had difficult times in the past; we will have difficult times in the future. It is not the end of violence; it is not the end of lawlessness; it is not the end of disorder."[42] Within days, rioting had broken out across the country and National Guard troops patrolled the streets around the White House. Less than two months later, the nation would learn that this moment indeed was "not the end of violence" when gunmen assassinated Kennedy in the kitchen of the Ambassador Hotel in Los Angeles.

On April 8 in Memphis, Coretta Scott King joined marchers in the demonstration that Dr. King had hoped to lead. Among the participants was a delegation from the United Farm Workers union that included Dolores Huerta, Frances Ryan, and other volunteers from the New York City UFW boycott committee. Ryan recalled:

> I had been following Martin Luther King's recent actions closely because he was helping another union, that of the sanitation workers, in Memphis. Just before a big planned sanitation workers march, King was killed. The New York Labor Council paid for a charter plane to send supporters to the march that King was supposed to have led. So our New York farm workers' group flew to Memphis and were well received that evening at several African-American churches, where we talked about the UFW organizing efforts to standing room-only crowds. On the big day of the march, we joined the other thousands on the streets. It was truly intimidating to march past the oversized armored personnel carriers that were strung along the route. Nearby, the National Guardsmen looked young and scared. Once again, when I needed it, Dolores Huerta boosted my spirits. She had brought along an oversized "Huelga" flag and enlisted us in helping to keep it unfurled so it would make a good TV shot.[43]

On April 9, King was buried in Atlanta. Among those in attendance were Reies López Tijerina, Corky Gonzales, Stokely Carmichael, Bobby Kennedy, Richard Nixon, and Vice President Hubert Humphrey. After the post-funeral procession arrived at Morehouse College, its president Benjamin Mays said of King, "He would probably say that, if death had to come, I'm sure there was no greater cause to die for than fighting to get a just wage for garbage collectors."[44] The April 15 issue of the United Farm Worker's newspaper, *El Malcriado*, showed a drawing of Dr. King in front of the Memphis sanitation workers with their "I Am a Man" signs and the caption "Killed helping workers to organize." Inside the paper was the text of King's 1963 "I have a dream" speech, the 1968 telegram King sent to Chavez, and the telegram Chavez sent to Coretta Scott King after Dr. King's assassination. "We owe so much to Dr. Martin Luther King that words alone cannot express our gratefulness," Chavez wrote. "[H]is non-violence was that of action—not that of one contemplating action."[45] In the article entitled "Who Killed King," the author argued that it was not a lone madman who had acted alone but an agent of American racism writ large. "He acted for every member of Congress who ever allowed this nation to withhold the natural rights of a man because he was poor or black or brown. He acted for every employer who ever drew a penny of profit by exploiting the group differences between men," the author stated.[46] Chavez, still weakened from his fast and suffering various physical aliments even as he attended to the daily details of managing a labor strike, would not travel to Atlanta for King's funeral or to Washington DC, for the Poor People's Campaign despite several entreaties from Ralph Abernathy and others.[47]

On June 4, the California presidential primary began to shape up as a decisive battle in the struggle for the Democratic Party nomination. Eugene McCarthy and Robert Kennedy both competed for the antiwar vote against Vice President Hubert

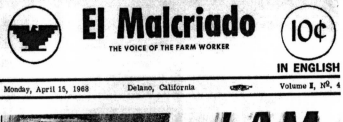

9. Martin Luther King Jr. on the cover of the United Farm Workers'
newspaper, *El Malcriado*, April 15, 1968. Drawing by Andy Zermeño.
Used by permission of the Board of Trustees, Farmworker Movement
Documentation Project.

Humphrey. Before his death, King had not made a public endorsement but Chavez and the farm workers called a temporary halt to all strike activities and began to mobilize on behalf of Kennedy. Kennedy advisor Frank Mankiewicz was amazed by the intensity and the effectiveness of the union's get out the vote drive. "Our turnout was tremendous," he noted, "we were getting 90–95 percent turnouts. And in some of the Mexican areas we had 100 percent turnout by 4 or 5 o'clock in the afternoon. I mean Chavez's guys went around to precincts to say, 'Cesar Chavez says today's the day to vote for Robert Kennedy,' that was the line. And by 4 and 5 o'clock in the afternoon they were phoning back in and saying we had 100 percent turnout. I couldn't believe it!"[48]

In reality, it was not that Chavez dictated to Mexican American voters but that the union enjoyed tremendous support in the barrios. Chavez himself remembers the effort this way: "We used to say, 'I'm from Delano with the farm workers.' 'Oh, the farm workers!' Just like that. 'Yes,' in Spanish. And we'd say, 'We're going to ask you to work for Kennedy,' 'Oh, wonderful. Sure. Sure.'"[49] As the results poured in, Kennedy chided civil rights activist John Lewis, telling him: "You let me down today. More Mexican Americans voted for me than Negroes." By midnight it was clear that Kennedy had narrowly won the primary with 46% to Eugene McCarthy's 42%. From the podium in the Embassy ballroom at the Ambassador Hotel, he thanked "Cesar Chavez and Bert Corona. . . . [A]nd Dolores Huerta who is an old friend of mine."[50] As he moved off the stage on his way to a press conference, Kennedy was shot three times at close range. He died the following day.

Too exhausted to stay for the victory celebration, Chavez had hitched a ride to his lodgings with Father John Luce, an Episcopalian priest with deep ties to the Chicano community. At a brief stop at Assemblyman Richard Calderon's election headquarters, they learned of the shooting.[51] During the

CBS coverage, reporter Mike Wallace reflected on the murders of Malcolm X, John Kennedy, Dr. King, and Bobby Kennedy. He posed the stunning question, "What kind of curious strain of violence is there in the American people?" For the Chicano community, the words written by attorney and novelist Oscar Zeta Acosta captured the moment: "We drive and listen to the live broadcast from the Ambassador Hotel. The reports make it pretty clear that Kennedy has only a few hours of life left. . . . I drive in the darkness and I know, I can feel it in my bones, that the ante has been upped."[52] Senator Kennedy would survive some twenty-four hours longer, bullet fragments dispersed throughout his brain. He was declared dead at 1:44 a.m. on June 6th. That evening in the California grape fields near Delano, farm workers attended a mass in his honor.

Notes

Author's Note: On the morning of March 5, 1968, the author accompanied his parents, Ralph and Irene Mariscal, to the Greyhound bus station in Long Beach, California. That afternoon he was inducted into the U.S. Army and transported to Fort Ord, California, for basic training. He spent 1969 in South Vietnam.

1. Jacques E. Levy, *Cesar Chavez: Autobiography of La Causa* (Minneapolis: University of Minnesota Press, 2007), 270–71.

2. See Steve Estes, *I Am a Man!: Race, Manhood, and the Civil Rights Movement* (Chapel Hill: University of North Carolina Press, 2005), chap. 6.

3. Lyndon B. Johnson, Statement by the President Summarizing Actions on the Recommendations of the Inter-Agency Committee on Mexican American Affairs; John T. Woolley and Gerhard Peters, *The American Presidency Project* (Santa Barbara CA: University of California [hosted], Gerhard Peters [database]), available at http://www.presidency.ucsb.edu/ws/?pid=29391 (accessed March 31, 2009).

4. "Our Nation Is Moving Toward Two Societies, One Black, One White—Separate and Unequal," excerpts from the Kerner Report, *History Matters*, http://historymatters.gmu.edu/d/6545/ (accessed April 4, 2009).

5. Report of the Select Committee on Assassinations of the U.S. House of Representatives, Findings in the Assassination of Dr. Martin Luther

King Jr., National Archives, http://www.archives.gov/research (accessed April 4, 2009).

6. Quoted in Roy Wilkens, *Standing Fast: The Autobiography of Roy Wilkins* (New York: Da Capo Press, 1994), 328.

7. A video clip of Cronkite's editorial can be viewed at http://www.youtube.com/watch?v=JdOb_183d10 (accessed March 16, 2009). For a general overview of 1968, see the documentary *1968: The Year that Shaped a Generation* (Oregon Public Broadcasting Corporation, 1998), http://www.youtube.com/watch?v=6vVZP2T6owI&NR=1 (accessed May 1, 2009).

8. See Carlos Muñoz Jr., *Youth, Identity, Power: The Chicano Movement, Revised and Expanded Edition* (London: Verso, 2007); Ian F. Haney López, *Racism on Trial: The Chicano Fight for Justice* (Cambridge MA: Harvard University Press, 2003).

9. "Lessons of Dr. Martin Luther King Jr." http://www.ufw.org/ (accessed March 31, 2009). An earlier telegram from King to Chavez was sent on September 22, 1966, shortly after the UFW merged with the AFL-CIO: "As brothers in the fight for equality, I extend the hand of fellowship and good will and wish continuing success to you and your members. The fight for equality must be fought on many fronts—in the urban slums, in the sweatshops of the factories and fields. Our separate struggles are really one—a struggle for freedom, for dignity, and for humanity. You and your valiant fellow workers have demonstrated your commitment to righting grievous wrongs forced upon exploited people. We are together with you in spirit and in determination that our dreams for a better tomorrow will be realized." Levy, *Cesar Chavez*, 246.

10. Andrew Young, *An Easy Burden: The Civil Rights Movement and the Transformation of America* (Waco TX: Baylor University Press, 2008), 445. According to Reies López Tijerina, Dr. King had sent him a telegram on March 5 as well inviting the New Mexico land grant movement leader to a planning meeting for the Poor People's Campaign. Reies López Tijerina with José Angel Gutiérrez, *They Called Me "King Tiger": My Struggle for the Land and Our Rights* (Houston: Arte Público, 2001), 101.

11. Chavez told Jacques Levy: "Although I met some of the people that were working with King and saw him on television, I never talked with him except on the phone." Levy, *Cesar Chavez*, 289. There is some confusion in the historiography regarding the Chavez-King relationship. Although the evidence is overwhelming that two men never met, Michael Honey incorrectly writes that King briefly met Chavez. See Honey, *Going Down Jericho*

Road: The Memphis Strike, Martin Luther King's Last Campaign (New York: W. W. Norton, 2008), 290.

12. LeRoy Chatfield, The Farm Worker Documentation Project, "Cesar Chavez and His Farmworker Movement," interview with Professor Paul Henggeler, Question 15, http://www.farmworkermovement.org/essays/essays.shtml (accessed March 31, 2009).

13. The Farm Worker Documentation Project, Jerry Cohen/UFW Legal Department 1967–1980, audio interview: Jerry Cohen Discussion about Cesar Chavez and the UFW, Part I; The Farm Worker Documentation Project, Panel Discussion: "Cesar Chavez 1968 Fast for Nonviolence," 2008, http://farmworkermovement.org/media/oral_history (accessed March 31, 2009); The Farm Worker Documentation Project, John Duggan Autobiography, 46, http://www.farmworkermovement.org/essays/essays (accessed March 31, 2009).

14. *El Malcriado*, March 15, 1968; Mark Day, *Forty Acres: Cesar Chavez and the Farm Workers* (New York: Praeger, 1971), especially chap. 3.

15. The most complete study of Kennedy's relationship with Chavez is Steven W. Bender, *One Night in America: Robert Kennedy, César Chávez, and the Dream of Dignity* (Boulder: Paradigm Press, 2008). See also, Thurston Clarke, *The Last Campaign: Robert F. Kennedy and 82 Days That Inspired America* (New York: Henry Holt, 2008), 36.

16. Oral History interview with Cesar Chavez (with Dennis J. O'Brien), Robert F. Kennedy Oral History Program of the Kennedy Library, The Farm Worker Documentation Project, Part I, http://farmworkermovement .org/media/oral_history; The Farm Worker Documentation Project, A. V. Krebs, "La Causa: The World Made Flesh," http://www.farmworker movement.org/essays/ (both accessed March 31, 2009).

17. The Farm Worker Documentation Project, Jerry Cohen/UFW Legal Department 1967–1980, audio interview: Jerry Cohen Discussion about Cesar Chavez and the UFW, Part II; Clarke, 115–16.

18. Oral History interview with Cesar Chavez (with Dennis J. O'Brien). See also Wallace Turner, "Head of Farm Workers Union Ends 25-Day Fast in California" and "A Farm-Bred Unionist: Cesar Estrada Chavez," March 11, 1968.

19. Chatfield, The Farm Worker Documentation Project, Question 18. In his question to Chatfield, Henggeler refers to the possible invitation of King as a "small, but curious matter."

20. See Philip S. Foner, *U.S. Labor and the Viet-Nam War* (New York: International Publishers, 1989).

21. Oral History interview with Cesar Chavez (with Dennis J. O'Brien); Levy, *Cesar Chavez*, 197.

22. Stan Steiner, *La Raza: The Mexican Americans* (New York: Harper and Row, 1969), 295; Taylor Branch, *At Canaan's Edge: America in the King Years, 1965–68* (New York: Simon and Schuster, 2007), 723. The most complete account of the March 14 meeting and of Chicano participation in the Poor People's Campaign is Gordon Mantler, "Black, Brown, and Poor: Martin Luther King Jr., The Poor People's Campaign, and its Legacies" (PhD diss., Duke University, 2008).

23. Bert Corona with Mario T. García, *Memories of Chicano History: The Life and Narrative of Bert Corona* (Berkeley: University of California Press, 1994), 216; Gordon K. Mantler, "Grassroots Voices, Memory, and the Poor People's Campaign," American Radioworks, http://american radioworks.publicradio.org/features/king/mantler.html (accessed April 4, 2009); Mantler, "Black, Brown and Poor," 59–60.

24. Tijerina, *They Called Me "King Tiger,"* 103; Branch, *At Canaan's Edge*, 715 ; George Mariscal, *Brown-Eyed Children of the Sun: Lessons from the Chicano Movement, 1965–1975* (Albuquerque: University of New Mexico Press, 2005), especially chap. 5.

25. King's "Two Americas" speech, news reports, and photos of his Grosse Pointe appearance can be viewed at http://www.gphistorical.org/mlk/index.htm (accessed April 4, 2009).

26. Levy, *Cesar Chavez*, 292. Jacques Levy's research materials related to subsequent assassination plots against Chavez are currently for restricted use only in the Jacques E. Levy Research Collection on Cesar Chavez, Yale Collection of Western Americana, Beinecke Rare Book and Manuscript Library, Yale University, MSS S-2406, Series X, *Assassination Plot, 1971–1974* (boxes 44–49).

27. Branch, *At Canaan's Edge*, 707. See also Ernesto Vigil, *The Crusade for Justice: Chicano Militancy and the Government's War on Dissent* (Madison: University of Wisconsin Press, 1999), 54.

28. Branch, *At Canaan's Edge*, 717; Report of the Select Committee on Assassinations of the U.S. House of Representatives, Findings in the Assassination of Dr. Martin Luther King Jr., National Archives, http://www.archives.gov/research (accessed April 4, 2009).

29. Mariscal, *Brown-Eyed Children of the Sun*, chap. 4; Peter Matthiessen, *Sal Si Puedes (Escape If You Can): Cesar Chavez and the New American Revolution* (Berkeley: University of California Press, 2000).

30. Branch, *At Canaan's Edge*, 696; Martin Luther King Jr., *Where Do*

We Go From Here: Chaos or Community? in *A Testament of Hope: The Essential Writings and Speeches of Martin Luther King Jr.*, ed. James M. Washington (San Francisco: Harper Collins, 1986), 601–2.

31. Full speech available at AFSCME Memphis Sanitation Strike, March 18, 1968, http://www.afscme.org/about/1550.cfm (accessed February 2, 2011). See also the AFSCME-produced short film "I Am A Man: Dr. King & the Memphis Sanitation Strike": http://www.youtube.com/watch?v=HBDgH435oaU (accessed February 2, 2011).

32. Cesar Chavez, "Letter from Delano," Good Friday, 1969, http://farmworkermovement.org/essays/ (accessed March 31, 2009).

33. Douglas Perry, "Court Documents Related to MLK Jr. and Memphis Sanitation Workers," ERIC # ED462357 (Washington DC: National Archives and Records Administration, 2000), http://www.eric.ed.gov:80 (accessed April 4, 2009).

34. Nick Kotz, *Judgment Days: Lyndon Baines Johnson, Martin Luther King Jr., and the Laws that Changed America* (New York: Houghton Mifflin Harcourt, 2006), 403; Stewart Burns, *To the Mountaintop: Martin Luther King Jr.'s Mission to Save America 1955–1968* (San Francisco: Harper, 2004), 430.

35. *Public Papers of the Presidents of the United States: Lyndon B. Johnson, 1968–69*, vol. I, entry 170, 469–76 (Washington DC: Government Printing Office, 1970). The speech can be viewed at http://www.youtube.com/watch?v=2-FibDxpkbo (accessed March 31, 2009)

36. Chatfield, The Farm Worker Documentation Project, Question 7.

37. Quoted in Honey, *Going Down Jericho Road*, 184.

38. King quoted in Washington, *Testament of Hope*, 280 (first quotation), 285 (second quotation); Branch, *At Canaan's Edge*, 759–66; Burns, *To the Mountaintop*, 447; Chavez quote on Kind in Levy, *Cesar Chavez*, 289. The CBS Evening News broadcast of April 4, 1968 can be viewed at http://www.youtube.com/watch?v=cmOBbxgxKvo (accessed April 4, 2009).

39. Stokely Carmichael with Ekwueme Michael Thelwell, *Ready for Revolution: The Life and Struggles of Stokely Carmichael (Kwame Ture)* (New York: Scribners, 2003), 658.

40. Randy Shaw, *Beyond the Fields: Cesar Chavez, the UFW, and the Struggle for Justice in the 21st Century* (Berkeley: University of California Press, 2008); Frank Bardacke, "Cesar's Ghost: Decline and Fall of the U.F.W.," *The Nation*, January 21, 2006, http://www.thenation.com/doc/19930726/bardacke (accessed March 31, 2009).

41. Clay Risen, *A Nation on Fire: America in the Wake of the King*

Assassination (New York: Wiley, 2009), 89. See also Risen, "The Unmaking of the President," *Smithsonian Magazine*, April 2008, http://www.smith sonianmag.com/history-archaeology/president-lbj.html (accessed April 4, 2009).

42. Kennedy's remarks to the stunned crowd can be viewed at http:// www.youtube.com/watch?v=MyCWV_NoEsM (accessed April 4, 2009).

43. Farm Worker Documentation Project, Frances Ryan, http://www .farmworkermovement.org/essays/ (accessed March 31, 2009).

44. Risen, *A Nation on Fire*, 212.

45. *El Malcriado* 2, no. 4 (April 15, 1968): 5.

46. *El Malcriado* 2, no. 4 (April 15, 1968): 12.

47. Mantler, "Black, Brown, and Poor," 183.

48. Frank Mankiewicz Oral History interview—RFK #9, December 16, 1969, http://www.jfklibrary.org/ (accessed February 2, 2011).

49. Oral History interview with Cesar Chavez (with Dennis J. O'Brien), part 2.

50. John Lewis and Michael D'Orso, *Walking with the Wind: A Memoir of the Movement* (San Diego: Harcourt Brace, 1998), 415. Kennedy's final speech on June 5, 1968 can be viewed at http://www.youtube.com/ watch?v=vXuHcQ1Mrqs&feature (accessed June 5, 2009).

51. Oral History interview with Cesar Chavez (with Dennis J. O'Brien), part 2.

52. Mike Wallace's televised comments on June 5, 1968 can be viewed at http://www.youtube.com/watch?v=qu3t3QosGFI&feature=related (accessed June 5, 2009); Oscar Zeta Acosta, *Revolt of the Cockroach People* (New York: Vintage, 1973), 64.

SEVEN

Black, Brown, and Poor

Civil Rights and the Making of the Chicano Movement

GORDON MANTLER

Early in the morning of May 15, 1968, Gloria Arellanes boarded a chartered Greyhound bus in South Central Los Angeles, ready to make the nearly three-thousand-mile journey to Washington DC. The nineteen-year-old Arellanes had never visited the nation's capital. She knew few Chicana or Chicano activists outside of her immediate world in East Los Angeles and El Monte, California. She had heard about but never seen anyone beaten by the police. Nor had she seen white people so poor that their children hardly had shoes. But this all began to change when she and her fellow Brown Berets—a Chicano youth organization from Los Angeles—heard about Dr. Martin Luther King Jr.'s vision for a new multiethnic alliance of poor people. Two months later, her life as an activist in the Chicano movement forever would be transformed.[1]

Unveiled by King in late 1967, the Poor People's Campaign (PPC) aimed to transform the African American freedom struggle into a larger class-based liberation movement that included not just blacks and whites, but also people of Mexican descent, American Indians, and Puerto Ricans. Together, King declared, they would dramatize the plight of poverty by bringing "waves of the nation's poor and disinherited to Washington DC . . . to demand redress of their grievances by the United States government and to secure at least jobs or income for all," adding that the poor would "stay until America responds."[2] This early rainbow coalition, he believed, would transform fully the struggle for civil rights into one for human rights—and in the process, restore the credibility of nonviolence in social justice organizing, a strategy that had seemingly lost ground amid the rhetoric of Black Power and the urban rebellions that erupted each summer.

Chicano activists responded with great enthusiasm, and for marchers such as Gloria Arellanes, the few weeks that she spent among the poor and their allies in Washington became a turning point personally. "I always told people, I learned more about people on that march than ever. I saw so many things," she recalled. It was an experience that changed her life permanently.[3] At times, Arellanes witnessed the best of people—the kindness of "the most wonderful" African American hosts in St. Louis or the "singing, laughing," and "festive kind of atmosphere" on the buses crossing the country. But she also saw the worst, from a black woman "clutching her daughter with . . . fear in her eyes" during a bomb threat in El Paso to the hypocrisy of a Chicano leader "trying to live like a king" by eating steak while everyone else ate canned rice and beans. All were invaluable lessons that she took home and that helped her become an increasingly sophisticated member of the Chicano movement. From land rights activists and students from New Mexico and Texas to Rodolfo "Corky" Gonzales and the Denver-based Crusade for Justice, Chicano participants in the PPC earned her respect and affection—and inspired her emergence as a leader, first in the Brown Berets and then as a leading voice of Chicana feminist nationalism.[4]

Gloria Arellanes's experience during the PPC was not unusual. Whether they went for months, weeks, or just a day or two, many marchers left Washington enlightened, if not transformed. Yet historians of both the modern African American freedom struggle and the Chicano movement largely have ignored the experiences of Arellanes and hundreds of other Chicanos. Scholars have dismissed the PPC as an inconsequential or destructive afterthought and have called it everything from a "disaster" to "an almost perfect failure."[5] Dismissing the PPC as "a shambles," one prominent scholar argues that Resurrection City, the tent city on the Washington Mall that was home to many of the marchers and emerged as the campaign's dominant symbol, "[B]ecame a gang-infested jungle—an eyesore and an embarrassment . . . having achieved virtually nothing. The Southern Christian Leadership Conference (SCLC) never recovered from the fiasco."[6] Others liberally quote SCLC executive director Bill Rutherford, who later branded the campaign as "the Little Bighorn of the civil rights movement"—an eye-catching albeit imprecise analogy.[7]

Indeed, the campaign did not achieve what Martin Luther King Jr. had set out to do. It did not reinvigorate nonviolent strategy. It did not produce a national multiracial alliance of the poor. And it did not extract a renewed commitment from the federal government to the War on Poverty. As a result, scholarly assessment of the campaign has focused exclusively on *why* the campaign failed. Historians' explanations range from a disorganized SCLC leadership incapable of filling King's shoes and an FBI-coordinated "dirty tricks" operation to the PPC's imprecise policy objectives and Middle America's discomfort with a class-based movement.[8] Most ignore the participation of anyone but blacks and whites.[9] Yet despite the validity of these factors in the PPC's failure to reach its lofty goals, the Poor People's Campaign represents a more complicated moment—particularly in how it illustrates the complexity of black-brown relations.

This essay argues that the campaign offers a compelling snapshot of both the potential of black-Chicano cooperation and the very real obstacles that stood in the way of such an alliance in the late 1960s. Such class-based cooperation "captured the imagination" of many marchers, leading to numerous instances of interethnic, interracial bonding.[10] But more often than not, this attempted alliance in the spring of 1968 highlighted the cultural and political differences between many black activists and their Chicano counterparts—what I call their contrasting social constructions of poverty and the solutions to combat it. Thus, the campaign produced several unintended but noteworthy consequences, the most prominent being its contributions to the then-burgeoning Chicano movement. The time spent by activists of Mexican descent in Washington helped build and deepen relationships with each other. In turn, these experiences empowered individuals, complicated their analyses, and strengthened the interregional networks that became the backbone of the Chicano struggle into the 1970s. Moreover, the PPC raised the prominence of Denver leader Rodolfo "Corky" Gonzales, whose El Plan del Barrio and overall message emphasized ethnic Mexican *mestizaje* and Brown Power, and diminished the class-based efforts of land grants agitator Reies López Tijerina. The notion of another brown race gained that much more traction. Thus, ironically, one of the greatest legacies of this class-based alliance was to reinforce ethnic and racial difference between African Americans and ethnic Mexicans on the eve of the 1970s.

Although King had included Spanish-speaking people from the campaign's first announcement, he and his aides did not know how to mobilize—or even contact—most activists of Mexican descent. Other than a telegram exchange with the United Farm Workers' Cesar Chavez and brief encounters with lesser-known Chicano leaders Gonzales and Tijerina in 1967 at the Conference for New Politics in Chicago, King and his organization had little interaction with ethnic Mexicans.[11] A few of King's aides questioned the wisdom of including such new constituencies in the campaign, including Chicanos. Dripping paternalism, one staff member later said that Tijerina "didn't understand that we were the parents and he was the child."[12] But as PPC national coordinator Bernard Lafayette recalled, he asked King early on, "Do you mean all the poor people? . . . What about the Mexican Americans?" and King responded emphatically, "Yes, of course, we want to get them involved."[13] Therefore, for the first two months of 1968, King's aides scoured the country for Chicano participants, often relying on third parties such as the American Friends Service Committee to make contact. And despite widespread respect for King and civil rights efforts in general, many ethnic Mexicans remained wary of the campaign's structure, goals, and rhetoric. According to José Angel Gutiérrez, a founder of the Mexican American Youth Organization (MAYO) in San Antonio, he and his fellow activists were interested but assumed that the campaign had not been designed for them. "Is this another black-white thing, or are we involved?" he asked.[14] That question was only answered after King invited activists to Atlanta to discuss the upcoming campaign.[15]

The so-called Minority Group Conference was just one day at a motel, but in many ways, it proved to be one of the triumphs of King's last weeks and of the campaign itself. In what Jesse Jackson called "exciting but tense," activists from several dozen organizations gathered to discuss the merits of King's proposed campaign and what exactly, as a unified group, they wanted to achieve.[16] Almost every sort of social justice organization from the era imaginable was represented in the room, from civil rights and student groups to labor, peace, religious, and welfare rights organizations. About a dozen male activists, including Gonzales, Gutiérrez, Tijerina, Bert Corona of California's Mexican American Political Association (MAPA), and Baldemar Velásquez, founder of the Ohio-based Farm Labor Organizing Committee (FLOC), represented the emerging Chicano movement.[17] For King and his aides, the conference provided a unique setting to hear other ethnic minorities' solutions to fight economic inequality that often differed substantially from SCLC's "jobs or income" agenda.[18] Although SCLC leaders appeared receptive to their issues—Ralph Abernathy, speaking for King, told nonblack participants that "we are with you 100 percent"—observers saw King and company as still "unsophisticated in understanding the multi-forces at work" in the room.[19]

Despite such qualms, Chicano activists such as Tijerina departed the conference with high hopes. A passionate and eccentric evangelical preacher who had founded the Alianza Federal de Mercedes, or Alianza, in 1963 to fight for Mexican land grant rights under the 1848 Treaty of Guadalupe Hidalgo, Tijerina had gained notoriety for a citizen's arrest turned violent at a northern New Mexico courthouse in June 1967.[20] In Atlanta, Tijerina mesmerized the room with the land grant movement's dramatic story and left believing his crusade would become a central demand of the campaign. "'We do not want scraps or charity,' I said to Dr. King," wrote Tijerina. "'We want justice. . . . We want the return of the land stolen from our populations. We want our culture respected, and we want the foreign, compulsory education removed.' Dr. King accepted our proposals."[21]

Chicanos also credited the conference with opening their eyes to new strategies and facilitating new connections. Velásquez said King's words about strategy resonated with him. "His comment was when you impede the rich man's ability to make money, anything is negotiable," Velásquez recalled. "I came away with that line branded in my brain."[22] For Gutiérrez, the gathering allowed him and other members of MAYO to meet their fellow student activists in the Student Nonviolent Coordinating Committee, with whom they stayed while in Atlanta.[23] And by publicizing King's invitation as a tacit endorsement, Tijerina also used his participation in the conference to blunt criticism at home. "The more I was accepted by the world as a voice of the oppressed people of the United States, the more that [U.S. Senator Joseph] Montoya's bosses became irked," Tijerina wrote later, referring to the white supporters of New Mexico's ethnic Mexican senator. "Anglos in power in the United States did not want me to be seen next to King." [24]

When the Atlanta meeting ended after much discussion, the conference appeared to have accomplished its main objective: to persuade leaders of the nonblack poor that campaign organizers understood their issues—especially the importance of land and treaty rights—and took them seriously. Myles Horton, longtime labor and civil rights organizer and founder of the Highlander Folk School, was cautiously optimistic, writing, "I believe we caught a glimpse of the future . . . [and] the making of a bottom-up coalition."[25]

Tragically slain in Memphis just three weeks later, King did not live to see such a coalition emerge. His successor Ralph Abernathy, however, immediately assured PPC organizers and participants, including those in the Chicano movement, that "we are going to carry through on Dr. King's last great dream—the poor people's campaign."[26] Ironically, King's death offered an unusual window of opportunity, motivating many people to volunteer their support and services to the campaign. SCLC staff members remembered the phones at Washington's PPC headquarters ringing nonstop, while tens of thousands of people showed up for King's funeral.[27] From Black Panther Party members to moderate leaders such as Roy Wilkins and Bayard Rustin, black activists changed their positions on the campaign, which they initially had seen as either an outmoded form of protest or an unwise provocation of the government. Lauren Watson, chairman of Denver's Black Panther Society and an advocate of "any means necessary" to achieve black freedom, "felt that as my personal tribute to Dr. King that I would go ahead and do it." His participation in the PPC—as a key regional coordinator for SCLC no less—did not mean he was confident that the campaign would succeed, he said, but "there's always room for (my) kind of thinking."[28]

Chicano activists, for the most part, also rallied to the campaign, with more than five hundred eventually making the trip across the country.[29] The reasons as to why they went varied. Tijerina had a recent history of reaching out to African Americans, most notably through the "mutual assistance treaty" with Black Power leaders from the Black Panther Party, SNCC, and Ron Karenga's Us organization at the Alianza's October 1967 convention.[30] In addition to seeing his inclusion in the SCLC-led campaign as vindication of him personally, Tijerina viewed the PPC as a valuable national stage to publicize land grant rights. To Tijerina—as with several generations of ethnic Mexicans before him—restoring the land to its rightful heirs represented a core objective of the Chicano movement and an essential step to combat poverty, particularly in northern New Mexico and southern Colorado. The chance to lobby in the seat of government was too good to pass up, despite King's death.[31]

Indeed, rarely did ethnic Mexican activism reach the nation's capital. Nevertheless, people of Mexican descent had challenged discrimination-spawned inequality throughout the twentieth century.[32] By the 1960s, amid Americans' growing protests against the Vietnam War and for free speech and civil rights, a new generation of Chicano activists offered a sharper, more vocal appraisal of American society and the so-called "Mexican American" generation Chicanos often saw as a champion of whiteness and assimilation.[33] This tougher critique first emerged in the early 1960s through the movement culture developed by the National Farm Workers Association (NFWA)— later renamed the United Farm Workers—under Cesar Chavez and Dolores Huerta in the fields of central California. While Chavez became the most well-known Chicano leader, the movement included many strains and activists unrelated to farm labor. On the community level, a unique Chicano critique based upon a *mestizo* identity and culture, one often connected to the land and symbolized by the mythic Aztlán, began to manifest itself.[34] Students, through groups such as MAYO and the Brown Berets, combined direct action protest with education-centered concerns, leading to such events as the East Los Angeles "blowouts," in which thousands of ethnic Mexican students walked out of schools in March 1968. Other organizations, such as Denver's Crusade for Justice, blended the concerns of urban ethnic Mexicans—such as police brutality, limited jobs and services, and educational inequality—with the cultural rhetoric of Aztlán and an invigorated Chicano identity.[35]

Corky Gonzales—veteran of local Democratic Party politics, former War on Poverty coordinator, and founder of the Crusade in 1966—saw the PPC as an opportunity to bring these disparate strains together and unify a still-fractured movement. To the political establishment that dominated media coverage and federal policy, Chicanos remained nearly invisible. As a result, Gonzales began to consider seriously a conference in which Chicano activists from across the country would come to a central location, such as Denver, to meet, hash out ideas, and build bonds in order to construct a more truly national movement. After receiving King's invitation to Washington, Gonzales delayed such an event in order to go to the nation's capital with thousands of other poor people and their allies. Perhaps in Washington, Gonzales believed, fruitful contacts could be made with their black counterparts, other Chicano activists, or maybe even sympathetic members of the white power structure, be they journalists or public officials. Either way, Gonzales also believed that, "The real work, building bases of power, would remain when the activists returned."[36]

More idealistic Chicanos belie Gonzales's strategic approach. Indeed, scholars have placed too much emphasis on the strategic motives of Tijerina and Gonzales and have silenced less-prominent individuals. For instance, Leo Nieto, a young Methodist minister with the Migrant Ministry of the Texas Council of Churches, saw the campaign as offering the potential of "seeing real democracy at work" and transforming a "glimmer of hope" into a greater federal commitment to the nation's poor, no matter what color. Nieto, who had journeyed one thousand miles to attend King's funeral, also "felt that (blacks) were listening" to Chicano needs, perhaps for the first time since he had begun organizing in west Texas.[37] Other activists saw a chance to make more specific, personal demands on the government—ones they might not be able to make without SCLC paying the way. "Since I was a kid, my grandfather used to tell me how we were robbed of land by the U.S. government," said Rafael Duran, who was sixty-seven at the time. "I was always looking for a way to come to Washington to get it back. It was taken by fraud."[38] Owning the land was inextricably linked to poverty among ethnic Mexicans, argued others, including Roque Garcia of Santa Fe. But Garcia also viewed the trip to Washington as an opportunity to protest urban renewal efforts back home and a welfare system seemingly hostile to clients like himself. East Los Angeles activist Alicia Escalante sought bilingual forms for welfare benefits—an issue which the African American-dominated National Welfare Rights Organization had been slow to prioritize.[39] Still others, like the Crusade's Ernesto Vigil, then nineteen years old, were attracted to King's militant language—tough talk promising "to dislocate the city's functioning, if necessary."[40]

Missing from the campaign's Chicano contingent were a few of the country's most prominent farmworker advocates. Velásquez of FLOC pulled out after King's death. "To pull together a cross-racial, cultural united front around class," he said, "it was going to take an extraordinary ability to articulate that. . . . I didn't think anyone else had that."[41] Even more conspicuous was the absence of Cesar Chavez, who had admired Martin Luther King Jr. greatly. "[M]uch of the courage which we have found in our struggle for justice in the fields had had its roots in the example set by your husband and by those multitudes who followed his non-violent leadership," he wrote Coretta Scott King after her husband's assassination. "We owe so much to Dr. Martin Luther King that words alone cannot express our gratefulness."[42] Yet Chavez, weakened by physical ailments and hesitant to leave a precarious strike situation, declined to attend the PPC. As he later told Eleanor Eaton of the American Friends Service Committee, "he had felt it would be immoral for him just to go and make a speech and then go back to California, that if he had come to the Poor People's Campaign he would have to stay and be part of it."[43] That he also disapproved of Tijerina's sometimes bombastic behavior and worried that a failure in Washington DC, could have cost Chavez goodwill among middle class supporters of UFW boycotts also probably played a role in his decision not to attend. Thus, the pleas of Abernathy and others to come to Washington did not dissuade Chavez from staying home.[44]

Whatever their motives, most Chicano activists climbed aboard charter buses without knowing quite what to expect from the upcoming adventure—starting with the transcontinental journey. The Western Caravan, one of seven organized caravans traversing across the country, carried most of the campaign's ethnic Mexicans from Los Angeles and stopped to pick up scores of new marchers in cities along the way. Most stops spawned a festive and hospitable atmosphere—from fiestas and rallies in Albuquerque and Denver to simple home-cooked meals and warm beds in St. Louis. It was during these breaks when Gloria Arellanes's education began. She recalled the generosity of her hosts: Corky Gonzales, who invited her and fellow Brown Berets to bond with members of the Crusade for Justice on their buses, to the older African American couple in Missouri who graciously opened up their home to her. She also remembered the fear: the hard glint in the eyes of Texas

Rangers, drinking beer as marchers were hustled into an El Paso arena because of a bomb threat; and the panic when a Chicano girl went missing for several hours in Louisville. Yet, overall, Arellanes and others stressed the multiethnic camaraderie, singing, and spirit on those buses—perhaps overshadowed only by their anticipation of what the nation's capital held.[45]

At times, the multiethnic façade showed cracks, especially when Reies Tijerina dramatically challenged SCLC officials over funding and the role of American Indian participants.[46] Similarly, when the Western Caravan arrived in Washington, its members did not join the other, predominantly African American participants living in Resurrection City on the Washington Mall. This tent city quickly had become the most enduring symbol of the campaign, but not necessarily a good one. Although it held about 2,500 people at its peak and sported an energy one journalist described as a "revival meeting within a carnival within an army camp," the shantytown was ravaged by disorganization and poor weather.[47] By the time most Chicanos had arrived, two days of steady rain had transformed the town into a sea of mud, slowing construction of the city's A-frame tents and fraying residents' nerves. Most SCLC officials, including Abernathy, Jesse Jackson, and Andrew Young, had yet to move into Resurrection City themselves and instead stayed in a motel. "We didn't see what we had hoped to see," said Vigil of the Crusade for Justice, adding that it was "[C]learly for understandable reasons. Martin Luther King had been assassinated." But: "[W]e figured, well okay, if they don't have their shit together, we wish them the best of luck. Meanwhile, we have to get on with what we want to do during the time that we're here."[48] Instead, most ethnic Mexicans lived in the Hawthorne School, an experimental high school about two miles away, which the Crusade's Richard Romero secured as temporary housing. A few Chicanos eventually moved into Resurrection City, often joining the campaign's small Puerto Rican contingent, but they proved to be exceptions.[49]

10. Resurrection City was a muddy bog for much of its existence. It rained heavily for more than half of the shantytown's six weeks, climaxing with more than two inches of rain in a twenty-four-hour period on June 12–13. The city's physical challenges contributed to the campaign's overall problems, including the segregation of ethnic Mexicans in the Hawthorne School. Ollie Atkins Photograph Collection, Special Collections and Archives, George Mason University Libraries.

Journalists at the time dismissed Hawthorne as little more than a segregated bunker to which Tijerina and his followers retreated after confrontations with SCLC officials over campaign decision making. Although not altogether inaccurate, such portrayals overly simplified Hawthorne's significance. In fact, choosing Hawthorne was perhaps the most critical decision made by Chicanos in the two months that they lived in Washington. In this space, much of the campaign's constructive relationship-building occurred, so much so that several activists independently called it "a successful multi-ethnic community."[50] Sometimes these connections were with people of other backgrounds, particularly whites from Appalachia or American

Indians, for whom control of ancestral land proved an essential issue of economic survival. Chicanos even bonded with rank-and-file black marchers, including Black Panthers, who proved more receptive to issues such as land rights than SCLC's middle class leaders.[51]

But the most important contacts Chicanos made in Hawthorne were with other people of Mexican descent and Latinos more generally. As Carlos Montes, another Brown Beret from Los Angeles, put it: "When would we have gotten together with the Crusade (for Justice)?" he asked. "Lived with them? Shared bread with them? Marched every day with them?"[52] Indeed, the opportunity to spend a month or more together, getting to know each in both exciting and mundane moments, was a golden opportunity for these mostly young activists and key to their later activities in the movement. Vigil rattled off all the people he met for the first time during the campaign, including Brown Berets, UFW activists, Ernesto Cortes of the Industrial Areas Foundation, Tijerina and members of the Alianza, and SNCC veterans María Varela and Betita Martinez (Elizabeth Sutherland), to name just a few. Based on their contact there, Alicia Escalante went to Denver to work with the Crusade for Justice, while Corky Gonzales's eldest daughter, Nita, met a Puerto Rican campaigner she would eventually marry—expanding the family's ties into a larger Latino alliance. *LADO*, Chicago's Latino newspaper published by an organization of the same name, concluded that, "The Poor People's Campaign, if it did nothing else, provided the chance for both Mexican-Americans and Puerto Ricans to come together, and begin to work together in fighting for our rights."[53]

Another result was the development of a more sophisticated way of viewing poverty—a direct product of interacting with Appalachian whites. Of course, Corky Gonzales, a seasoned and well-read activist, knew about the rich organizing tradition poor whites had in the Appalachian area. But for younger activists it gave them something to think about. "It was the first time that a lot of us had any contact with Puerto Ricans, with Appalachian whites," recalled Ralph Ramirez, a Brown Beret. "When you never have been . . . over one hundred miles from where you were born, to come in contact with all these people and these different cultures and these different subcultures," Ramirez concluded, it was an education far beyond any classroom.[54] Rudy Gonzales, one of Corky's sons, found it invaluable in his later years to have played with kids of many backgrounds and ethnicities during their stay at Hawthorne. "I had never seen poor whites before," he recalled. "I mean dirt poor. Some hardly had shoes."[55] Many other marchers echoed this sentiment. One initial response Chicanos had was to gather the extra shoes and jackets they brought and to give these items to their white counterparts.[56] To most of the Chicanos there, whites were typically rich elites who suppressed the rights of minorities and ran the nation's power structure. They certainly were not *more* impoverished than ethnic Mexicans, these activists had believed. For Carlos Montes, it helped crystallize a developing class consciousness. Rather than vilifying white men, he began to criticize the capitalist structure and its most common defenders, *rich* white men.[57]

Many of the direct-action demonstrations in which Chicanos participated also helped cement bonds—from the infamous rally at the U.S. Supreme Court building, in which activists broke several windows and were arrested, to the myriad protests outside federal agencies and inside congressional offices. Spearheaded by American Indian activist Hank Adams and only reluctantly endorsed by Abernathy, the boisterous demonstration outside the Supreme Court challenged a recent ruling against several tribes' rights to fish protected waters in Washington state.[58] The four hundred ethnic Mexicans, Indians, and blacks who participated considered the protest a moral victory—and not just because a handful of marchers met the court's clerk for a three-hour meeting. While marching back to Hawthorne, Washington DC, police officers on motorcycles nearly ran over several children, sparking a small melee, in which police beat Ernesto Vigil, Danny Tijerina, son of the Alianza leader, and several others. "It was the first time I . . . ever saw anybody brutally beaten," said Gloria Arellanes. "[L]ooking into the faces of these police officers, you could see so many different emotions. I remember one young man, just so embarrassed. You could see his pain."[59]

The aftermath proved particularly memorable in how it strengthened Chicano camaraderie. Commenting on the hours he spent behind bars with young Chicanos from New Mexico and California, Vigil stated, "You really find common cause when you sit in the same god-damned jail cell." Several blacks also had been arrested. After authorities released them later that evening, a multiethnic crowd at the Vermont Street Baptist Church greeted them as heroes. We "received a thunderous reception, black folks standing up . . . after we were bonded out and marching in," Vigil recalled. "[I]t was really a tremendous time which we could have capitalized on." Unfortunately, the moment for multiethnic unity proved fleeting after several Black Panthers from Denver challenged Abernathy and his aides, arguing that they had paid too much attention to the Chicanos. After considerable awkwardness, Abernathy smoothed over their differences, at least publicly, but the damage had been done. Yet, ironically, this "power play," as Vigil described it, ended up strengthening bonds among Chicanos, who concluded they could not count on some of their black brethren—even those from their hometown—when the chips were down.[60]

During the next several weeks, Chicanos took their message to the government for land and treaty rights, and against police brutality, education inequality, racial discrimination, and the Vietnam War. María Varela, who photographed much of the campaign and worked extensively with the Alianza members in

Washington, described the interactions she witnessed between younger Chicanos as "critical in forming some of the New Mexico folks who" once "were more isolated than the others."[61] Luís Diaz de León recalled how he received his "Vietnam antiwar education" after Sal Candelaria, a member of the Black Berets from San Jose, California, came back bloodied from an antiwar protest.[62] At the climactic Solidarity Day march on June 19, Corky Gonzales brought these varied demands together in El Plan del Barrio, which became a model for later movement documents. Declaring that "poverty and city living under the colonial system of the Anglo has castrated our people's culture, consciousness of our heritage, and language," Gonzales offered a coherent list of demands in the areas of housing, education, job development and economic opportunities, law enforcement, farm labor, and land reform.[63]

While Chicanos nurtured and strengthened many relationships, some began to question the skills of at least a few black and brown leaders during their time in Washington. Disgusted with Abernathy and SCLC officials for their seeming unwillingness to share decision making or fully comprehend Chicano issues, Gonzales wrote off the venerable civil rights organization as a reliable partner. The campaign also began Tijerina's marginalization as a Chicano movement spokesman. While his declarations about stolen land and cultural pride may have animated Chicanos from afar, many were left unimpressed given the opportunity to work closely with the land rights activist. María Varela quit working with him halfway through the campaign, convinced he was racist, sexist, and not a good organizer. Gloria Arellanes recalled him eating steak in the Hawthorne School while most everyone else ate beans and rice. Miguel Bárragan called him "hard to reach. . . . He was pretty much into his pontificating."[64] Corky Gonzales refused to criticize Tijerina publicly, saying that, "Any fights within our family, we keep within the family."[65] But behind the scenes, he came to believe

195

11. Reies López Tijerina speaks to a group at the Hawthorne School, where the campaign's southwestern contingent stayed while in Washington. Looking on are (*from left*) Corky Gonzales, American Indian activists Hank Adams and Al Bridges, and SCLC's Ralph Abernathy. Karl Kernberger Pictorial Collection, PICT 2000–008–0130, Center for Southwest Research, University Libraries, University of New Mexico.

that Tijerina's harangues and public spats—including a public shouting match with SCLC's Hosea Williams—were counterproductive. Even the children who had traveled with their families called him Reies López "TV-rina" because of his penchant to chase television cameras. By the early 1970s, many activists considered him an afterthought.[66]

During the last week of June 1968, increasingly impatient authorities pulled the plug on Resurrection City, flattening the shantytown and, with it, much of the energy of the PPC—at least in Washington. Many Chicanos, including Tijerina, stayed on for another month, using the Hawthorne School as a home base for further lobbying and the development of a multiethnic Poor

People's Embassy (PPE). Designed to represent poor people's interests in the capital but remain disentangled from the liberal establishment, the PPE became more of a clearinghouse to provide informational, networking, and strategic support to local community groups interested in class-based, multiethnic alliances at home. Nita Gonzales, Corky's eldest daughter, stayed to work with the embassy. But despite substantial multiethnic support from activists initially, the embassy never secured enough funding to influence policy.[67]

Corky Gonzales returned to Denver to pick up where he and members of the Crusade for Justice had left off, but he did not return empty-handed. Rather, Gonzales could count many more friends and followers after the campaign. "SCLC knew about us now . . . the Puerto Ricans knew about us now, and it allowed for those alliances at times on issues [that] . . . before we didn't have," said Nita Gonzales. Her brother, Rudy, added that although the Crusade did not maintain close relations with SCLC, the Chicano organization did foster important connections with people like Father James Groppi of Milwaukee's open housing movement and fishing rights activists Suzette Bridges and Roxanne Allen, who visited Denver in the months after the campaign.[68]

Corky Gonzales also recognized that, as important as such alliances were, it was essential to organize themselves as Chicanos first. Ironically, perhaps the most important lesson activists drew from the PPC was that Chicano strength relied on a certain level of intraethnic unity and that although poverty and oppression were shared by many people, African Americans, Chicanos, and Indians constructed their solutions to poverty differently. Ethnically and racially driven culture, such as the importance of land and Aztlán, resulted in dissimilar but not necessarily competing needs from African Americans. Therefore, Gonzales returned to his idea of a regional event for Chicano students to be held in the spring of 1969 in Denver.

Undoubtedly, the Crusade would have held the first Chicano Youth Liberation Conference whether or not Gonzales attended the PPC. Yet for some activists, the difference between going and not going was their personal interactions with Gonzales and other Chicano youth. For participants such as Carlos Montes, Ralph Ramirez, and Lorraine Escalante, spending a month or more with the Chicano leader and his family in the Hawthorne School influenced their response to his call. "The fact that we knew Corky and Ernesto Vigil real well, as soon as they told (us), we were there," Montes recalled. "It was no question of that."[69] Escalante also found herself in Denver with her activist mother, Alicia, who had settled in Denver for a time after meeting Gonzales in Washington. For "[t]he young people, there was a lot of impact," María Varela said. "Again, many of them had never traveled. Here they were in Washington DC. Here, they were meeting people from other places. The kids from the Crusade hung with the guys from New Mexico. There were connections made there."[70]

The conference proved to be a key turning point in the rhetoric and direction of the student movement and Corky Gonzales's role with it. The roughly 1,500 participants—a number that far surpassed the Crusade's expectations—embraced what one scholar calls a "foundational blueprint for the Chicano movement."[71] *El Plan de Aztlán*, a document compiling the many resolutions passed during the five-day conference, trumpeted Chicano self-determination, ethnic pride and unity, and an emphasis on cultural values of "life, family, and home," in contrast to alleged societal values of hyperindividualistic materialism and whiteness. Declaring themselves free of persistent feelings of inferiority, conference participants "publicly and proudly linked their political crusade to their cultural inheritance" by declaring, among other things, that "brown was beautiful"— an echo of "black is beautiful" sentiments seen and heard during the campaign in Washington and elsewhere.[72]

The Brown Berets that went to Denver already had made a lasting impression on their fellow activists at the campaign, serving as models of different sorts for student activists from across the country. For instance, the youth organization inspired Gilberto Ballejos, an Alianza member and PPC organizer, to form one of the Brown Berets' most effective chapters in Albuquerque.[73] In the form of Gloria Arellanes and her fellow Chicanas in the feminist *Las Adelitas de Aztlán,* the Berets spawned a distinctly Chicana nationalism, articulated by women tired of their marginalization in the movement.[74] And following the youth conference, the Berets became a key antiwar voice, helping establish the Chicano Moratorium Committee. On August 29, 1970, that committee sponsored a rally–turned–police riot that scholars and activists routinely see as the peak of the Chicano movement.[75]

That the PPC, directly and indirectly, helped seed these events alters not only our understanding of Dr. Martin Luther King Jr.'s last crusade, but also places in sharp relief the inherent complexity of black-brown organizing and relations. SCLC's attempt at building a class-based, multiethnic alliance in the spring of 1968 had several subtle and not-so-subtle consequences. It highlighted very real cultural and political differences between African Americans and ethnic Mexicans, particularly in how each group constructed their own poverties. While many blacks such as King and Abernathy sought "jobs or income" to combat poverty, the Chicano activists in Washington emphasized land and language rights. Chicanos found that some rank-and-file blacks understood their issues, especially the economic and cultural significance of the land, but that their black middle class counterparts—including those among the SCLC leadership—rarely comprehended such differences or took them seriously.

Both of these phenomena contributed to the PPC's most striking consequence: that the campaign experience strengthened ethnic identity—particularly among people of Mexican descent—and thus the Chicano movement. When activists such as Arellanes, Vigil, and Ballejos returned home to Los Angeles, Denver, and Albuquerque, they were energized by their experiences in Washington, by the other Chicanos they met, and by the lessons they learned. They were that much more serious and informed about what it took to make elites in Washington and at home listen. And the result was a more unified, energized movement in the years to come. Ironically, the interethnic efforts of the PPC, prompted by the nation's most prominent African American civil rights leader, became a key building block to concrete intraethnic gains for Brown Power and the burgeoning Chicano movement.

Notes

1. Gloria Arellanes, interview by author, November 9, 2006, El Monte CA. All interviews by author are in his possession, unless otherwise noted. A note about terminology: I use the term "Chicano" to describe those people of Mexican descent who identified with the specific political movement of the 1960s and 1970s called the Chicano movement. "Ethnic Mexican" describes anyone of Mexican descent living in the United States, Chicanos and otherwise. I also refer to black-brown relations as "interethnic"—in contrast to the term interracial, which presumes the racial binary of black and white.

2. Martin Luther King Jr., press conference transcript announcing Poor People's Campaign, December 4, 1967, Martin Luther King Jr. Papers Project, http://www.stanford.edu/group/King/ publications/papers/unpub/671204-003_Announcing_Poor_Peoples_campaign.htm (accessed September 9, 2005).

3. Arellanes, interview by author, November 9, 2006.

4. Arellanes, interview by author, November 9, 2006. Dionne Espinoza distinguishes between Arellanes's feminist nationalism as a Chicana and the feminism of middle class white women. Espinoza, "'Revolutionary Sisters': Women's Solidarity and Collective Identification Among Chicana Brown Berets in East Los Angeles, 1967–1970," *Aztlán* 26, no. 1 (2001): 17–58.

5. Quotes in Peter Ling, *Martin Luther King Jr.* (New York: Routledge, 2002), 297; and Gerald McKnight, *The Last Crusade: Martin Luther King Jr., the FBI and the Poor People's Campaign* (Boulder CO: Westview, 1998),

107. By privileging King's life, biographers Taylor Branch and David Garrow discuss the planning stages for the PPC but not the campaign itself. Branch, *At Canaan's Edge: America in the King Years, 1965–1968* (New York: Simon & Schuster, 2006), 659, 661, 670–73, 679, 688–91, 707, 720–21, 754–55, 764–65; and Garrow, *Bearing the Cross: Martin Luther King Jr. and the Southern Christian Leadership Conference* (New York: William Morrow, 1986), 589–601, 606–9, 611–18, 622–23. See also Michael K. Honey, *Going Down Jericho Road: The Memphis Strike, Martin Luther King's Last Campaign* (New York: W. W. Norton, 2007), 173–90, 500–501; Harvard Sitkoff, *King: Pilgrimage to the Mountaintop* (New York: Hill & Wang, 2008), 223–31; Nick Kotz, *Judgment Days: Lyndon Baines Johnson, Martin Luther King Jr., and the Laws that Changed America* (Boston: Houghton Mifflin, 2005), 379–403; and Adam Fairclough, *To Redeem the Soul of America: The Southern Christian Leadership Conference and Martin Luther King Jr.* (Athens: University of Georgia Press, 1987), 394–97. Scholars of the ethnic Mexican experience in the United States are a bit less harsh, but rarely do they offer the PPC more than a passing mention. See Rodolfo Acuña, *Occupied America: A History of Chicanos* (New York: Longman, 2000), 370–71; Lorena Oropeza, *¡Raza Si! ¡Guerra No!: Chicano Protest and Patriotism During the Viet Nam War Era* (Berkeley: University of California Press, 2005), 73–74; Rudy V. Busto, *King Tiger: The Religious Vision of Reies López Tijerina* (Albuquerque: University of New Mexico Press, 2005), 62; Ernesto Chávez, *'¡Mi Raza Primero!': Nationalism, Identity, and Insurgency in the Chicano Movement in Los Angeles, 1966–1978* (Berkeley: University of California Press, 2002), 51; Armando Navarro, *Mexican American Youth Organization: Avant-Garde of the Chicano Movement in Texas* (Austin: University of Texas Press, 1995), 26, 39–40, 153; Mario T. Garcia with Bert Corona, *Memories of Chicano History: The Life and Narrative of Bert Corona* (Berkeley: University of California Press, 1994), 216; Juan Gómez-Quiñones, *Chicano Politics: Reality and Promise, 1940–1980* (Albuquerque: University of New Mexico Press, 1990), 114–15; Carlos Muñoz, *Youth, Identity, Power: The Chicano Movement* (London: Verso, 1989), 66; and José Angel Gutiérrez, *The Making of a Chicano Militant: Lessons from Cristal* (Madison: University of Wisconsin Press, 1998), 221. Two exceptions are Ernesto Vigil's book on the Crusade for Justice and George Mariscal's larger study of the Chicano movement. Offering a short chapter on the campaign mostly reliant on FBI surveillance files, Vigil's study contends that the campaign at least helped publicize the Chicano movement outside of the Southwest. Mariscal, who

201

devotes a lengthy chapter to black-brown relations more generally, portrays the PPC as a failure. Vigil, *The Crusade for Justice Chicano Militancy and the Government's War on Dissent* (Madison: University of Wisconsin Press, 1999), 54–63; and Mariscal, *Brown-Eyed Children of the Sun: Lessons from the Chicano Movement, 1965–1975* (Albuquerque: University of New Mexico Press, 2005), 196–200. Daniel Cobb offers a more sympathetic account of the campaign through the American Indian experience. Cobb, *Native Activism in Cold War America: The Struggle for Sovereignty* (Lawrence: University of Kansas Press, 2008), chaps. 7–8.

6. Adam Fairclough, *Better Day Coming: Blacks and Equality, 1890–2000* (New York: Viking, 2001), 321. "Fiasco" proves a popular label among historians, including Harvard Sitkoff and John D'Emilio. Sitkoff, *The Struggle for Black Equality, 1954–1980* (New York: Hill & Wang, 1981), 222; and D'Emilio, *Lost Prophet: The Life and Times of Bayard Rustin* (Chicago: University of Chicago Press, 2003), 464–65.

7. *Voices of Freedom: An Oral History of the Civil Rights Movement from the 1950s through the 1980s*, ed. Henry Hampton and Steve Fayer (New York: Bantam, 1990), 480. At least in 1876 the Sioux decisively "won" the Battle at Little Bighorn before losing the eventual war against federal soldiers.

8. Charles Fager, *Uncertain Resurrection: The Poor People's Washington Campaign* (Grand Rapids MI: William B. Eerdmans, 1969); McKnight, *The Last Crusade*; Robert T. Chase, "Class Resurrection: The Poor People's Campaign of 1968 and Resurrection City," 40 *Essays in History* (1998); and Mariscal, *Brown-Eyed Children of the Sun*, 178–99.

9. While Thomas Jackson downplays failure, he also misses the campaign's multiethnic character. *From Civil Rights to Human Rights: Martin Luther King Jr. and the Struggle for Economic Justice* (Philadelphia: University of Pennsylvania Press, 2007), 329–59.

10. Quote in Al McSurely, "What Have We Done and What Should We Do?" undated [July 1968?], Box 32, Folder 5, Reies López Tijerina Papers, Center for Southwest Research, University of New Mexico, Albuquerque NM (hereafter RLT).

11. King telegram to Cesar Chavez, September 19, 1966, in Box 21, Folder 5, Martin Luther King Jr. Papers, Martin Luther King Jr. Center for Nonviolent Change, Atlanta, Georgia (hereafter KP); Tijerina letter to King, September 7, 1967, Box 34, Folder 20, and King telegram to Tijerina, January 8, 1968, both in RLT; and Vigil, *The Crusade for Justice*, 53. In 1966 an SCLC contingent showed their support for striking Mexican farm workers

by joining the end of a two-month, four-hundred-mile march from the Rio Grande Valley in Texas to Austin. King aide Andrew Young was reported to have led the black contingent at a march-ending rally. *New York Times*, September 5, 1966.

12. Garrow, *Bearing the Cross*, 607.

13. Bernard Lafayette, national coordinator of the PPC, interview by author, June 13, 2005, by telephone. See also Branch, *At Canaan's Edge*, 716.

14. José Angel Gutiérrez, interview by author, January 8, 2006, by telephone.

15. Lafayette, interview by author; and Tom Houck, minority groups coordinator, July 19, 1968, and Ernest Austin, Appalachian leg coordinator, July 9, 1968, both interviews by Kay Shannon, Washington DC, in Ralph Bunche Oral History Collection, Moorland-Spingarn Research Center, Howard University, Washington DC (hereafter MSRC).

16. Quote from Jesse Jackson, "Resurrection City: The Dream, The Accomplishments," *Ebony* (October 1968): 66.

17. "American Indians, Poor Whites, Spanish-Americans Join Poor People's Washington Campaign," SCLC release, March 15, 1968, Poor People's Campaign folder, Box 2101, unprocessed Papers of the National Welfare Rights Organization, MSRC (hereafter NWRO); "Participants of Minority Group Conference," March 14, 1968, Box 179, Folder 11, Subseries 1, Reel 27, frames 01009–01016, Records of the Southern Christian Leadership Conference (hereafter SCLC); Baldemar Velásquez, interview by author, August 8, 2007, by telephone; and Tom Houck, interview by Shannon.

18. "Income" referred to a guaranteed annual income or negative income tax, in which the national government made a direct payment to every citizen whose income fell below a certain level. Economists ranging from John Kenneth Galbraith to Milton Friedman and a range of social justice groups endorsed this policy, including SCLC and the National Welfare Rights Organization, in the late 1960s and early 1970s. Felicia Kornbluh, *The Battle for Welfare Rights: Poverty and Politics in Modern America* (Philadelphia: University of Pennsylvania Press, 2007), 48–51.

19. Eleanor Eaton memo to Barbara Moffett, "Minority Leaders Conference," April 2, 1968, Community Relations Division (CRD) Folder 32556, "Poor People's Campaign: General, Planning Materials, 1968," American Friends Service Committee records, Philadelphia PA (hereafter AFSC).

20. Twenty followers of Tijerina's went to Tierra Amarilla, the dusty county seat of Rio Arriba County, New Mexico, in order to place District Attorney Alfonso Sánchez under citizen's arrest. Sánchez had pursued

assault charges against Tijerina, who, in the name of ethnic Mexican land rights, attempted to place two park rangers at the Kit Carson National Forest in northern New Mexico under citizen's arrest for trespassing. Sánchez, however, was not at the courthouse and in their frustration the Alianza members wounded the jailer. Tijerina's role in the raid has come under dispute, but he became a wanted man by authorities and a hero in the eyes of black activists like the Us organization's Ron Karenga and SNCC's Ralph Featherstone. For narratives of Tierra Amarilla, including the courtroom case to come later, see Richard Gardner, *Grito! Reies Tijerina and the New Mexico Land Grant War of 1967* (Indianapolis IN: Bobbs-Merrill, 1970); Patricia Bell Blawis, *Tijerina and the Land Grants: Mexican Americans in Struggle for Their Heritage* (New York: International, 1971); and Peter Nabokov, *Tijerina and the Courthouse Raid* (Albuquerque: University of New Mexico Press, 1969). Unhappy with these accounts, Tijerina provides his own retelling, first published in Spanish, and then in English. Tijerina, *Mi Lucha por La Tierra* (Mexico City: Fondo de Cultura Economica, 1978), later translated into Reies López Tijerina, *They Called Me "King Tiger": My Struggle for the Land and Our Rights*, trans. José Angel Gutiérrez (Houston: Arte Publico, 2000). See also Busto, *King Tiger*; and Lorena Oropeza, "The Heart of Chicano History: Reies López Tijerina as a Memory Entrepreneur," *The Sixties* 1, no. 1 (2008): 49–67.

21. Tijerina, *They Called Me "King Tiger,"* 103.

22. Velásquez, interview by author.

23. Gutiérrez, interview by author.

24. Quote in Tijerina, *They Called Me "King Tiger,"* 102, 104. Reis López Tijerina letter to Bob Brown, editor, *Albuquerque Journal*, April 26, 1968, Box 31, Folder 28, RLT; and Tijerina, *They Called Me "King Tiger,"* 102, 104. Also, "Poor March Subdues Militant 'Bandido,'" *Washington Post*, June 4, 1968; and Roque Garcia, Alianza member, interview by author, August 17, 2005, by telephone.

25. Quote in Myles Horton letter to Andrew Young, April 5, 1968, in Box 177, Folder 20, Reel 26, frame 00614, SCLC. Horton dictated the letter immediately after the conference, originally written to King, but did not mail the letter, readdressed to Young, until after his friend's death. His optimism had turned to despair, at least temporarily: "I am too numbed by Martin's death to think clearly and I am sending it as dictated in the hopes that you who are his heirs may still find these ideas of some value. . . . The lights are dim in my world today." Also, Tom Houck, interview by Shannon.

26. *Los Angeles Times*, April 5, 1968.

27. James Edward Peterson, administrative assistant to the PPC's national deputy coordinator, interview by Kay Shannon, July 3, 1968, and Kay Shannon, interview by Claudia Rawles, Washington DC, both in MSRC; and Andrew Young, *An Easy Burden: The Civil Rights Movement and the Transformation of America* (New York: Harper Collins, 1996), 476. In fact, police estimated 150,000 to 200,000 people participated in King's funeral procession and services on April 9, 1968. *Atlanta Constitution*, April 10, 1968.

28. Lauren Watson, interview by author, June 27, 2005, Denver CO.

29. Estimates of how many participated in the PPC range widely. Overly optimistic SCLC reports suggested as many as one thousand ethnic Mexicans, while more skeptical press accounts and a detailed demographic study by Albert Gollin, a sociologist, public opinion researcher, and chair of the PPC's General Administration and Services Committee, concluded the total was much lower. Gollin, *The Demography of Protest: A Statistical Profile of Participants in the Poor People Campaign* (Washington DC: Bureau of Social Science Research, 1968), 2–3; *New York Times*, May 26 and 28, 1968, and March 31, 1999; Tom Houck memo to William Rutherford, April 20, 1968, Box 177, Folder 20, SCLC; *Albuquerque Journal*, May 10 and June 3, 1968; *Denver Post*, May 16 and 20, 1968; *Washington Post*, May 27, 1968; and FBI memo, Albuquerque, May 14, 1968.

30. Maulana Ron Karenga, "Gente de Color: Vamos a Sobrevivir—People of Color: We Shall Survive," 1967, in Box 34, Folder 24, and FBI file, SAC-Abq, December 27, 1967, Box 2, Folder 23, both in RLT. Tijerina shared the stage with African Americans several times in 1967 and 1968, including an event to support the Black Panthers' Huey Newton in February 1968 in Los Angeles. FBI memo, "Stokely Carmichael—Internal Security," February 26, 1968, Box 3, Folder 4, RLT. See also George Mariscal's chapter in this volume.

31. Reies López Tijerina, interview by James Mosby, June 12, 1968, Washington DC, MSRC; and Tijerina, *They Called Me "King Tiger,"* 101, 103–4, 115, 117.

32. Many earlier organizations provided a foundation for the Chicano movement, including the Congress of Spanish-Speaking Peoples and the Mexican American Movement during World War II and the National Farm Workers Association and Asociación Nacional México Americana in the 1950s. George Sánchez, *Becoming Mexican-American: Ethnicity, Culture and Identity in Chicano Los Angeles, 1900–1945* (New York: Oxford

University Press, 1993); and Mario T. García, *Mexican Americans: Leadership, Ideology and Identity, 1930–1960* (New Haven: Yale University Press, 1989).

33. For the coining of this somewhat misleading generational moniker, see Garcia, *Mexican Americans*, 1–2.

34. The Southwest, including the territory ceded to the United States in the 1848 Treaty of Guadalupe Hidalgo, became known to activists as Aztlán, referring to the mythical place of origin of the pre-Columbian Aztec people. It represented many things to Chicanos, from an identity independent of European influence to a culture of economic independence based upon herding, weaving, and communal property. The loss of that land not only translated into a decline in wealth but also endangered a cherished way of life. Acuña, *Occupied America*, 14–15.

35. Gómez-Quiñones, *Chicano Politics*, chaps. 2–3. On the Crusade, see Vigil, *The Crusade for Justice*; and Tom Romero II, "Our Selma is Here: The Political and Legal Struggle for Educational Equality in Denver, Colorado, and Multiracial Conundrums in American Jurisprudence," *Seattle Journal for Social Justice* 3, no. 1 (2004): 73–142.

36. Quote in Vigil, *The Crusade for Justice*, 56. Nita Jo Gonzales, daughter of Corky, interview by author, June 27, 2005, Denver CO; Ernesto Vigil, interview by author, December 10, 2005, by telephone; Gerry Gonzales and Rudy Gonzales, Corky's son and wife, interview by author, June 26, 2005, Denver CO; *Crusade for Justice Newsletter*, May 1966, Box 3, "Prison Info," unprocessed Papers of Rodolfo "Corky" Gonzales, Denver Public Library, Denver; *El Gallo*, June 23, July 28, and August 31, 1967, April and May 1968; and Vigil, *Crusade for Justice*, 26–27, 56, 63.

37. Quote in Leo Nieto, interview by author, March 9, 2006, by telephone. See also Leo Nieto, letter to Ralph Abernathy, April 23, 1968, Box 49, Folder 3, SCLC, "The Poor People's Campaign, 1968," unpublished chapter, in author's possession, and "The Chicano Movement and the Churches in the United States," *Perkins Journal* 29 (1975): 32–41. Here, he lays out a theological statement for the Chicano experience, one which explicitly identifies with the poor.

38. *Washington Post*, May 28, 1968.

39. Escalante founded the East Los Angeles Welfare Rights Organization, later named the Chicana Welfare Rights Organization, after her children's state health benefits were cut. Alicia Escalante, interview by author, September 19, 2005, by telephone; Garcia, interview by author; (San Francisco) *People's World*, May 18, 25, and June 1, 1968; and *The (New York)*

Worker, June 2, 1968. On the NWRO, see Felicia Kornbluh, *The Battle for Welfare Rights: Politics and Poverty in Modern America* (Philadelphia: University of Pennsylvania Press, 2007).

40. SCLC internal memo, "Statement of Purpose: Washington DC, Poor People's Campaign," January 1968, SCLC.

41. Velásquez, interview by author.

42. *El Grito del Norte* (Española, New Mexico), Spring 1968.

43. Eleanor Eaton memo to Barbara Moffett, "Cesar Chavez," in CRD Folder 51910, "Economic Security and Rural Affairs 1968-Comms and Orgs: United Farm Workers Organizing Cmte," AFSC. Please note that AFSC uses folder numbers exclusively, not box numbers, in its archives.

44. Chavez and Larry Itliong telegram to SCLC, April 29, 1968, and Abernathy, Young and Lafayette telegram to Chavez, June 4, 1968, both in Box 69, Folder 11; Leo Nieto telegram to Chavez, May 2, 1968, Box 70, Folder 1, all in Office of the President Files, Part I, Papers of the United Farm Workers, Archives of Labor and Urban Affairs, Walter P. Reuther Library, Wayne State University, Detroit (hereafter UFW). Chavez routinely cited his health for not attending out-of-state events, including SCLC conventions, but documents suggest an active travel schedule in May 1968 that included fundraisers and other trips to the East Coast. May 16–21 itinerary, May 3, 1968, and Marion (?) letters to Cesar Chavez and Jim Drake, administrative assistant, May 1, 3, and 9, 1968, all in Box 6, Folder 25, UFW Administration Department Files.

45. *People's World*, May 25 and June 1, 1968; *Albuquerque Journal*, May 16 and 18–19, 1968, in Box 61, Folders 7–8, and Katherine Hattenbach and Shirley Hill Witt form letter to New Mexico hosts, May 29, 1968, Box 31, Folder 21, both in RLT; *Denver Post*, May 19–20, 1968; *Rocky Mountain News*, May 19–20, 1968; Blawis, *Tijerina and the Land Grants*, 116–17; Tom Houck, interview by Kay Shannon; Juanita Malouf Dominguez, interview by author, December 2, 2007, Taos NM; and Arellanes and Escalante, interview by author.

46. When the caravan first arrived in Albuquerque, Tijerina threatened to pull the Alianza from the coalition if SCLC officials did not meet their earlier commitment to fund ethnic Mexican marchers in their entirety. Later, Tijerina insisted that reluctant caravan organizers allow American Indian marchers to march across the Mississippi River first. Reies López Tijerina, interview by James Mosby; FBI memo, May 20, 1968, Denver CO; *St. Louis Post-Dispatch*, May 20–21, 1968; Ralph Ramirez, a Brown Beret member, interview by author, September 11, 2005, by telephone; Tijerina, *They*

Called Me 'King Tiger,' 103, 106–7; and Blawis, *Tijerina and the Land Grants*, 120–22.

47. *Time*, May 31, 1968.

48. Vigil, interview by author. María Varela, a former SNCC organizer and an assistant to Tijerina during the campaign, recalls how shell-shocked Abernathy and his aides were, although at the time she had not been as understanding. "I don't know how they got up in the morning. . . . They all looked awful. Bags under their eyes. They all looked, just terrible." María Varela, interview by author, June 18, 2005, Albuquerque NM. See also *Washington Post*, May 25, 1968.

49. Richard Romero, interview by James Mosby, June 11, 1968, Washington DC, MSRC.

50. Quotes by Michael Clark, in letter to Chuck Fager, "Resurrection City Comments," 5, Box 105, Folder 12, Highlander Research and Education Center Records, Part II, State Historical Society of Wisconsin, Madison, Wisconsin; Vigil, interview by author; and Luís Diaz de León, interview by José Angel Gutiérrez, 1999, Tejano Voices: University of Texas at Arlington Center for Mexican American Studies Oral History Project, CMAS No. 135.

51. Carlos Montes, interview by author, August 8, 2005, Los Angeles CA; *Southern Patriot* (June 1968); and Ernesto Vigil, e-mail correspondence, August 30, 2007, in author's possession. Crusade members remember Albert King, a native of Missouri they met on the caravan, who lived with the Chicanos in Hawthorne for the duration, participated in their protests, and was even arrested after the Supreme Court rally.

52. Montes, interview by author.

53. Quote in LADO (August 1968). Also, R. Gonzales, G. Gonzales, N. J. Gonzales, Ramirez, Vigil, Escalante, and Montes, all interviews by author. LADO was part of the Chicano Press Association and founded by an ethnic Mexican, Obed Lopez, but served Chicago's large Puerto Rican community.

54. Ramirez, interview by author.

55. R. Gonzales, interview by author.

56. Montes, R. and G. Gonzales, Vigil, and N. J. Gonzales, interviews by author.

57. Montes, interview by author.

58. For the small Puyallup, Quinault, Muckleshoot, and Nisqually tribes, fishing rights had become a central issue of their survival. Federal treaties long had guaranteed Indian rights to fish in traditional places off

the reservation. But state and local governments had chipped away at their ability to do so legally. By the early 1960s game officials routinely arrested Indians fishing in federally sanctioned "usual and accustomed grounds and stations." Indian activists began using "fish-ins"—deliberate provocations to get arrested—to dramatize their cause. See American Friends Service Committee, *Uncommon Controversy: Fishing Rights of the Muckelshoot, Puyallup and Nisqually Indians* (Seattle: University of Washington Press, 1967; 1970); and Charles Wilkinson, *Messages from Frank's Landing: A Story of Salmon, Treaties and the Indian Way* (Seattle: University of Washington Press, 2000).

59. Quote by Gloria Arellanes, interview by author. Also *Washington Post*, May 30–31, 1968; *El Grito del Norte*, October 31, 1968; and Vigil, R. Gonzales, and Varela, interviews by author.

60. Vigil, interview by author; and Craig Hart, Crusade for Justice chaplain, interview by author, November 29, 2007, Denver CO.

61. Varela, interview by author.

62. Luís Diaz de León, interview by José Angel Gutiérrez.

63. *Denver Post* and *Rocky Mountain News*, June 20, 1968; and (Los Angeles) *La Raza*, July 10, 1968.

64. Miguel Bárragan, interview by author, October 27, 2006, by telephone.

65. *Denver Post*, June 10, 1968.

66. Varela, Arellanes, and G. and R. Gonzales, interviews by author.

67. "Proposal Draft for Developing National Cooperation and Communication Among Minority Group Leadership," undated [September 1968?], Folder 20, Alianza press release, July 20, 1968, Folder 28, Minutes of Poor People's Coalition, July 17, 1968, Folder 24, all in Box 31, RLT; Roger Wilkins memo to Attorney General Ramsey Clark, undated [late 1968?], Box 73, "Poor People's Campaign—Arrest Statistics" folder, Papers of Ramsey Clark, Lyndon Baines Johnson Presidential Library, University of Texas, Austin; and N. J. Gonzales, interview by author.

68. *El Gallo* (March 1969); and G. Gonzales, R. Gonzales, N. J. Gonzales, and Vigil, interviews by author.

69. Montes, interview by author.

70. Varela, interview by author.

71. Oropeza, *¡Raza Si, Guerra No!*, 86.

72. Quote in Oropeza, *¡Raza Si!, ¡Guerra No!*, 87. Also, "El Plan Espiritual de Aztlán," 1969, in *Testimonio: A Documentary History of the Mexican American Struggle for Civil Rights*, ed. F. Arturo Rosales (Houston:

Arte Publico, 2000), 361–63; *El Grito del Norte,* April 14 and May 19, 1969, in Box 68, RLT; and Carlos Muñoz Jr., *Youth, Identity, Power: The Chicano Movement* (New York: Verso, 1989), 75–78.

73. Emerging as Reies Tijerina's influence began to wane, Ballejos's chapter led direct action protests against police shootings, formed multi-ethnic alliances with blacks and Indians in town, and called for stronger state minimum wage laws, school community control boards, bilingual education, respectful welfare regulations, and reforms of state corporate tax laws. SAC-Albuquerque to FBI Director, August 21, 1968; SAC-WFO to FBI Director, September 13, 1968; *Albuquerque Tribune,* August 20 and October 22, 1968; *El Grito del Norte* (Española NM), August 24, September 15, and December 18, 1968, all in Box 68, RLT; *Albuquerque Journal,* November 18, 1968; *El Papel* (March 1969); and Gilberto Ballejos, interview by author, December 6, 2007, Albuquerque NM.

74. See Espinoza, "Revolutionary Sisters."

75. The antiwar march and rally attracted approximately twenty thousand Chicano activists and their supporters to East Los Angeles. Police responded to a small dispute near Laguna Park, which erupted into a full-blown riot. Three died, including *Los Angeles Times* columnist Ruben Salazar. See Chavez, *¡Mi Raza Primero!,* chap. 3.

EIGHT

Brown-Eyed Soul

Popular Music and Cultural Politics in Los Angeles

LUIS ALVAREZ AND DANIEL WIDENER

In May of 1970 the East Los Angeles–based band El Chicano hit number 28 on the *Billboard Top 100* pop music chart
with their song "Viva Tirado." Exhibiting El Chicano's eclec-
tic mix of rock and jazz, the tune was the first ever to attain positions in every category of the *Billboard* chart except country and western. It may seem odd that a band that had recently
changed their name from the generic sounding "VIPs" to El Chicano—a reflection of the Chicana/o Movement's radical critique
of racism, poverty, and political neglect in the United States—
appealed to such a diverse American audience. Despite "Viva
Tirado's" popularity, there was some confusion over who El
Chicano was and how their music should be classified. When on
tour in New York, for instance, band member Bobby Espinosa
remembers, "[T]hey didn't know where to book us. We ended
up playing a show at the Apollo Theater with the O'Jays, Jerry
Butler, the Last Poets, all these black groups. They didn't know
what we were. They'd say, 'What are you guys, Indians? What's
a Chicano?'"[1] Closer inspection of "Viva Tirado" however,
helps explain why El Chicano achieved such crossover appeal
and ended up playing gigs alongside African American artists.

"Viva Tirado" was originally written by Gerald Wilson, a black trumpeter, composer, and jazzman, who was born in Mississippi, grew up in Chicago, and practiced his trade as part of the big band scene in World War II era Los Angeles. Wilson's original "Viva Tirado" paid homage to a Mexican matador named Jose Ramon Tirado, a salute inspired by Wilson's affection for the Mexican music and culture he became enthralled with after moving to Southern California. The history of "Viva Tirado" thus helps reveal the interracial and polycultural past of El Chicano, Gerald Wilson, and post–World War II Los Angeles.[2]

Using "Viva Tirado" as a starting point, this chapter examines how the popular music of El Chicano and other artists that were part of the brown-eyed soul scene of the 1960s and early 1970s illuminates the contours of African American–Chicana/o cultural identity and politics in Los Angeles. We argue that brown-eyed soul, which included a wide-range of Mexican American and African American artists who combined elements of rock, soul, jazz, R&B, country western, Mexican, and Caribbean rhythms, grew from the city's interracial past to challenge the segregated and culturally nationalist streams of the era's ethnic politics. Brown-eyed soul, and the many social relationships that grew from the music and the night club, house party, and concert scenes where it was played, served as a cultural terrain where African Americans and Chicanas/os experimented with social and political relationships that were not always possible in other arenas of struggle or cultural expression. Moreover, the brown-eyed soul scene provides important clues as to how the often overlooked interracial cultural and political energy of the civil rights movement continued to shape Los Angeles long after the 1960s. As much as it was embedded in the political tumult of the sixties and early seventies, brown-eyed soul drew from and contributed to a much longer legacy of black-brown relations in Los Angeles and California.

As a vibrant site of African American and Chicana/o cultural and political collaboration, brown-eyed soul disrupts urban, race, and social movement historiographies that too often frame race relations in a black-white binary or in how single ethnic or racialized groups engaged the white majority. Unlike the assimilationist or conflict models employed by so many academics and policymakers who sought to address race relations in the sixties and seventies, these musicians built upon the rich history of Los Angeles's diverse urban landscape by articulating cultural and political identities that were at root about cultivating relationships across, between, and among racialized groups rather than simply carving out space to exist alongside one another. Moreover, brown-eyed soul reveals as much about World War II and contemporary Los Angeles as it does the civil rights years. The multiethnic character of the music underscores that the Chicana/o and black civil rights movements share many political and cultural connections with both earlier and later periods. Scholars often consider the ethnic radicalism and militancy of the sixties and seventies to be a distinct political break with the accommodation of previous years and the liberal multiculturalism that followed, yet brown-eyed soul highlights the continuities between the culture and politics of the extended postwar period in profound ways.

To address the longer history of brown-eyed soul and the light it sheds on our understanding of African American and Chicana/o relationships, we follow the methodological lead of cultural critic George Lipsitz, who underscores how "reading popular music as history and interpreting history through popular music" helps reveal the experiences, perspectives, and politics of aggrieved groups that are often excised from dominant historical narratives.[3] We thus consider how brown-eyed soul reveals three often-obscured historical narratives, including: (1) the history of interracial cultural politics in postwar Los Angeles; (2) the history of the relational and transregional character of the civil rights and Chicana/o movements; and (3) the more recent history of interracial politics and cultural expression in Los Angeles since the 1990s. Although brown-eyed soul artists did not pretend to be historians or claim to provide an empirical account of postwar conditions, their seemingly apolitical songs acquired deeply political and social meanings that, as Lipsitz reminds us about popular music more generally, serve as "alternative archives of history, the shared memories, experiences, and aspirations of ordinary people."[4] Despite being circulated, bought, and sold as commodities, sometimes articulating new forms of sexism, misogyny, and racism, and rarely meant to be taken literally, brown-eyed soul demonstrates how people connected to the past, struggled in the present, and thought about the future in creative ways.

The Los Angeles that Wilson settled in after a stint in the U.S. Navy during World War II was a city undergoing fundamental demographic, economic, cultural, and political changes. Southern California, especially L.A., experienced a population explosion in the 1930s and 1940s of Mexican, African American, Filipina/o, and Japanese American communities as a result of the wartime economic boom and related Great Migration, immigration from Asia and Mexico, and a rise in the number of first-generation U.S.-born children. One important by-product of the advent of the war was close-knit spatial relations. Sharing residential areas, frequenting the same night spots, and, in some neighborhoods like the Eastside, attending integrated high schools led to a myriad of contacts among Angelinos of different colors. Although geographic proximity did not always lead to social interaction, the dramatic changes during World War II set the stage for city dwellers from a variety of ethnic and racial backgrounds to socialize, share workplaces and political struggles, and create musical styles together in subsequent decades.[5]

During the 1940s a unique music scene, intertwined with zoot suit fashion and dancing, grew from the shared experiences of many of L.A.'s nonwhites. According to one journalist:

[I]t was no accident that Los Angeles and Southern California became the birthplace of R&B. People had been migrating there from all over the United States since before the Depression. When they came, they brought along their music. During the war the defense industry concentrated in the area soaked-up thousands of workers, and thousands of blacks moved in from the South and Northeast to get those jobs. Money was plentiful for a while, but leisure time hours were short. The need for entertainment was satisfied by hundreds of nightclubs, juke joints, saloons, and theaters featuring live music and dancing. The blues from the Deep South, brittle New York jazz, hot string jive, and Chicago jump blended into a new music.[6]

Black, Mexican American, Filipina/o, and Japanese American youth frequented hot spots in the heart of L.A.'s African American neighborhood on Central Avenue to hear big band music; Mexican American pachuco artists like Don Tosti and Lalo Guerrero made the black tradition of scat singing their own by doing it in Spanglish; and Cuban composers and musicians influenced sojourners like Dizzy Gillespie, while jazz, mambo, and Mexican rhythms merged to form what one historian calls "Hollywood Latin."[7]

All of this cultural borrowing and collaboration served as a dress rehearsal for similarly diverse, if uneven and shifting, political coalitions that grew from wartime urban conditions throughout the city. As historians Scott Kurashige, Kevin Allen Leonard, and others have shown, interethnic politics emerged in a variety of forms during the course of the Second World War as many Angelinos struggled to make sense of an intensifying public debate about race following the bombing of Pearl Harbor at the same time they sought equal economic and political participation in the city's war effort. For instance, though the voices protesting Japanese American internment were sporadic and often overshadowed by individuals ambiguous about internment or those who sought economic or political clout from the situation, they did include those like African American lawyer and activist Hugh Macbeth, who actively campaigned against the disenfranchisement of Japanese Americans. African Americans, Mexican Americans, and Jewish Americans participated in labor organizing efforts spearheaded by the Congress of Industrial Organizations (CIO) and the local Communist Party. Many leaders in these same communities actively participated in the Citizens Committee for the Defense of Mexican American Youth, the Sleepy Lagoon Defense Committee, and the Council for Civic Unity, among other wartime organizations, which were formed to free a group of young Mexican American boys erroneously convicted and imprisoned on charges of murder and conspiracy in 1942. These groups also responded to the infamous zoot suit riots in 1943.[8]

During the decade after World War II in Southern California efforts for racial justice inevitably and increasingly linked spatial and cultural issues. Led by former Marine officer William Parker, a reorganized Los Angeles Police Department busily tried to prevent white patrons from visiting nightclubs in the predominantly black Central Avenue area at precisely the moment when white musicians like Chet Baker, Shorty Rogers, Shelly Manne, and Dave Brubeck were popularizing postbop "cool jazz" as a form of more or less improvised music shorn of its previous associations with blackness and vice. To the northeast of Central Avenue, Brooklyn's perennially underachieving baseball team took possession of a stadium erected upon the foundations of one of the city's oldest Mexican American neighborhoods. Despite the presence of a thriving local community, municipal leaders used the power of eminent domain—financed by Federal Housing Administration funds—to raze the bungalows of Chavez Ravine. In each case, new freeway construction allowed increasingly suburbanized white populations to pass between points of interest with less direct interpersonal contact with nonwhite people than before. Thus, rather than progress toward desegregation, the interval between the end of the Second World War and the explosion of the 1965 Watts riot saw efforts at increasing urban resegregation, exemplified most aptly by California voters' overwhelming approval of a ballot initiative upholding restrictive housing covenants and their subsequent support for the openly racist gubernatorial candidacy of Ronald Reagan.[9]

Unsurprisingly, the same interval witnessed new openings for points of contact between communities of color. In the early 1950s, for example, building upon an earlier event sponsored by the Nisei Student Club of Los Angeles City College, more than two thousand people attended a four-day festival of ethnic culture held at the Soto-Michigan Jewish Community Center in East Los Angeles. Jointly sponsored by the National Association for the Advancement of Colored People (NAACP), the Japanese American Citizen's League (JACL), and the Jewish Centers Association, the festival showcased presentations of "traditional" Japanese, African American, Jewish, and Mexican cultures in an effort to "establish lasting bonds of friendship and understanding through the democratic American way of greater equality." Flanked by NAACP chairman E. I. Robinson and JACL regional director Tats Kushida, City Councilman Ed Roybal presided over the event.[10] These cultural galas helped cement the growing bonds between the NAACP, the JACL, and the predominantly Mexican American League of United Latin American Citizens (LULAC). On the surface, these events suggest episodic forerunners of what would later be termed "multiculturalism." The relationship between presentations of cultural difference and ongoing political projects, however, illustrates an ongoing relationship between black, Japanese American, and Mexican American civic groups that extended to the NAACP, the American Jewish Congress, and the JACL's participation in the landmark school segregation lawsuit brought by Mexican American families to desegregate schools in Westminster, Orange County, in 1946.[11]

The interracial sensibility present in the postwar politics found novel aural outlets as well. On the heels of the Mexican American pachuco songs of the late 1940s, a number of black jazz artists in the early 1950s, including saxophonists Joe Houston, Big Jay McNeely, and Chuck Higgins, who had city-wide hits with his "Pachuko Hop," "Pancho Villa," and "Wetback Hop," generated a huge following among Mexican Americans on the Eastside. Higgins remembers that "Pachuko Hop" "didn't have a Spanish flavor, but when we released the record, all the [Mexican American] gangs around here [Los Angeles] would just follow us around, wherever we played."[12] After legendary deejay Hunter Hancock, whose show featured black music but was wildly popular among Mexican Americans, played "Pachuko Hop" on the radio, Higgins began to play live versions of the song for Mexican American audiences that lasted close to two hours.[13] "Little" Julian Herrera also had a big hit in 1956 among East L.A. Mexican Americans with his Johnny Otis produced "Lonely Lonely Nights," an early Chicana/o rock record sung in the style of black soul singers. Otis, who considered himself "black by persuasion" despite being the son of a Greek immigrant, figured Herrera to be Mexican American, but soon learned that he was a Hungarian Jewish runaway from New Jersey who had been taken in and raised by a Mexican American woman in Boyle Heights. In a scenario emblematic of the diverse roots of brown-eyed soul, a Greek American who considered himself African American produced a pop hit sung by a Hungarian Jew who considered himself Mexican American.[14]

Aspects of what would become brown-eyed soul also pervaded the outlying areas of Los Angeles. Historian Matt Garcia notes that in the 1960s, on the rural outskirts of L.A. where many Mexicans worked in the citrus groves, El Monte Stadium and clubs like Rainbow Gardens, where the house band was a multiracial group called the Mixtures, drew fans to see performances by McNeely and other black and Mexican American artists like Ritchie Valens who were central in the birth of rock 'n' roll in Los Angeles.[15] In fact, these rural venues drew large crowds in part because they faced fewer restrictions on underage gatherings and segregation than Los Angeles proper.

At the same time, the members of what scholars have labeled the "Mexican-American" generation were cutting rugs in venues across the breadth of Los Angeles. Historian Anthony Macias provides an exhaustive archaeology of the musical interactions between African American and Mexican American musicians and fans, "from the zoot suit and the jitterbug to neighborhood jazz instructors and high schools, from boogie woogie and jump blues to doo wop, Motown and Afro-Latin music."[16] Significantly, jazz musicians formed a critical part of this musical moment, whether in the guise of mixed black and brown school bands like the Jordan High Junior Hep Cats, the big band swing competitions that pitted the Sal Cervantes Orchestra against the George Brown Orchestra, or in the case of avant-garde saxophonist and composer Anthony Ortega, who studied music alongside Eric Dolphy in the private classes of legendary local music teacher Lloyd Reese. These figures—and Macías finds many—point to the existence of intersecting jazz world alongside the rhythm and blues and pre–rock 'n' roll worlds that would give rise to brown-eyed soul.

Such connections only hint at the mutuality of Chicano and black connections. Brothers Coney, William, and Britt Woodman all recalled family musical gigs for Mexican neighbors in Watts, as did trumpeter Art Farmer and saxophonist Buddy Collette.[17] Wilson summarized his feelings by noting, "I have been into the Mexican culture for a long time. Just listening can get you somewhere, but you have to be exposed to the people."[18]

Personal exposure formed part and parcel of jazz composer Charles Mingus's experience as well. Raised in a multiethnic Watts community populated by blacks, Latinos, Japanese Americans, and a smattering of whites, Mingus made repeated efforts to develop interpretive fusions of African American and Latino sounds. Among these efforts, his 1957 recording "New Tijuana Moods" stands out. A conceptual album based upon his impressions of the border city, the record begins with an adaptation of a Dizzy Gillespie tune Mingus reshaped during the car ride from L.A. to the border. The record then moves through a number of impressionistic sketches of border life, including a nightclub, a gift shop, and a bevy of street musicians. In one tune, "Los Mariachis," Mingus sought to capture the sensibility of musicians forced to anticipate the tastes of prospective clients by linking a series of stylistically divergent sections through a recurring melody meant as a Mexican riff on the blues. Imagining a young Carlos Santana (then a recent arrival in Tijuana) as a busker playing B. B. King and Little Richard tunes in the streets of Tijuas, gives a good sense of the back and forth of musical interaction during this time. Of course, Ramon Ruiz reminds us that African Americans drawn to Tijuana by advertisements published in L.A.'s black newspaper, the *California Eagle*, often encountered incidents of bigotry and patterns of segregation.[19] Still, by the time of Mingus's sojourn, African Americans had been traveling to Tijuana for at least three decades, and the city was familiar to figures like Jack Johnson, Sonny Clay, and Jelly Roll Morton.[20]

These linkages help us to recall that the brown-eyed soul of the 1960s and 1970s stood on cultural foundations built during a time when Chicano and African American urban cultures were deeply and inextricably linked to one another. Far from pointing to a popular culture that was in any way derivative, the development of an identifiably Chicano music, in particular, during the decades before the full explosion of the Chicano movement remained contingent upon a complex urban terrain in which borrowing, innovation, and the reworking of extant cultural forms like *rancheros* and *corridos* as well as boogie woogie and jump blues formed an integral part of a citywide search for dignity and fun. This created the conditions for a popular culture capable of extending hundreds of miles, from El Monte to Venice Beach, from Santa Barbara to Tijuana. Back in the day, this geography of sound and dance constantly contested the racist spatial parameters of Southern California; today, it illustrates the limits of scholarly and popular accounts that take unincorporated East Los Angeles as the sine qua non of Mexican American culture in the greater Los Angeles area.

At the same time, successive interethnic musical scenes attest to the limited manner in which African American cultural history has yet to grapple fully with what Jelly Roll Morton called "the Latin Tinge." If we are serious in proposing California as a center of black cultural production—whether in the pioneering jazz of Kid Ory and Morton, the avant-garde of Ornette Coleman, Bobby Bradford, and Horace Tapscott, the boogie woogie and rock 'n' roll era, or contemporary hip hop—we must do more to extend Peter Narvaez's path breaking examination of "the influences of Hispanic music cultures on African American blues musicians" to new places and new musical genres. Here, the pioneering work of Gaye Johnson points us toward a new sonic mapping of relational black and Chicana/o studies. In describing the influence of Mexican military bands on the burgeoning jazz and blues music scenes of late nineteenth century Louisiana, Johnson reminds us that the questioning of ostensible ethnic boundaries often serves as a precursor to the rethinking of stylistic and generic conventions as well.[21] Narvaez and Johnson are both path breaking and evocative in that their investigations illustrate how the sorts of musical crossings of brown-eyed soul possessed antecedents going back more than a century. Perhaps new research will reveal a rhythm and blues equivalent to Lighting Hopkins's offhand but serious warning to "always watch out for them Mexicans with the six-string guitar. They can do so much on it they'll kill you with it." Or perhaps groups like Los Lobos from East L.A. will finally find their way into the blues canon. At the very least, greater attention to the possibilities of interethnic musical milieus along the U.S.-Mexico borderlands would reveal a fuller picture of the earlier links that underscore the undeniably common aesthetic and political sensibilities that have arisen time and again.

El Chicano's "Viva Tirado" not only helps excavate the roots of brown-eyed soul, the group and 1960s scene reveal the complexity of the period in which brown-eyed soul flourished. When they shed the moniker "VIPS" and renamed themselves El Chicano, the band mirrored the thousands of young people who increasingly self-identified with the Chicana/o movement of the late sixties and early seventies. Chicanos rejected assimilation, whiteness, and a status quo long associated with the term "Mexican American" in favor of the political empowerment, indigeneity, radicalism, and cultural expression encapsulated by the label Chicana/o. On the one hand, then, the broader fragmentation of the civil rights movement into strands of black, brown, red, yellow, gay, and women's power, along with the intensification of racial violence and rebellion in Watts and other urban areas across the country, resulted in deeply seeded cultural nationalism and often divisive gender and sexual relations that often bifurcated not only interracial relationships, but intraracial interactions as well. On the other, however, even though the L.A. music scene reflected the hardening of racial and ethnic divisions in the city, brown-eyed soul did otherwise by combining new sounds, styles, and rhythms in ways that articulated a Chicana/o and black politics that drew from one another and cultivated connections between the two.

By the mid 1960s Chicano bands like Thee Midnighters, Cannibal and the Headhunters, The Jaguars, The Premiers, and

The Village Callers remained popular among Mexican Americans and African Americans in Los Angeles, but also increasingly experienced national success. Part of this growing reach of the L.A. Chicano sound stemmed from the intensified commercialization of popular music, the phenomenal growth in popularity of rock 'n' roll, and diverse urban experiences that marked L.A. and other cities in the sixties. Led by Little Willie G (for Garcia), Thee Midnighters, for example, had city-wide hits with "Land of a Thousand Dances" in 1964 and its first studio single "Whittier Boulevard" in 1965. Cannibal and the Headhunters re-covered "Whittier Boulevard" a year later, to national acclaim. "Whittier Boulevard" became something of an anthem among young Mexican Americans in L.A. because it was essentially a shout out to one of the most popular cruising spots for car customizers on the Eastside. Though "Whittier Boulevard" was more of an up tempo rock tune, Thee Midnighters also incorporated rhythm and blues, soul, funk, salsa, and more traditional Mexican forms of music in their songs and in the hundreds, if not thousands, of live performances they gave across Southern California during the 1960s. Not only did numerous Mexican American bands draw heavily from music often associated with African Americans, but, as with Chuck Higgins, Big Jay McNeely, and others a decade prior, black artists had massive followings among Mexican Americans as well. One such singer in the 1960s was Brenton Wood, who had his own local hits with the likes of "Gimme Little Sign," "Baby You Got it," and "Can You Dig It." Though Wood was little known outside of L.A., Cannibal and the Headhunters and The Premiers (whose "Farmer John" went to number 19 in 1964) had hits that climbed the national charts.

Moreover, L.A.'s brown-eyed soul shared qualities with other regional and international music scenes that together formed a Cold War and civil rights movement era soundscape that stretched from L.A. to San Antonio to Detroit to Kingston,

Jamaica and many points in between. As Manuel Peña and others have shown for San Antonio and across South Texas, for example, from the late 1940s on the influence of black jazz and blues artists like T-Bone Walker and Gatemouth Brown mixed with the western swing of the German influenced Adolf Hofner and his San Antonians to shape the fifties and sixties music of Tejano groups like Freddy Fender, Sunny Ozuna and his Sunliners, Charlie and the Jives, and the Lyrics. The Tejano artists mixed a range of styles, including R&B, jazz, blues, doo-wop, and soul and, in many instances, borrowed from black vocal styles.[22] Once Motown began cranking out hits, the black American soul and R&B sound found eager listeners in Kingston, Jamaica, where ska, rock steady, and then reggae crooners like Ken Booth and Alton Ellis borrowed style, lyrics, and music from Sam Cooke, Otis Redding, Marvin Gaye, and countless others after listening to their hits via radio from Miami and New Orleans. Along with the Tex-Mex scene, the rock steady/reggae scene, and the Motown scene, the brown-eyed soul scene in L.A. demonstrated that interracial, multiethnic, and cross-cultural flows were local, regional, and even transnational. Such musical expressions spoke to urban areas with shared economic and political conditions and across time and space.

Just as the music of the Chicana/o and African American generation of sixties Los Angeles was a piece of a much broader soundscape, so too did politics in the city increasingly engage what Cynthia Young, Laura Pulido, and others call the United States "third world left."[23] Some racialized black, Chicana/o, Latina/o, Asian American, and Native American groups in the United States claimed third world identities for themselves in an effort to connect to international streams of leftist and anti-imperialist politics. This third world identity reinforced the often seething critiques of racism and poverty these groups aired at home. Pulido makes evident the cross-cutting and international character of organizing efforts in Los Angeles and Southern

California during the era by analyzing how area Black Panthers, the predominantly Japanese American East Wind, and El Centro de Accion Social y Autonomo (CASA) traversed interconnected activist terrains and shared a range of political principles. Lorena Oropeza, Ernesto Chavez, and others have detailed how the biggest protest of the L.A. area Chicana/o movement occurred when tens of thousands of anti-Vietnam War protesters turned out for the Chicano Moratorium in East Los Angeles in May of 1970.[24] Moreover, George Mariscal elucidates that in San Diego, as in L.A. and elsewhere, the Cuban Revolution dramatically shaped how local Chicana/o and black university students and activists constructed a transcendent international political imaginary.[25] We might also point to the Black Panther support of the Chicana/o high school blowouts in L.A. in 1968 and the ongoing links between the BPP and the UFW. On the "cultural front," to paraphrase Michael Denning, George Lipsitz notes the internationalist sensibilities of Chicana/o poster art, while Cynthia Young suggests pushing the periodization of the sixties forward into the next decade to include the revolutionary third cinema developed by black, Latino, Asian American, and Middle Eastern student filmmakers affiliated with the ethnocommunications program at UCLA.[26] Such events and activity not only reveals the extent of the worlds which many Los Angeles black and Chicana/o activists saw themselves, but reminds us that Cold War ideologies never fully contained the interracial, cross-cultural, and oppositional vibe of politics in the postwar period, especially when it came to cultural expression and music.

If we listen carefully to the shifting nature of brown-eyed soul in the late 1960s and early 1970s, we can hear and feel in the music the same range of political and cultural exchange that animated the period's activism. By the late 1960s, several newer groups on the L.A. scene, including El Chicano, Tierra, Mark Guerrero, and War, increasingly politicized the brown-eyed soul sound by sometimes engaging on-the-ground peace and protest movements, anti-colonial struggles, and U.S.-based third world organizing in their music. Many of these late 1960s and early 1970s bands consciously made politics a more central feature in their music in ways that did not simply echo popular notions of cultural nationalism and ethnic solidarity, but embraced the longer fetch of L.A.'s interracial and multiethnic history. Thus, Chicana/o and black cultural politics drew much from one another and the relational and internationalist impulses of the Chicana/o and larger civil rights movements, providing a soundtrack to political change unbound by ethnicity, culture, or nationalism.

Brown-eyed soul registered the political changes of the era at the same time it indexed the multicultural history of Los Angeles. Around the time the civil rights and Chicana/o movements and urban life more generally in Los Angeles began to be eclipsed by the grim realities of economic restructuring, deindustrialization, failure to enforce new civil rights laws, and deliberate abandonment of inner cities and their inhabitants, brown-eyed soul continued to regenerate the interracial and multicultural relationships of years past. El Chicano, Mark Guerrero, Tierra, Yeska, and other bands continued the tradition of combining sounds, aesthetics, and influences from everything from black jazz to Mexican cumbias at the same time that they responded to the constricting racial policies of the Nixon, Ford, and Carter administrations. They reversed the trend of Mexican American bands from the Eastside claiming English-language names, sang more in Spanish, and performed songs about overtly politicized topics. Of course, they still sang about love, sex, and good times, but also about the Chicana/o movement's demand for equal education, against police brutality, or against the Vietnam War. Songs like "Chicano Power" and "The Ballad of Cesar Chavez" by Thee Midnighters and Mark Guerrero's "Radio Aztlan," "The Streets of East L.A.," "Pre-Columbian Dream," or "I'm Brown" (which told the story of a down-on-his-luck Chicano who hijacked a plane with a toy gun to bring attention to the plight of Chicanos); El Chicano's and Tierra's rock covers of Mexican classics like "Sabor a Mi" and "Gema;" Tierra's involvement in a Chicano-led boycott against the Coors beer company for discriminatory hiring practices in the early seventies; and the emergence of Chicano-controlled production companies like Brown Bag Productions that promoted many of the Eastside bands at Cinco de Mayo and Mexican Independence Day celebrations at Cal State Los Angeles and other venues across the city after 1970 all demonstrate that music became more politicized because of the Chicana/o and civil rights movement's focus on ethnic pride and cultural nationalism.[27] As much as this politicization drew from commitments to ethnic revitalization and nationalism, it was also part and parcel of brown-eyed soul's organic connection to the history of Mexican Americans and African Americans sharing public space, politics, culture, and music in Los Angeles. Bassist Freddie Sanchez, as if conjuring up the longer history of brown-eyed soul, put it like this: "We're Chicanos. That means American as well as Mexican. Our music is a combination of everything we've heard and felt."[28]

Just as Big Jay Mcneely and Brenton Wood in earlier years borrowed from Mexican American musicians, African American artists in the post-1968 era continued to connect with Chicana/o music fans in L.A. Perhaps the best example of this continuing phenomenon was War, a group initiated by British pop star Eric Burdon when he joined the largely African American ensemble Night Shift, the former back-up band of football star Deacon Jones.[29] After parting ways with Burdon, War's fusion of Latin jazz, soul, and rhythm and blues cemented their popularity among Chicanas/os in L.A. War cuts like "The World is A Ghetto," "Fidel's Fantasy," and "Why Can't We Be Friends" explored the economic and political conditions of early seventies urban America and the possibilities of hemispheric

revolution. Others like "Spill the Wine" and their now classic tribute to car customizers, "Low Rider," made heavy use of
Latin rhythms. War's interracial appeal and variant influences, recalled guitarist Howard Scott, grew from coming of age
in mixed black and Latino neighborhoods, getting their "Latin
thing" from playing with lots of different groups and musicians,
and, according to one journalist, a "mood of cultural exchange
common during the late 1960s and early 1970s."[30] War further
strengthened its relationship to Chicana/o audiences by playing
legendary free Cinco de Mayo shows in downtown L.A., participating in *Low Rider Magazine*'s Fiesta Tours, and playing reg-
ularly at car shows. War's popularity fit well with their all-en-
compassing, if slightly romantic and utopic, approach to their
music, a music defined by conga player Pappa Dee as a "univer-
sal fight against 'Unlove.'"[31]

Brown-eyed soul did not just reflect the politics of the Chi-
cana/o and civil rights movements after 1968. Rather, bands like
Tierra and War constituted a critical element of a novel concep-
tion of Chicanisma/o and blackness, one not circumscribed by
singular notions of race or ethnicity and one integrally tied to
both the long history of African American–Mexican American
relations in L.A. and the transregional and internationalist seg-
ments of 1960s leftist politics. These artists and many of their
fans turned on its head the typical identity politics of the day by
not simply getting their politics from their race or ethnic identity, but by crafting their own identity from complicated and interconnected political struggles and cultural expressions.

On a July Saturday in 1992, more than twenty years following the heyday of the brown-eyed soul scene, War played an afternoon concert in MacArthur Park in Los Angeles. The hundreds of people in attendance, many of them African American
and Latina/o, enjoyed what were by then considered the "old-
ies" for which War was so well known. Songs like the aforemen-
tioned "Why Can't We Be Friends," "The World Is a Ghetto,"

and the anthemic "Low Rider" with its ubiquitous twelve-note hook, offered a testament to the longevity and continuing resonance of brown-eyed soul. Beyond this, the event showcased a number of much younger Latino rappers who had together contributed to a recent compilation CD entitled "Rap Declares War" in which L.A.-area Chicano hip hop artists, including Kid Frost, A Lighter Shade of Brown, and Proper Dos, and African American artists De La Soul, 2Pac Shakur, and Ice-T, put forth a call for social justice expressed by new lyrics set within a medley of beats based around samples of classic War songs.

The timing and location of the "Rap Declares War" event were significant. The concert took place three short months after the explosion of popular rage that followed the police acquittals in the Rodney King case. The most serious urban disturbance since the U.S. Civil War, the riots were described by historian Mike Davis as "a postmodern bread riot" that simultaneously encompassed a radical democratic protest of aggrieved African Americans, an interethnic conflict between African Americans and Korean and Korean Americans, and an explosion among the city's multiracial poor. As a formerly elegant urban oasis that demarcates the intersection of Koreatown, the northernmost fingers of a predominantly "black" Vermont and Hoover Avenue corridors, and the overwhelmingly Central American and immigrant Mexican Pico-Union district, the city blocks surrounding MacArthur Park are a polyglot area that saw widespread looting—often of food staples, consumer goods, and other basic necessities—and large numbers of arrests during the riots. With the memory of National Guard armored cars fresh in the minds of many Los Angelenos, including those whose homes were invaded by soldiers searching for stolen articles, it takes little imagination to see the selection of MacArthur Park as a site for the concert as part of a continuing contest over public space pitting soldiers and police against the black and brown youth of Southern California.[32]

In the subsequent interval between the Rodney King riots and the present day, MacArthur Park has emerged as an important center within the musical and political renaissance that has helped reshape Los Angeles into one of the most important sites of labor, immigration, racial justice, and youth organizing in the United States. MacArthur Park serves as the site for an annual May 1 march coordinated by Multiethnic Immigrant Worker Organizing Network (MIWON).[33] Predating the larger immigrant rights mobilizations that spread during the spring of 2006, the May 1 rallies continue despite a vicious police riot in 2007 and notwithstanding the demise of larger political coalitions led by popular radio personalities, the Democratic Party, Latino elected officials, and the Catholic Church. In another illustration of the park's central place in the city's recent political history, visitors today can take a short walk from the park's eastern edge to a building that served as the main coordination point for the protests that accompanied the 2000 Democratic Party Convention held in downtown L.A. As was the case with the anti-WTO protests in Seattle a few years prior in 1998, moreover, the 2000 protests against the DNC were accompanied and shaped by the contributions of musicians and cultural activists who helped provide the energy, momentum, and context for the strength of the movement.[34]

The efforts of these Chicana/o and African American artists and activists, moreover, have been far from episodic. Across a wide sweep of Northeast Los Angeles, from MacArthur Park through Echo Park–Silverlake and East Hollywood and over the hills into Highland Park and El Sereno, one finds an archipelago of cafes, bookstores, and performance spaces, all of which speak to a broad structure of feeling that suggests a present-day incarnation of the sorts of musical configurations present in brown-eyed soul. Although Chicana/o and Latina/o Studies scholars have tended to assess this moment and cultural geography using the language of a "greater Eastside," that accompanies the demographic expansion of diverse locales linked by the predominance of Spanish-speaking populations, we argue that the musical production of groups like Quetzal, Burning Star, East L.A. Sabor Factory, and Ozomatli speaks to a left-inflected, sonic blending that represents a profound coming together of African American and Latin music. Furthermore, as with brown-eyed soul, members and collaborators with these bands have included Chicanos, Latinos, Japanese Americans, and African Americans.[35]

As was the case during World War II and again during the Vietnam era, the contemporary incarnation of brown-eyed soul emerges from a particular political, demographic, and cultural milieu. After 1992 Latinos emerged as a diverse majority within a city that counted nearly a million African Americans and Asians. Los Angeles became poorer during this time as well, despite the efforts of a resurgent, immigrant-led labor movement. On a wider level, new activists confronted a bevy of racist ballot initiatives, the economic dislocation of NAFTA, and two American wars in the Near East. On the local level, then, Josh Kun's description of Ozomatli as "a band synonymous with a post-urban-uprising Los Angeles, justice-seeking-janitors-striking-down-Westside-Wilshire Los Angeles, MTA-bus-strike Los Angeles, DNC-rubber-bullets Los Angeles, Rampart-frame-ups-that-put-innocent-bodies-in-jail-and-in-hillside-Tijuana-*dompes* Los Angeles" seems on the mark.[36] As Victor Viesca notes, the band's genesis was political. Core members of Ozomatli coalesced around a struggle to unionize the Los Angeles Conservation Corps. Although their organizing drive failed, activists managed to occupy the headquarters of their worksite for more than a year, founding a Peace and Justice Center that served as an activist clearinghouse and performance space for a generation-in-formation of young radicals.[37]

In the decade since the closure of the Peace and Justice Center, groups like Quetzal, Quinto Sol, and Ozomatli have become fixtures at demonstrations, benefits, and fundraising events. Several of the bands formerly affiliated with the Peace and Justice Center, moreover, have regenerated the international flavor of brown-eyed soul's cultural politics by reestablishing the connection to Mexico made evident by previous generations of L.A. area musicians. The music of Quetzal and others, for instance, is profoundly shaped by the Zapatista uprising in Chiapas, Mexico. Group members have explored the possibilities of zapatismo influenced organizing for labor and immigrant rights in Los Angeles and south of the border. This was most evident in their support and participation in Afro–Mexican cultural and political struggles in Veracruz and elsewhere. In a manner not dissimilar from El Chicano a generation earlier, musician/activists like Quetzal Flores and Martha Gonzalez are part and parcel of a new urban landscape defined less by a politics of identity than by an identity of politics. This is not a music that represents radical politics as much as it is a terrain of political activity in its own right.

As did their predecessors, the political and cultural tapestry of these more recent musicians and artists can be seen in the transformative aesthetics of the music as well. Much as War, Santana, and El Chicano obliterated distinctions between jazz, rock, and R&B, Ozomatli and their ilk offer sonic variations that cross ostensibly national, ethnic, and racial music styles. Audiences at Ozomatli concerts may hear as many musical styles as they do songs, and "Mexican" rancheras, "Dominican" meringues, "Brazilian" sambas, and "African American" hip hop maybe included in a given song.[38] Quetzal's music, beyond combining a dizzying array of regional Mexican styles grounded foremost in the Caribbean son jarocho, incorporates hip hop and Lucumi sacred music, while the ska-funk-reggae-clave offerings of Quinto Sol and Burning Star lack a generic name. This is a musical milieu that stitches together Robert Fogelson's famously "fragmented metropolis," most particularly through the coming together of the nominally separate categories of "black" and "Latino."[39] This, ultimately, is both the lesson and the promise of this moment, a kind of Baraka-esque "changing same" in which black and Chicana/o communities create and recreate musical forms that speak to the dialectic between the porous nature of ethnic affiliation and the ongoing reality of external and internal racialization within ongoing efforts to ensure not that we survive, but that we *live*.

Notes

1. Don Snowden, "Latino Bands—High-Riders of the Future?" *Los Angeles Times*, January 8, 1984, N-60.

2. Snowden, "Latino Bands"; Steven Loza, *Barrio Rhythm: Mexican American Music in Los Angeles* (Urbana: University of Illinois Press, 1993), 102–4; Jim McCarthy, *Voices of Latin Rock: The People and Events that Created this Sound* (Milwaukee WI: Hal Leonard, 2004), 16–17; El Chicano official website, http://www.elchicanomusic.com/ (accessed July 18, 2009).

3. George Lipsitz, *Footsteps in the Dark: The Hidden Histories of Popular Music* (Minneapolis: University of Minnesota Press, 2007), xvi.

4. Lipsitz, *Footsteps in the Dark*, xi.

5. For recent discussions of the interracial and multiethnic nature of residential patterns, cultural expression, labor relations, and politics in wartime Los Angeles see, for example, Luis Alvarez, *The Power of the Zoot: Youth Culture and Resistance during World War II* (Berkeley: University of California Press, 2008); Anthony Macias, *Mexican American Mojo: Popular Music, Dance, and Urban Culture in Los Angeles, 1935–1968* (Durham NC: Duke University Press, 2008); Allison Varzally, *Making a Non-White America: Californians Coloring Outside Ethnic Lines, 1925–1955* (Berkeley: University of California Press, 2008); Kevin Allen Leonard, *The Battle for Los Angeles: Racial Ideology and World War II* (Albuquerque: University of New Mexico Press), 2006.

6. Pete Grendysa, "The Making of Rhythm and Blues," *Collecting Magazine* (1985).

7. Daniel Widener, "Perhaps the Japanese Are to Be Thanked? Asia, Asian Americans, and the Construction of Black California," *Positions* 11, no. 1 (2003): 135–81; Anthony Macias, "Rock con Raza, Raza con Jazz:

Latinos/as and Post–World War II Popular American Music," in *Musical Migrations, Volume 1: Transnationalism and Cultural Hybridity in Latin/o America*, ed. Frances Aparicio and Candida Jaquez (New York: Palgrave, 2003).

8. Scott Kurashige, *The Shifting Grounds of Race: Black and Japanese Americans in the Making of Multiethnic Los Angeles* (Princeton NJ: Princeton University Press, 2008); Greg Robinson, "The Great Unknown and the Unknown Great: African American Attorney was Defender of Japanese Americans During World War II," *Nichi Bei Times Weekly* (Los Angeles), June 7, 2007, 1, 5; Kevin Allen Leonard, "In the Interest of All Races: African Americans and Interracial Cooperation in Los Angeles During and After World War II," in *Seeking El Dorado: African Americans in California*, ed. Lawrence B. De Graaf, Kevin Mulroy, and Quintard Taylor (Seattle: University of Washington Press, 2001), 309–40.

9. Gerald Horne, *Fire This Time: The Watts Uprising and the 1960s* (New York: Da Capo, 1997); Lisa McGirr, *Suburban Warriors: The Origins of the New American Right* (Princeton NJ: Princeton University Press, 2002); Matthew Dallek, *The Right Moment: Ronald Reagan's First Victory and the Decisive Turning Point in American Politics* (Oxford: Oxford University Press, 2000).

10. "2009 Persons Attend Cultural Programs at Soto, Michigan," *California Eagle*, November 23, 1952.

11. George Sanchez, "What's Good for Boyle Heights Is Good for the Jews: Creating Multiculturalism on the Eastside during the 1950s," *American Quarterly* 56, no. 3 (2004): 633–61.

12. David Reyes and Tom Waldman, *Land of a Thousand Dances: Chicano Rock 'n' Roll from Southern California* (Albuquerque: University of New Mexico Press, 1998), 13.

13. Reyes and Waldman, *Land of a Thousand Dances*, 13.

14. Bill Millar, "Chicano Rock: Down Mexico Way," *Let It Rock* (September 1975): 16–17; George Lipsitz, *Time Passages: Collective Memory and American Popular Culture* (Minneapolis: University of Minnesota Press, 1990), 140–43.

15. Matt Garcia, *A World of Its Own: Race, Labor, and Citrus in the Making of Greater Los Angeles, 1900–1970* (Chapel Hill: University of North Carolina Press, 2001).

16. Macias, *Mexican American Mojo*, 4–5.

17. Clora Bryan, et. al., eds., *Central Avenue Sounds: Jazz in Los Angeles* (Berkeley: University of California Press, 1998).

18. Macias, *Mexican American Mojo*, 159–60.

19. Ramon Ruiz, *On the Rim of Mexico: Encounters of the Rich and Poor* (Boulder co: Westview, 1998), 51.

20. Michael Balkan, "Way Out West on Central: Jazz in the African-American Community of Los Angeles before 1930," in *California Soul: Music of African Americans in the West*, ed. Jacqueline Cogdell DjeDje and Eddie Meadows (Berkeley: University of California Press, 1998), 43–45.

21. Gaye Theresa Johnson, "'Sobre Las Olas': A Mexican Genesis in Borderlands Jazz and the Legacy for Ethnic Studies," *Comparative American Studies* 6, no. 3 (2008): 225–37.

22. Martin Hawkins, "Tex Mex Makes Your Feet Smile," *Melody Maker*, March 22, 1980; Manuel Peña, *Musica Tejana* (College Station: Texas A&M University Press, 1999), 155–58.

23. Cynthia Young, *Soul Power: Culture, Radicalism, and the Making of a U.S. Third World Left* (Durham nc: Duke University Press, 2006); Laura Pulido, *Black, Brown, Yellow, & Left: Radical Activism in Los Angeles* (Berkeley: University of California Press, 2006).

24. Lorena Oropeza, *¡Raza Si! ¡Guerra No!: Chicano Protest and Patriotism during the Vietnam War Era* (Berkeley: University of California Press, 2005); Ernesto Chavez, *¡Mi Raza Primero! Nationalism, Identity, and Insurgency in the Chicano Movement in Los Angeles* (Berkeley: University of California Press, 2002).

25. George Mariscal, *Brown-Eyed Children of the Sun: Lessons from the Chicano Movement, 1965–1975* (Albuquerque: University of New Mexico Press, 2005).

26. George Lipsitz, "Not Just Another Social Movement," in *American Studies in a Moment of Danger* (Minneapolis: University of Minnesota Press, 2001); Young, *Soul Power*.

27. Robert Hilburn, "Chicano Rock on Bill at Cal State L.A.," *Los Angeles Times*, September 16, 1972, A-6; Snowdin, "Latino Bands." For a brief overview of the politicization of brown-eyed soul during the heyday of the Chicano Movement see, for example, Reyes and Waldman, *Land of a Thousand Dances*, 103–9.

28. Robert Hilburn, "Chicano Rock on Bill at Cal State L.A.," *Los Angeles Times*, September 16, 1972, A-6.

29. Dennis Hunt, "War: Warriors in Recording Industry Combat," *Los Angeles Times*, August 19, 1973, O-50; Sharon Lawrence, "Burdon Tries New Musical Direction with War Group," *Los Angeles Times*, July 17,

1970, D-15; Mike Jahn, "Eric Burdon Bows with New Group," *New York Times*, September 27, 1970, 84.

30. Ann Powers, "Broken Barriers and Disk Generosity," *New York Times*, November 13, 1992, C-7.

31. Keith Altham, "War: The Battle Against 'Unlove'," *New Musical Express*, July 21, 1973.

32. Mike Davis, "Uprising and Repression in L.A.," *Covert Action Information Quarterly* (Summer 1993); reprinted in Robert Gooding-Williams, ed., *Reading Rodney King/Reading Urban Uprising* (New York: Routledge, 1993), 142.

33. MIWON is a coalition of four immigrant rights organizations, the Coalition for Humane Immigrant Rights (CHIRLA), Korean Immigrant Workers Organization (KIWA), Instituto de Educacion Popular del sur de California (IDEPSCA), the Garment Workers Center and Pilipino Workers Center. MIWON has been active since 1999.

34. Daniel Widener, "Another City Is Possible: Interethnic Organizing in Los Angeles," *Race/Ethnicity: Multidisciplinary Global Contexts* 1, no. 2 (2008): 188–219.

35. Yvette Doss, "Choosing Chicano in the 1990s: The Underground Music Scene of Los(t) Angeles," *Aztlan* 23, no. 2 (1998): 191–202; Josh Kun, *Audiotopia: Music, Race, and America* (Berkeley: University of California Press, 2005); Victor Hugo Viesca, "The Battle of Los Angeles: The Cultural Politics of Chicana/o Music in the Greater Eastside," *American Quarterly* 56, no. 3 (2004): 719–39.

36. Kun, *Audiotopia*, 219.

37. Viesca, "The Battle of Los Angeles," 731.

38. Daniel Widener, "Radical Rhythms: A Band Whose Time Has Come," *Against the Current* 13, no. 6 (1999): 25.

39. Robert Fogelson, *The Fragmented Metropolis: Los Angeles, 1850–1930* (Berkeley: University of California Press, 1993).

NINE

Raising a Neighborhood

Informal Networks between African American and Mexican American Women in South Central Los Angeles

ABIGAIL ROSAS

In the fall of 1978 Elena Santiago, her husband Antonio, and their daughter and son decided to leave their hometown in Mexico to make the arduous journey north to the United States. The family did not know they would end up settling and living in the heart of the African American community in Los Angeles. They left their modest middle class home in Mexico to move to what they thought would be a smaller version of their hometown on the other side of the border, which promised to have many more opportunities and mobility. Fellow compatriots from their town lived in East Los Angeles, and like many immigrants before them the Santiago's settled in this area temporarily. But shortly thereafter the family relocated to their permanent home in South Central Los Angeles.[1] In the summer of 1980, when Elena and Antonio purchased their home in the "hood" they were among the few Mexican immigrant families that began to move into this community.[2] In a similar pattern of migration, Ruth Smith, like many African American migrants before her, made the journey west in search of better housing and employment opportunities. She arrived in Los Angeles in the aftermath of the Watts uprising in 1965 and temporarily settled into a community devastated by days of unrest. As the conditions in Watts worsened in the late 1960s, she and her husband decided to purchase a home blocks away from Central Avenue—once the heart of the black cultural and arts movement—the same street that ten years later Elena would also call home.[3]

Both women's migration experience, while separated by time and place of origin, culminated in their settlement and calling of the same residential street home. Their commitment to the well-being of their community, and their shared sense that only by working together could they make South Central Los Angeles a desirable home for themselves and their families, shaped these women's interaction and friendship for the last three decades. Their stories at first appear to run different courses, yet their migration, settlement, and commitment to the longevity and progress of the community in South Central Los Angeles united them in unforeseeable ways. By examining these women's attitudes, commitments, and activism, we can appreciate how female residents in South Central Los Angeles worked across racial, gender, class, and ethnic lines to cope with this region's continuous economic restructuring, immigration, and dehumanizing government services and policies. Such serious issues bolstered the importance of establishing an inclusive multiracial and multiethnic notion of solidarity.

Ruth and Elena's activism operated outside of traditional understandings of community organizing. Their commitment to their community was fueled by an understanding of how motherhood and family was a driving force for civic engagement and civil rights. Ruth Wilson Gilmore, in her discussion of the origins and politics of Mothers Reclaiming Our Children (Mothers ROC), a group that formed in Los Angeles in response to the growing crisis of incarceration of youth of color, argues that through "cooperative self-help, the mothers transformed their care giving or reproductive labor into activism, which then expanded into the greater project to reclaim all children, regardless of race, age, residence, or alleged crime."[4] Ruth and Elena's collaboration thus reveals the importance of historically interpreting how the most disenfranchised of residents created and nurtured a sense of unity and belonging while simultaneously crafting an understanding of community that made room for two racial and ethnic groups with distinct yet interconnected trajectories of migration and settlement. Their devotion to family and community, and their desire to improve their neighborhood, guided the activism of Elena and Ruth. Thus, Elena and Ruth's lives provide an example of black and Latino relations that does not fit the narrative of interracial tension, but rather illustrates the importance of uncovering the day to day neighborly and collaborative interaction between black and Latino residents. These two women further reveal how these groups learned to cooperatively adapt and cope with demographic, economic, political, and social change.

South Central lies just south of Downtown Los Angeles. Since the nineteenth century it has been the home of diverse groups of people. Early twentieth-century Los Angeles was characterized by its multiracial character, as whites, Asian Americans, African Americans, and Mexican Americans lived, worked, and participated in similar activities in South Central. As Anglos left the urban core, communities of color were increasingly segregated in older housing and communities around downtown.[5] The multiracial and multiethnic landscape that once defined downtown and Central Avenue increasingly became more segregated. The racially determined real estate restrictive covenants ensured that as African American migrants arrived to Los Angeles they settled into South Central. Bronzeville and Central Avenue, two communities defined by their multiracial character before this period, increasingly became African American during the 1940s and 1950s. Despite the Supreme Court's decision in 1948 in *Shelley v. Kraemer*, which made racially restrictive real estate covenants illegal, realtors continued to deter people of color from renting and purchasing homes in all-white neighbor-hoods. Los Angeles housing arrangements were divided along racial and class lines, and African American migrants arriving to the Los Angeles basin were steered almost exclusively into South Central.[6] Realtors continued to deter communities of col-or from renting and purchasing homes in all-white neighbor-hoods for decades to come.

The postwar period offered a window of opportunity for Af-rican American men and women in the defense, aerospace, and rubber industries. The black population in the West grew from 1 to 8 percent almost overnight, and by 1950 more than 85 per-cent of the African Americans settling in Los Angeles had come from metropolitan areas. From 1940 to 1970 the African Amer-ican community in Los Angeles grew faster than in other metro-politan area, increasing from 63,744 to almost 763,000.[7] Blacks actively organized to be included in employment unions and at-tain higher wages, which in turn offered opportunities for work-ing class and middle class African Americans to purchase homes in the area. The proportion of African American men employed in white-collar positions rose from 16 percent in 1950 to 28 percent in 1970. More impressively, the proportion of African American women employed in white collar occupations rose from 17 percent to 50 percent during the same years.[8] By the late 1960s South Central, Watts, and Compton had become the heart of African American Los Angeles.

The Watts uprising illustrated that a particular sector of the community was not experiencing mobility. Ruth recalls when she arrived to Los Angeles she could see the devastation of the violence in Watts and realized that living in Los Angeles was a double-edged sword.[9] The uprising represented the culmina-tion of decades of struggle against police violence and labor, housing, and public inequities. By the 1960s, a new generation of African Americans called Los Angeles home. The children of World War II migrants "compared their opportunities not to what African American people in other cities had, nor to the opportunities their parents had, but rather to the opportunities enjoyed by their white peers in L.A.," a place where police harassment, lack of employment, poor schooling, and housing segregation made them painfully aware of their second-class status throughout the city.[10] Youth responded negatively to the lack of opportunity in South Central, which pushed dual-earning African American families to move into middle class neighborhoods in Los Angeles. The upward mobility experienced by African Americans in the 1970s and 1980s facilitated middle class African American families' migration west to affluent neighborhoods like Baldwin Hills and Ladera Heights, and more recently to farther counties like Riverside or even back to the South.[11] These middle class communities were defined by strong homeowner associations that aimed to protect the new community from the same deterioration plaguing Compton, South Central, and Watts. The out-migration of middle class black people ensured that South Central, Watts, and Compton's African American community was increasingly working class and working poor.

From the late 1970s to the present the combination of upwardly mobile African Americans, the Watts uprising, economic deindustrialization from an auto and aerospace industry to a reindustrialization in low-wage, nonunion garment and service sector work, and transformations in immigration policy laid the groundwork for the ways that South Central's racial and economic demographics were dramatically altered.[12] Also, the 1965 Hart-Cellar Act dramatically transformed the racial make up Los Angeles, and the nation as a whole. From 1970 to 1990 the Latino population increased to more than 2.2 million people, an increase of 238 percent in Los Angeles alone.[13] Latinos settled across the Los Angeles basin, a growth that meant that Latinos settled in communities outside of East Los Angeles barrios. The massive demographic shift meant that South Central experienced a growth in the Latino population. Demographic shifts changed the ethnoracial character of South Central, while the economic transformations of the 1970s and 1980s laid the foundation for a poverty rate of 30 percent by 1990.[14]

The demographic and economic transformations defined interactions between and amongst African Americans and Mexican immigrants in South Central. Albert Camarillo notes that considering the realities of "cities of color"—urban spaces where "contemporary ethnic and race relations are increasingly defined by interactions among and between non-whites"—requires an awareness of conflict, misunderstanding, and tension as well as (and less obviously) the "resourceful ways diverse people are working together to overcome the history of marginalization."[15] Camarillo helps us frame the lives of women like Elena and Ruth because their interaction for the last three decades has been determined and mediated by the resources and the ways they make ends meet in their community. The demographic and economic statistics previously mentioned act as the structural constraints that attempt to define the lives of South Central residents; however, Ruth and Elena's lives illustrate how South Central residents found creative ways to craft a sense of community in the midst of worsening economic conditions and decreasing economic opportunities.

The 1980s were pivotal in the racial transformation of South Central. The 1970 and 1980 census reported that the African American population was 93 and 83 percent respectively, but by 1990 it had dropped dramatically to 55 percent in South Central. Mexican and Central American immigrants occupied homes left vacant by blacks as they left the city. In 1980 Latinos accounted for 14 percent of the total population. By 1990 that number had grown to 45 percent.[16] More recently, in 2006 the racial demographics had changed with Latinos comprising 62 percent of the population compared to the 31 percent of African Americans, with the remainder Asian American and white. Ruth had moved to her home on 53rd Street a decade before

this demographic change. She recalled, "I loved this street because there was a Baptist Church at the corner, I am still a pa-
rishioner there, also everyone was middle class or at least
everyone was working . . . it also was a beautiful street . . . it
was a much prettier street than my home in Watts."[17] The allure
of both a beautiful and calm street, along with the proximity of
the parish, facilitated Ruth's transition to her new home. She
immediately became active in the affairs of the church by helping to organize church events and upkeep church grounds. Her
participation in the church facilitated her engagement and concern over her neighbors' lives, especially the well-being of their
children. Having no children of her own, Ruth made sure to remind the kids on her block of the importance of schooling since
she is a firm believer in the promise of education. She remembers the late 1970s as a pivotal period in which she began to see
the onset of dramatic change: "[M]y friends and husband grew
concerned over the closure of the Goodyear plant, and other
factories. . . . Elena's home was once my closest friend's home
. . . I was sad to see her go, she moved further west, but you see
where all the Mexicans are now, there used to be Black people there."[18] Ruth witnessed how the economic bedrock of African American financial stability and immigration created the
conditions for a major change in the community. She was anx-
ious about what this dramatic change would mean for family,
neighbors, and block. But she remained steadfast in helping ease
her neighbors' apprehension over their economic and housing
vulnerability.

Elena was one of the migrants who helped change South
Central. Elena was among the many Mexican immigrants who
moved into the area in the 1980s, as the "flurry of moving vans,
pickup trucks and station wagons" lined streets across the
South Central area as Latino immigrants unloaded their modest
belongings.[19] Elena's realtor found a beautiful three-bedroom
home on 53rd Street, a house vacated by a middle class African

American family leaving the area. Elena stated that street and home appealed to her because it had a "middle class feel," with wide streets beautifully lined by palm trees and manicured lawns. Moving to 53rd Street meant she had to leave the comforts of a predominantly Mexican and Chicano East Los Angeles neighborhood. But the appeal of owning a home, the beauty of the street, and the fact that the day she went to view the home she noticed a Latino family move into another house convinced her to settle in South Central. The realtor also promised that the neighborhood was undergoing a demographic change, and that African Americans were increasingly getting accustomed to having Latino neighbors. For Elena, this meant there would be no racial strife.[20]

In the 1980s the African American community's receptiveness to Latino immigrants in the region was varied and complex. For example, long-term African American resident Gertrude Blanche has lived in the neighborhood for twenty-two years and directed the neighborhood watch program on her block on 56th Street. Like other black residents, Gertrude had concerns about the dramatic changes her "sophisticated ghetto" experienced. Gertrude viewed the Mexican immigrant families moving into her neighborhood with a great deal of apprehension. She described how her new neighbors, an extended family comprised of brothers and sisters, lived in an apartment designed for two adults and child. Blanche would "watch 'em . . . you should have seen the way they'd sneak around so nobody would see how many there were. They'd be quiet as a mouse, quiet as a mouse!"[21] Recently arriving immigrant families commonly shared a small living space, but Blanche could not understand the logic of their living arrangements. Moreover, many Mexican families settled for what Blanche considered an unhealthy quality of life because of financial difficulties and because it helped them avoid detection, detention, and deportation from the Immigration and Naturalization Service

(INS). Blanche's fear that Mexican immigrants were taking over African American housing and employment opportunities was heightened by her inability to communicate with her new neighbors. This exacerbated her fear, anxiety, and misunderstanding.

Not all neighbors expressed apprehension toward Mexican immigrants in the 1980s. Leon Jones, an auto repair shop worker, noted that "[Y]ou've got so many poor blacks and poor Mexicans and we're just gonna all have to get along . . . we blacks can't afford to go nowhere. If I could, I'd get out. Not because of the Mexicans. I'd just like to get out of the area."[22] Leon's sentiments regarding his inability to leave the community were based on his own limited economic opportunities, not racial prejudice. More important, his feelings reflect how both black and recent Mexican immigrants were both plagued by the same circumstances: poverty. Economic vulnerability could serve as a source of coalition building, but also led to much of the tension, apprehension, and misunderstanding between these two groups as limited opportunities made cross-racial relationships all the more fragile. Language barriers heightened misunderstanding and tension. As a black resident adeptly put it, both "groups don't quite know what to make of it yet." African Americans did not know what to make of these demographic shifts. Clearly the transformation of South Central would result in changes to the racial character of their residential streets, but also to the political, social, and economic environment of the community.[23]

It was in this milieu of racial understanding and misunderstanding that Ruth and Elena became friends. They both relished the ability to call something their home and only wanted the best for their residential street and overall community. Despite the larger narratives of South Central, which focus on urban decline and disinvestment, Ruth and Elena saw their community as something to be proud of and worth preserving. Both women became important to the overall operation of their block. They became community matriarchs who watched over the neighborhood and its children, holding the community together. For instance, Elena attempted to befriend all her Mexican neighbors because she knew that they had a difficult time settling into the region due to the looming threat of INS officials, job exploitation and insecurity, and poor knowledge of local school options. Elena took it upon herself to ensure that all the children on her block enrolled in school. She remembered, "[M]y neighbors want the best for their children . . . that's why we make the dangerous trip over here. I just wanted to help them and make sure they knew where the closest school was, how to enroll their kids, because it's a community effort . . . we help each other equally, we have to help each other. . . . [I]f we don't do it who will?"[24]

Elena took her role in the education of local children very seriously. In the morning and afternoon she walked her children and her neighbors' kids to the nearby junior high and high school. She did this with great pleasure. Ensuring the children's safety when crossing the street or simply making sure they got to school on time was a great priority for her. This was one way she sought to build a good community. Little by little, she also began to grow concerned for the African American children on her block. Whenever she saw the neighborhood kids she would ask them, in her limited English, if they had done their homework, gone to school, or participated in school pageants. She thus became known by both Mexican and African American parents as the enforcer of education. As one of her Latino neighbors recalled, "[Y]ou couldn't get past her. I felt bad for the kids because she would keep tabs on them . . . and even the parents, she would remind us when parent teacher meetings were coming up and Christmas shows . . . she was on top of it all. . . . I am thankful for her, because I never worried about my kid not going to school or ditching because when I wasn't around she was."[25] In a similar fashion, Ruth also played the same vital role as community leader and activist in South Central. She was more attentive to the needs of the African American children on her block, ensuring they went to school, played safely on the block, and most especially kept the kids away from some of the hazards of living in an impoverished community like South Central. Ruth disliked the "prevalence of crack" which "became an epidemic in the 1980s—it was and continues to plague the community—you could feel it. I wanted to make sure the kids didn't get into any trouble."[26] Both women understood that if they allowed racial differences to create a wedge between them they would be doing their community a disservice; thus, they actively pursued their vision of community activism, accountability, and social justice.

Elena and Ruth's concern over helping youth in their community was in response to the closing of teen service centers and the demise of African American political organizations like the Black Panthers. This decline facilitated the growth and prevalence of gangs and drugs in the community. From 1978 to 1982 the number of gangs increased to over one hundred and fifty, mostly consisting of factions of Bloods and Crips.[27] The prevalence of gangs and drugs intensified South Central Los Angeles's exposure to crime. Gangs engaged in escalated warfare in pursuit of territory expansion, in the process killing rival gang members and innocent bystanders alike. The homicide rates across the State of California dramatically increased in the late 1970s and peaked in 1980. In the early 1980s, Los Angeles had one of the highest homicide rates in the state. Homicide became a leading cause of death for men of color, in particular African American men. Black men were nine times more likely to be murdered than whites, and Latinos were four times more likely than whites.[28] In addition to the high homicide rates, youth violence in South Central combined with education inequalities. Over fifty percent of male and female youth of color did not receive a high school diploma in the 1980s.[29]

The growing youth gang and drug subculture, increased police aggression, and alarmingly high drop-out rates compelled Ruth and Elena to set up informal networks to ensure that their children would not succumb to the dangers of "the street." South Central neighbor Valeria Rodriguez reflects on the livelihood of her children: "having both Ruth and Elena around was like having a third authority figure . . . my kids stayed on track because of their help."[30] Ruth and Elena ensured that parents never forgot important school deadlines and translated information from the school board, serving as an unending resource for families on the block. Valeria's daughter Jennifer described Ruth and Elena's role in the community like this: "I was scared of them . . . they would tell on me . . . like, if they saw me ditching, hangout with friends, you know that stuff . . . they would tell on me . . . and I would get in trouble . . . like, we would say that we feared them more than our parents 'cuz they knew the principal, office staff, everybody."[31] Jennifer acknowledged an element of fear and accountability that Ruth and Elena inspired in the community children. She and her friends were doubly scared because they knew that unlike their parents, these two women knew everyone in the schools, making it more difficult to engage in the teenage antics Jennifer described. However, Jennifer elaborated that Ruth or Elena did not create a sense of fear by being particularly harsh or mean. Rather, they were genuinely concerned for the well-being of all the children. "I know they care about me," Jennifer stated. "[T]hey want me to go to college, have a future."[32] As a result of their community policing, and out of respect for their efforts, Jennifer committed herself to her studies. She also engaged in after-school community service. Jennifer learned Ruth and Elena's lessons well: she not only excels in school but also actively participates in the betterment of the community.

Elena and Ruth's neighbors acknowledge the benefit of having them concerned over the well-being of their children. The poor educational opportunities in South Central schools make Elena and Ruth's work and concern important. It was also what compelled Jennifer to work hard in school. She hoped to not only make good life for herself, but also to provide a healthier quality of life for her mother and sister. Elena and Ruth have had a positive impact on Jennifer as they guided her through school and neighborhood life. They take great pride and joy in helping children such as Jennifer reach their potential. Their only regret was not being able to help many more children and families. They never attempted to set up a formal community organization to assist these efforts as they felt that the informal relationships developed with children and parents was enough to keep them accountable, as well as manageable, in light of their other obligations. By the same token, they did not need such an organization because the women made up their own impromptu, two person organization.

Ruth and Elena's presence, activism, and commitment to the children in their neighborhood proves of critical importance. Instead of focusing on steering their own families and children away from the hazards of the inner city, they understood their struggle as not an individual issue but rather as a larger community struggle irrespective of race and class that could only be confronted with collective strategies. Their battle for community pride, civil rights, and social justice took place on a street by street basis and involved life and death. Ruth and Elena's story illustrates how these women, in the absence of an organized movement, played an important role in brokering relationships between the members in the community of different racial groups and thereby saved lives. It may seem like these two women would operate with two distinct communities marked by race. However, upon closer inspection we can appreciate the unique ways in which they consciously crossed racial lines and transcended ethnic differences and language barriers.

Ruth and Elena were very conscious in asserting their friendship and cooperation as their interaction and strategizing occurred primarily on the sidewalk and streets. The encounters on the street served as more than just a convenient place to talk, but rather served as a visual and physical marker for their neighbors to see the ways they worked across racial lines for the betterment of their community. In the 1980s, when mutual distrust and animosity between these two racial communities was commonplace, their interaction on the street represented a bold racial reconfiguration—an important symbolic gesture for how people can work across racial lines—as well as a model of the power of neighborly interaction and concern. They also educated each other about why black residents were apprehensive of recently arrived Mexican immigrants, and vice versa. Elena elaborates, "no ones owns anything here . . . I know that when I got here [immigrated to South Central] they [African Americans] didn't like my family moving in, but I think this part of a natural progression." Ruth helped her understand that African Americans were apprehensive because they "had worked really hard to get the little they have [political representation and the ability to own a home], so to see us move in proves to be a threat to their struggle."[33]

Both women understood that community building and education, civic pride, and neighborhood protection operated as a small-scale movement for civil rights and social justice. We live in an age in which many people do not get to know their neighbors intimately, yet these women's friendship, commitment, and service to the community helped them understand the evolution of the community—both African American and Latino— providing us with a window into the ways that actually getting to know each other can be beneficial to the overall operation of their neighborhood. Their lives also provide an example of how black and Latino communities are not always in conflict.

Rather if one investigates the day to day neighborly interaction between members of these communities one uncovers the unique, complex, and cooperative relationships that emerge in a working poor and working class neighborhood like South Central Los Angeles.

Elena and Ruth over the years created a mutual relationship of trust where they depended on each other to make sense of their changing community, landscape, and neighbors. While their initial encounter focused on the immediate concern of property and rights—two divisive subjects that the women struggled to deal with—over time they came to focus much more exclusively on children and education. They were able to rally around the issue of kids and schools without much division. As Chandra Talpade Mohanty explains, solidarity is best sustained when the "terms of mutuality, accountability, and the recognition of common interests is the basis for relationships among diverse communities."[34] Ruth and Elena both grew to understand that their stories overlapped—both were migrants who had similar goals for a better life for themselves and their families. Once they realized their similarities, they extended their goals to their neighbors and the community at large. Their willingness to think critically about the plight of the working class, most prevalently in a community like South Central, made their interaction possible. These women's connection, activism, and friendship is distinctive and worthy of examination.

Both women, and the families on 53rd Street, have found creative ways to work together in the absence of coordinated or identity-based movement. In a similar fashion, Ruth and Elena's activism and politics were rooted in their roles as mothers and caregivers. Ruth had no children of her own, which made her activism more important because her care for the children of other families made those children, in a fashion, her own. Both women believed that only through community support and self-help, and through their own mothering practices and politics, could they move beyond seeing motherhood as a politics relegated solely to the domestic sphere. Rather, motherhood became a larger organizing principle and the concept was, in many ways, their civil rights struggle. For these women, and like the women of Mothers ROC, motherhood was not an oppressive or pejorative term. Instead, it served as a method of exerting power, allowing them to work with the community as well as complicate negative representations of working class women of color as pathological and part of the undeserving poor. They challenged these images and discourses through their lived experience, education, and organizing. Indeed, even in the worst of circumstances they stayed hopeful and helped give their children and families a future.

Their interaction was based on mutual understanding that did not aim to erase their differences and different concerns, but rather operated within a framework that emphasized cooperation to ensure that the community functioned and operated safely. They could not thwart all the structural changes that took shape in their community in the 1970s and 1980s. In the midst of declining governmental social services, economic transformations, recessions, drug and youth violence, and declining school funding and opportunities, only through working together and collaborating across racial lines could they keep their families and neighbors safe. Certainly they could not help everyone. Nevertheless, their willingness and ability to work together illustrated the potential for organizing through an understanding of solidarity, civil rights, and the politics of womanhood and motherhood.

Elena and Ruth's experience, while unique, was not one of a kind. For example, historian Luis Alvarez in his study of youth of color argues that in the post–World War II period, interactions between young people of different ethnic groups should be understood through the politics of dignity. Alvarez makes a persuasive plea to understand Chicana/o youth culture as much more than a rebellious phase, but as an "identity that is deeply shaped by how Chicanos relate to other racialized groups." He argues that what binds Chicanos and other youth of color is "a profound connection between their efforts to reclaim dignity amidst difficult life conditions, including internment, discrimination, and poverty."[35] Both Ruth and Elena understand their role in the community in a similar light. They made sense of their shared history of migration into the region as part of a quest for better opportunity and dignity. Their migration experiences were attempts to reclaim the dignity of themselves and the people living in the inner city. This population was not composed of the undeserving poor, but was a community that in the face of adversity attempted to create a space of their own. The women helped the community maintain its dignity.

Ruth has seen the community change dramatically before her very eyes. That change was not only demographic, but also includes a loss of tradition and a hopelessness among the younger generation. She has seen over the course of her life working class people of color connected with negativity in the broader American public. As she states, "just because we are economically poor does not mean we are morally bankrupt."[36] She believes that we must continue to struggle for dignity. She hopes that her friendship, commitment, and work with Elena serves as an example for families across the community. Both women believe that black and Latino people must work together if the people in the community are to have a chance for a good future. Working across racial and class differences is not easy, most especially in the face of economic recessions, demographic transformations, and dwindling social resources. But these facts, they believe, should not thwart people's attempts to work together. In the end, their friendship and activism was not about understanding where they fit in a racial hierarchy, but had more to do with co-existence, cooperation, and community.

Notes

1. In 2004 South Central Los Angeles was renamed South Los Angeles as a way to move away from the negative representations and features attributed to the community. I continue to use South Central because that is how the people in this article refer to the region—for them the name change does very little to change the perception and/or realities of the community thus they continue to use the old terminology.

2. Elena Santiago (a pseudonym), interview with the author, Los Angeles CA, November 19, 2008.

3. Ruth Smith (a pseudonym), interview with the author, Los Angeles CA, November 21, 2008.

4. Ruth Wilson Gilmore, *Golden Gulag: Prisons, Surplus, Crisis, and Opposition in Globalization California* (Berkeley: University of California Press, 2008), 183.

5. Mark Wild, *Street Meeting: Multiethnic Neighborhoods in Early Twentieth-Century Los Angeles* (Berkeley: University of California Press, 2005).

6. For further information on the impact of the Great Depression on the Chicano community, the impact of Japanese interment on the reconfiguration of residential neighborhoods in Los Angeles, and the impact of real estate restrictive covenants on Chicano, Japanese, and African American residential opportunities see George J. Sanchez, *Becoming Mexican American: Ethnicity, Culture, and Identity in Chicano Los Angeles, 1900–1940* (Oxford: Oxford University Press, 1993); Scott Kurashige, *Shifting Grounds of Race: Black and Japanese Americans in the Making of Multiethnic Los Angeles* (Princeton NJ: Princeton University Press, 2008); Douglas Flamming, *Bound for Freedom: Black Los Angeles in Jim Crow America* (Berkeley: University of California Press, 2005).

7. Josh Sides, *L.A. City Limits: African American Los Angeles from the Great Depression to the Present* (Berkeley: University of California Press, 2003), 38, 4.

8. Sides, *L.A. City Limits*, 190.

9. Smith, interview with author, November 21, 2008.

10. Sides, *L.A. City Limits*, 172.

11. By the 2000 census, one-quarter of the African American population had moved out of the community. See Sides, *L.A. City Limits*, 201.

12. The reindustrialization of the city negatively impacted black employment opportunities, as undocumented and documented Latino and

Asian immigrants were the majority of the labor force in nonunion garment and service sector employment options. See Roger Waldinger and Mehdi Bozorgmehr, eds., *Ethnic Los Angeles* (New York: Russell Sage Foundation, 1997).

13. David M. Grant, "A Demographic Portrait of Los Angeles County, 1970 to 1990" in *Prismatic Metropolis*, ed. Lawrence D. Bobo, Melvin L. Oliver, James H. Johnson Jr., and Abel Valenzuala Jr. (New York: Russell Sage Foundation, 2000), 52.

14. Sides, *L.A. City Limits*, 203; Paul Ong et al., *The State of South Los Angeles* (Los Angeles: UCLA School of Public Affairs, August 2008), 4.

15. Albert M. Camarillo, "Cities of Color: The New Racial Frontier in California's Minority-Majority Cities," *Pacific Historical Review* 76, no. 1 (2007): 2, 28.

16. Hector Tobar, "Latinos Transform South L.A.," *Los Angeles Times*, February 16, 1992, A-1.

17. Smith, interview with author, November 21, 2008.

18. Smith, interview with author, November 21, 2008.

19. Hector Tobar, "Latinos Transform South L.A.," *Los Angeles Times*, February 16, 1992, A-1.

20. Santiago, interview with author, November 19, 2008.

21. William Overend, "South Central L.A.: Minority Meets Minority: Minorities Mix in South Central L.A.," *Los Angeles Times*, August 19, 1979, D-1.

22. Overend, "South Central L.A."

23. Overend, "South Central L.A."

24. Santiago, interview with author, November 19, 2008.

25. Valeria Reyes (a pseudonym), interview with the author, Los Angeles CA, December 13, 2008.

26. Smith, interview with author, November 19, 2008.

27. João H. Costa Vargas, *Catching Hell in the City of Angeles: Life and Meaning of Blackness in South Central Los Angeles* (Minneapolis: University of Minnesota Press, 2006), 179–80.

28. E. Richard Brown et al., "Inequalities in Health: The Sickness in the Center of our Cities," in *South-Central Los Angeles: Anatomy of an Urban Crisis* (Lewis Center for Regional Policy Studies, 1993), 77.

29. Brown et al, "Inequalities in Health," 102.

30. V. Reyes, interview with author, December 13, 2008.

31. Jennifer Reyes (a pseudonym), interview with the author, December 13, 2008.

32. J. Reyes, interview with author, December 13, 2008.

33. Santiago, interview with author, November 19, 2008.

34. Chandra Talpade Mohanty, *Feminism Without Borders: Decolonizing Theory, Practicing Solidarity* (Durham NC: Duke University Press, 2003), 7.

35. Luis Alvarez, "From Zoot Suits to Hip Hop: Towards a Relational Chicana/o Studies," *Latino Studies* 5, no. 1 (2007): 55.

36. Smith, interview with author, November 19, 2008.

TEN

A New Day in Babylon

African American and Mexican American Relations at the Dawn of the Millennium

MATTHEW C. WHITAKER

"We are all tied together in the single garment of destiny, caught in an inescapable network of mutuality. I can never be what I ought to be until you are what you ought to be. And you can never be what you ought to be until I am what I ought to be."
—MARTIN LUTHER KING JR., from "Remaining Awake through a Great Revolution," a speech delivered at the National Cathedral, Washington DC, March 31, 1968

On February 10, 2007, Barack Obama announced his candidacy for president of the United States in front of the state capitol in Springfield, Illinois. In 1858 Abraham Lincoln used this same site to deliver his historic "House divided" speech. The location not only historicized and gave meaning to Obama's message of unity and hope, but also signaled the progress Americans had made in the realm of race relations. Obama promised progressive change and a fundamental shift in America's political culture. Among other things, he vowed to bring Americans of all persuasions together in common cause for freedom and democracy. Obama's campaign stunned pundits and political experts with its broad-based appeal. His principal opponent during the primaries was the formidable New York Senator and former First Lady Hillary Rodham Clinton. The two candidates waged an epic battle for the Democratic Party's nomination, fighting to become either the first African American or woman nominated for president by a major political party. This was a difficult battle, as both Obama and Clinton proved to be serious contenders early in the primary season.[1]

On February's "Super Tuesday," the day that hosts the largest number of elections during the primary campaign, Obama won twenty more delegates than Clinton. He also won the remaining eleven primaries and caucuses scheduled for February. He and Clinton split delegates and states equally in the March 4 contests of Vermont, Texas, Ohio, and Rhode Island. He closed the month with victories in Wyoming and Mississippi. As Obama became the leading candidate for the Democratic nomination, American race relations at large became an explicit issue on the campaign trail and in media coverage of the election season. Despite his early attempts to present himself as a new-age candidate who transcended race, he and his staff were forced to address his racial identity, its meaning in a society in which race remained a highly emotional and volatile issue, and the extent to which other people of color, particularly Chicanos, who comprise America's larges Latino group, would support his bid.[2]

After a fair amount of internal dialogue and debate, the vast majority of black Americans decided to endorse Obama's candidacy. After Obama successfully courted large numbers of white voters in Iowa and New Hampshire, however, he faced an electorate that was increasingly Latino, and heavily Chicano, in Arizona, California, New York, and Nevada. Obama was compelled to confront the history of the often uneasy and competitive relations between African Americans and Chicanos, especially as they jockeyed for influence in cities like Houston, Los Angeles, New York, and Phoenix. Indeed, as Natasha Carrillo, a resident of East Los Angeles, argued: "Many Latinos are

not ready for a [black] person of color. I don't think many Latinos will vote for Obama. There's always been tension in the
black and Latino communities." Younger Chicanos, such as Los
Angeles resident Javier Perez, pointed out that older Chicanos,
like his grandmother, tended to "resist the notion of supporting an African American," a trend that he described as alive but
"changing" among younger Latinos.[3]

As Obama gained momentum and prepared to clinch the
nomination, National Public Radio, major newspapers, scholarly forums, Sunday morning news shows, and African American and Chicano leaders weighed in on the status of "black-
brown" relations. Many wondered aloud if the large numbers
of Latino voters who had pledged their support for Clinton
would cast their vote for Obama. Many black Obama supporters, who believed that the black freedom struggle helped inspire
the Chicano movement and paved the way for increased Latin
American immigration and upward mobility, felt betrayed by
what appeared to be significant discomfort among large numbers of Latinos with Obama's candidacy. In April, May, and
June, however, Obama won primaries in North Carolina, Oregon, and Montana, seizing the lead in the number of pledged
delegates and superdelegate endorsements. On June 3, he passed
the threshold, securing a slight majority of Chicano votes in the
process, to become the presumptive Democratic nominee. On
Thursday, August 28, 2008, a date marking the forty-fifth anniversary of Martin Luther King Jr.'s "I Have a Dream" speech,
Obama took the stage on Invesco Field at Mile High Stadium
in Denver, Colorado, alongside his running mate Senator Joe
Biden of Delaware, and accepted the Democratic Party's nomination for president. In doing so, he became the first person of
color and African American to lead a major party ticket. Obama
addressed a diverse group of an estimated eighty-four thousand
people, many of whom cheered, embraced, and cried as they
affirmed Obama's nomination and celebrated the transcendent

moment and one of the most historic and electric nights in U.S. history. His speech was viewed on television and the internet by over thirty-eight million people. Even Republican observers hailed the achievement. Former President Bill Clinton, however, described Obama's accomplishment as "a twenty-first-century incarnation of the old-fashioned American dream. His achievements are proof of our continuing progress toward the more perfect union of our founders' dreams . . . Barack Obama will lead us away from the division and fear of the last eight years back to unity and hope."[4]

After accepting the Democratic presidential nomination, Obama immediately turned his attention to Senator John McCain of Arizona, the Republican nominee for president, as well as the Republican ticket's running mate, Governor Sarah Palin of Alaska. In the end, McCain could not withstand Obama's momentum, message of redemption, and ability to tap into the American people's disappointment and yearning for a new direction. On November 4, 2008, Barack Obama won the election by a wide margin in the popular vote and with a slim edge in the Electoral College, becoming the forty-fourth president of the United States.

Several factors led to Obama's victory. The election transpired amidst a severe economic crisis, U.S.-led wars in Iraq and Afghanistan, eroding American prestige in international affairs, and an increasing polarization that fostered narrow cynicism about the nation's prospects for a brighter future. Obama also garnered the majority of young voters, labor, teachers, urbanites, women, liberal and moderate whites, and other people of color, including 67 percent of the Latino vote. His message of change resonated with the American public, and the diversity he embodied gave faith to many that his election would reaffirm the American dream.[5] Obama's election represented the substantive reflection of a seismic shift in American life, and his very person embodied America's promise. His rise to power, however, did not eradicate racial division in America, including those between African Americans and Chicanos. Rather, his election reveals a relationship between blacks and browns characterized by similar and distinct histories, competition, conflict, collaboration, and the efficacy of interracial alliances. The last three decades have particularly shaped the interactions between the two groups.

This chapter explores the history and legacy of African American and Mexican American relations in the United States since World War II. It primarily addresses the social, economic, and political nature of these interactions in select cities and local communities that have become multiracial and highly contested terrains in which blacks and Chicanos have cooperated and competed for educational opportunities, employment, housing, and political representation. Los Angeles, Phoenix, and Houston, for example, have emerged as places in which longstanding racial stereotypes; ongoing social, economic and political struggle; and competition for resources and power have made interracial coalition building between these historically marginalized groups difficult, but not impossible. In considering these issues, this chapter examines three fundamental aspects of African American and Mexican American relations: (1) the history and life of the positive and often retrograde perceptions that members of each group have held of the other; (2) the issues that have proved to be the most critical and divisive for black people and Chicanos; and (3) the areas and instances in which the two groups have often agreed and cooperated to secure social justice, enhanced mobility, and greater political power.[6]

The distinct relationship between African Americans and Chicanos, particularly in the American West, has a long history. African Americans and Mexican Americans had already settled in the region when many of its largest cities were founded. Unlike black Westerners, however, Americans of Mexican descent can trace their lineage in the region to at least 300 AD

Through a process called *mestizaje*, indigenous populations in the American Southwest and Mexico, through sexual liaisons with Spanish colonizers and Africans as well as through cultural exchange, produced persons of Spanish-Indian descent and Indians who adopted the language, religion, and customs of the Spanish. By the late 1530s, these people were referred to as *mestizos* in "New Spain." By the late nineteenth century *mestizos* constituted the majority population of what was by then the Mexican and the American Southwestern populations. Mexican Americans in the early West, therefore, were largely a *mestizo* people: acculturated, Spanish speaking, and persons with both Indian and Spanish ancestry. Since the nineteenth century, Mexican Americans with *mestizo* roots have been instrumental in the development of the United States, particularly the West.[7]

As with African Americans, Mexican Americans, despite their longstanding connections to American society, were subjected to white supremacy and racist segregation. Mexican American and African American workers were exploited, underpaid, and restricted to the most menial labor. Unlike black people, however, the dominant society often deemed Mexican Americans with fair skin and "European features" as white. This racial dynamic afforded some Mexican Americans more socioeconomic mobility than their black counterparts. Among the founders and early boosters of cities such as Albuquerque, Houston, Los Angeles, and Phoenix were former Southerners and others who embraced many of the antiblack attitudes that dominated race relations in the South. To them, blacks represented the antithesis of whiteness, while Mexican Americans, although they were deemed subordinate and inferior, were also viewed as partially European and exotic as early as the first decade of the twentieth century. Some Mexican Americans thought of themselves, and were viewed by others, as a white ethnic group such as the Irish or Italians. The fact that some Mexican Americans considered themselves a kind of white ethnic group caused much of the tension between African Americans and Mexican Americans throughout the twentieth century.[8]

Despite the fact that some Mexican Americans were deemed white or considered themselves white, most were subjected to the indignities of Jim Crow segregation. In fact, whites in Phoenix placed signs throughout the city declaring "No Mexicans Allowed" and "No Negroes, Mexicans, or Dogs allowed." Like most African Americans, the majority of Mexican Americans lived in segregated neighborhoods. Exclusion and inequity, coupled with inexpensive land and lodging, common language and cultural mores, bonds to family and friends, and the desire to maintain connections to their homeland and a link to American society, brought more people of Mexican descent to Phoenician "barrios."[9]

As Mexican Americans began to make inroads in employment, a Mexican American middle class developed. By the 1940s and 1950s this group began to call for better opportunities for themselves. These leaders laid the foundation for a more intensive Mexican American freedom struggle that would commence in the years to come. As they became politically active, moved up the socioeconomic ladder, and worked more closely with the white establishment, many black leaders became suspicious. They did not want the few resources available to minorities to be given disproportionately to Mexican Americans. They also knew that many Mexican Americans did not want to share some of the resources they had secured. For instance, in 1935 the Latin American Club of Arizona presented a resolution to the Phoenix City Commission requesting the exclusion of black people from Southside Park, a predominantly Mexican American neighborhood located at Second Avenue and Grant Street. Mexican Americans, some black observers noted, viewed themselves as superior to black people and were, therefore, their adversaries.[10]

African Americans were encouraged to adopt this competitive

outlook by a racial order that often reserved some of its most disparaging and violent attacks for people of African descent. The ability of Mexican Americans to make some advances in the realms of finance and public accommodations, at a time when African Americans could not, contributed to uneasy relations between the two groups. These advancements, coupled with the social construction of race in America, reflect a more fluid formation of racial conventions in the United States as they relate to Mexican Americans. "The conditions that led to the inequality of Mexican Americans," argues F. Arturo Rosales, "are steeped in a legacy of conquest and then labor exploitation." The oppressive treatment of African Americans, however, can be attributed to a more fixed, biological construction of race. This construction places black people, by virtue of their dark skin and African origins, at the bottom of the racial hierarchy. Mexican Americans were "cast as undesirable because of their Indian features," Rosales posits, but white Americans did not often perceived them to be another species altogether.[11]

Discrimination against Mexican Americans, like that faced by white ethnic groups such as the Irish, had much to do with white American stereotypes that portrayed Mexicans and Mexican Americans as poor, culturally divergent, and idle. These dissimilar racial constructions greatly influenced the courses of the Mexican American and African American freedom struggles. The social construction of race as it pertained to Mexican Americans was more fluid than that pertaining to African Americans. This more elastic construction of race caused many Mexican Americans to believe their problems were largely cultural and economic, rather than racial. African Americans, therefore, found it objectionable that Mexican Americans claimed status as a "race" when they benefited from race-conscious remedies to racial inequality, but an "ethnic group" when they sought to set themselves above and apart from African Americans. Since black people did not have an escape clause when it came to the "race problem," they looked at this Mexican American escape clause as an unfair advantage in the fight for rights.[12]

Prior to the emergence of the Mexican American civil rights movement (*el movimiento*) in the 1960s, Mexican American leaders did not focus on white supremacy and racial injustice in the way that African American leaders did. Nevertheless, the persecution of black people by the white majority kept the black freedom struggle at the forefront of American political culture, and eventually tapped into the frustration of oppressed Mexican Americans. The abuse of African Americans at the hands of white Americans outraged younger, more militant Mexican American leaders. As Rosales posits, this outrage helped raise the race "consciousness that was necessary for Chicanos to take the first step into activism."[13] Mexican American activism developed more slowly than black activism, but by the late 1960s and 1970s young individuals from the more oppressed Mexican American classes, particularly recent Mexican immigrants, became educated and began to identify with their *mestizo* heritage as well as the salience of race. Although race is a social construction, it has had real, detrimental, social, economic, and political effects on all Americans. As a result, these younger, more radical Mexican Americans, like their black counterparts, realized that they could not treat race simply as a specious theoretical phenomenon. Instead, they engaged it as a genuine verity that must be denounced to truly render it immaterial. By the late 1960s, these activists began to call attention to the negative ways in which racism adversely affected them as an oppressed racial group. They initiated a grassroots quest for civil rights, a struggle that evolved into the "Brown Power" or Chicano movement.[14]

While Mexican Americans and African Americans "fought for goodies" during the early 1960s, individual African American and Mexican American leaders began to collaborate in efforts to bring attention to the poor socioeconomic state of their respective communities. In Phoenix, Lincoln J. Ragsdale worked with members of the Mexican American Political Association (MAPA) and other activist organizations to promote increased voter registration and political activism. Manuel Peña Jr., future Arizona legislator, joined forces with Ragsdale in the Citizens Action (ACT) Phoenix City Council electoral campaign of 1963. Peña, owner of the Peña Realty and Insurance Company, was born in the agricultural community of Cashion, Arizona, in 1924. From 1953 to 1956, he served as president of the Phoenix Community Service Organization, and from 1956 through 1960, along with Ragsdale, was also a member of the Phoenix Urban League. When he and Ragsdale helped launch the ACT campaign, they were both members of the Phoenix Council for Civil Unity, an interracial band of antiracists who sponsored multiracial educational programming and lobbied the Arizona legislature and the courts for the abolition of Jim Crow laws and practices. Ragsdale and Peña bemoaned the lack of black and brown representation on the Phoenix City Council. Peña worked with Ragsdale and other leaders to improve educational opportunities for minorities in Phoenix. He argued that the problem faced by Mexican Americans and other minorities "lies in education, and it is our great hope that as more and more youngsters and adults become educated they will be able to take their rightful place within the larger community."[15]

The efforts of activists such as Ragsdale and Peña opened the door for more militant Chicano leaders to emerge in the late 1960s. Indeed, Mexican American students at Arizona State University in Tempe followed the lead of California activists and brought the Chicano movement to Phoenix. During the spring of 1968, students at ASU, led by Alfredo Gutierrez, who was inspired by the Chicano movement after visiting Los Angeles and working with Cesar Chavez and the farm workers' movement, extended an invitation to San Francisco leader Armando Valdez to speak on campus. His fiery oratory launched a wave of activism on ASU's campus and throughout the city. These young Chicanos soon organized under the banner of the Mexican American Student Organization (MASO). Gutierrez and his supporters, which included radical white students from the Young Socialist Alliance (YSA) and Students for a Democratic Society (SDS), demonstrated against discriminatory practices targeted at Chicanos. Gutierrez, along with Joe "Eddy" Lopez, Rosie Lopez, Manuel Dominguez, and Gustavo Gutierrez, also helped establish organizations such as Chicanos por la Causa (CPLC) in Phoenician barrios to combat racial discrimination in the city.[16]

Although the Chicano movement was inspired by the black freedom struggle, these two movements never formed an alliance. Chicano activists, however, had a more sophisticated race consciousness and were not as prone to harbor the same anti-black feelings as their predecessors. They understood that the white supremacy that had terrorized and oppressed African Americans was in many ways the same white supremacy that had subjugated them. Nevertheless, Chicano activists, like the more radical black leaders of the 1960s and early 1970s, were primarily interested in justice for *their* people, not integration with others. This approach helped to usher in positive change in the short term, but also continued to undermine the ability of these two groups to work together effectively in the future.[17]

Tensions between black and Chicano Phoenicians erupted during the fall of 1970 after competition over representation and resources at Phoenix Union High School (PUHS), located at First Street and Van Buren in downtown Phoenix. Gutierrez, Lopez, Manuel Dominquez, Earl Wilcox, a number of CPLC leaders, and the parents of numerous Mexican American students at the school, argued that the PUHS did not respond appropriately to the needs of the expanding population of black and Mexican American students. The school boasted few black and Mexican American teachers and activists accused the white teachers and administrators of running a school "full of discrimination and exploitation." One observer noted that the school's leaders "have failed miserably to provide equality and equitable education" for people of color. Others complained that PUHS counselors knowingly pushed Mexican American and African American students "toward manual rather than intellectual development, without consideration of the fact that such a choice produces and perpetuates economic-racial discrimination."[18]

The high school underwent racial demographic changes throughout earlier decades. The number of white students at PUHS declined steadily following Phoenix's 1953 desegregation ruling. The landmark decision triggered white flight. By 1967, whites were abandoning the area and the school in large numbers. From 1967 to 1970, the number of white students at PUHS dropped from 35.1 to 19.3 percent. Many observers had begun to refer to PUHS as a "minority's" school. Although racial segregation was illegal, the relative poor economic status and immobility of African Americans and Mexican Americans locked them into inner-city schools like PUHS. Chicanos and African Americans had virtually no power, however, to shape the school's curriculum, hiring, structure, and administration. This segregated, unequal, and unstable environment exacerbated the already tense relationship between the Mexican American and African American students and their parents by forcing them to compete for mediocre resources. Fistfights and other violent confrontations between blacks and Chicanos became almost daily events at PUHS. Each side blamed the other for the altercations. Mexican American students blamed black students for the violence and their leaders "protested harassment of their children by black students and the school system's failure to cope with the high drop-out rate of Mexican American students." Chicanos held regular marches and demonstrations, and demanded that PUHS leaders move to correct these problems.[19]

On October 9, 1970, Chicano leaders initiated a boycott of PUHS. The CPLC and the newly formed Parent-Student Boycott

Committee (PSBC) demanded that "law and order on the campus be restored." The PSBC and the CPLC also indicated that they would not end the boycott until the "unlawful activity by black students is addressed by authorities." PUHS administrators, Chicano leaders complained, were reluctant to deal with black Phoenicians because they feared escalating the conflict. These events disturbed and saddened some black activists. Black antiracists, with their white supporters, had managed to help desegregate the city's schools, only to have whites flee these previously racially restricted institutions. This left black and Chicano students in what became poorly administered schools that discriminated against them and placed them in adversarial positions that led to conflict. Chicano protesters also desired a more demanding and culturally sensitive curriculum. PUHS officials eventually settled this impasse by promising to hire more Latino employees and to execute programs that were more mindful to the instructional needs of Chicano students. While this helped resolve the crisis, it intensified alienation and anger between African Americans and Chicanos in Phoenix. Black leaders and their Mexican American counterparts had worked hard to form a substantive coalition, but the standoff at PUHS seriously undermined their efforts.[20]

Like African Americans, Chicanos made political advancements as educational and employment opportunities developed in the wake of the civil rights movement. With the support of their individual constituencies, Chicano and black leaders made progress in the political arena. Black leader Calvin Goode and Mexican American leader Rosendo Gutierrez won seats on the Phoenix City Council. Similarly, Mexican American Alfredo Gutierrez, and African American Art Hamilton won election to the Arizona Legislature during the 1970s and 1980s. Throughout this period, the percentage of Chicanos in the Los Angeles and Phoenician populations increased, and they became the dominant racial minority in these cities for the remainder of the twentieth century. The increase in the Latino community greatly affected the African American community. Once predominantly black neighborhoods now received large influxes of Chicanos, who put additional pressures on local services that had previously been geared toward African Americans. One Phoenician reporter observed: "African Americans complain that Hispanics are taking a bigger piece of that tiny slice of economic pie left for minorities. . . . It's the same piece African Americans say they have fought for generations to get." Leaders of the city's Chicano population answered by indicating that African Americans "don't have an exclusive on the legacy of suffering, and that civil rights in this country, though programs like Affirmative Action, have favored African Americans."[21] As African Americans and Mexican Americans continued to fight for insufficient resources, and as the number of Mexicans who migrated to the United States, particularly the urban Southwest, vastly outpaced the influx of people of African descent, tensions rose. Moreover, the rising Chicano population in the American West and other urban areas ushered in greater economic and political power for Chicanos, power that often surpassed what became a comparatively small black population.[22]

Much as in Arizona, tension and conflict also developed in California. Between 1970 and 1990, higher numbers of Chicanos and African Americans enjoyed professional and financial success in Los Angeles. Many who could afford it scattered throughout urban areas, leaving predominantly poor African American and Chicano communities behind. Like African Americans, however, the majority of Mexican Americans and other Latinos continued to be mired in poverty. Despite the fact that most African Americans and Mexican Americans lived in poverty born of historic and lingering racial discrimination, each group continued to have a difficult time relating to and assisting one another. In Los Angeles, three areas of conflict arose between African Americans and Chicanos: the struggle for

educational resources and representation on the districts' teachers and administrator; the fight for public sector jobs; and representation on the city council.

Between 1984 and 1989 the Latino student population in
Compton grew by 17 percent, while black student enrollment
decreased by 16 percent. By 1989, 12,393 Latino and 13,447
African American students were enrolled, reflecting almost
equally divided African American and Latino populations. The
increase in Latino students did not engender a parallel rise in
the number of Latino teachers and administrators in the district, however. In 1989, 3.6 percent of the 1,385 teachers and
administrators were Latino, while 77 percent were black. Many
Chicano activists accused black administrators of "racial discrimination," and many African American leaders charged Chicano activists with saber rattling and betrayal.[23] This battle over
teachers and administrators in the schools, then, transformed an
educational issue into a conflict over jobs.

The fight for public sector jobs in Los Angeles often brought
out the worst in the black and Chicano communities. Chicanos charged blacks, who occupied two-thirds of the city's public
sector jobs, with systemic discrimination, indicating that Latinos held 9.7 percent of the 514 full-time city jobs, while African Americans held 78 percent of the jobs. Black leaders shot
back, pointing out that they were working hard to recruit Latinos, and that in the private sector, particularly in manufactur-
ing, Mexican American owned and operated firms rarely if ever
hired non-Latino workers. While the latter was not a particularly sophisticated or just response, black leaders attempted to
ask a fundamental question: Were the Chicano activists who
drew attention to disparities in the public sector seeking equality or control?

The third contested terrain was the Los Angeles city council. By 1990, no Latino candidate had won election to the council for twenty years. Chicanos faced an uphill battle in securing

seats on the city council because many residents were new arrivals or undocumented immigrants. Indeed, by 1990, of Compton's forty thousand registered voters, merely one thousand eight hundred were Latino. Some black leaders were at best cautious and at worst unsupportive when it came to advocating for Latino representation on the city council. Marcy D. Filer, a city councilman, argued that when Chicano leaders such as Manual Carrea, the only member of the Compton School Board, Joe Ochoa, a former member of the Compton Personnel Board, and Ray Gonzales, a deceased school board member, had the opportunity to aid blacks who sought positions with the city, they neglected to come to their aid. "I don't remember any of them fighting for blacks," Filer argued. "Where were they when I was walking a picket line in Compton?"[24]

By the 1990s, the Chicano population had expanded rapidly. Latino students were now the majority in Compton schools, and the Latino percentage of the Los Angeles population grew from 21 to 30 percent. African Americans continued to dominate public positions, however, and few openly supported policies and programs that helped Latinos integrate themselves into city government or acclimate themselves into a largely English-speaking educational environment. Some blacks were blatantly antagonistic. John Steward, a Compton school trustee, declared that he had "no respect" for the language issue, stating: "This is America. Because a person does not speak English is not a reason to provide exceptional resources at public expense." Coalition building proved extremely challenging amidst these kinds of attitudes, competition for resources, and cultural distinction. The failure to find common ground was more than a minor concern. While some African American and Chicano leaders, in Los Angeles and elsewhere, wished to work harder to form a substantive alliance between 1990 and the present, many within these communities questioned the feasibility of a substantive and sustained alliance.[25]

El Sol, a Chicano newspaper in Phoenix, however, spoke
for many African American and Chicano activists when it announced that "[W]e've fought over limited resources, and we're
tired of doing that. We want to unite for a greater share of the
resources." Many people praised these ideals, but to create such
a coalition proved to be quite complicated. The relationship between Chicanos and African Americans remained fragile. The
competition to promote their unique cultures and socioeconomic problems instigated bitter conflicts between the two groups
during the last twenty years. In September 1990, for example,
African American parents called for the firing of Alexander Perez, the superintendent of the predominantly Mexican American and African American Phoenix, Arizona Roosevelt School
District. The parents accused Perez of being "insensitive" to
the needs of black students and African American personnel.
Leaders of the African American Parents for Quality Education
(AAPQE) also accused him of favoritism, charging him with hiring more Mexican Americans than African Americans in the
school district. The controversy lingered for months as African American leaders such as the Reverend George Brooks, and
a number of Mexican American leaders, participated in "educational politics." Ultimately the Roosevelt District Board,
headed by Brooks, purchased the contract of Perez and initiated a search for a new superintendent. The vote to buy out his
contract was three to two. The three African American board
members voted in favor of his departure, and the two Mexican
American board members voted for his retention.[26]

Some African American and Chicano leaders denied that a racial conflict existed between the two groups, but the competition
for jobs in urban areas, particularly in Houston, Los Angeles,
Phoenix, and New Orleans, which has received large numbers of
Mexican immigrants in recent years, was formidable. Predominantly African American and Chicano neighborhoods suffered
from economic deprivation and high unemployment. Jobs were

precious and each group wanted them. Moreover, ongoing demographic shifts, battles over illicit drug markets, and gang turf wars, intensified by xenophobia and lingering racist stereotypes, generated anxiety and dissonance between the groups. This angst and discord, often encouraged and exacerbated by ethnic leaders, not only cultivated conflict in the public sector but generated violence in schools, on the streets, and in prisons.[27]

Los Angeles has hosted some of the most violent confrontations between African Americans and Chicanos in the United States. Racially motivated brawls and shootings have occurred at several Los Angeles high schools, including Inglewood, Centennial, Luzinger, Jordan Downs, and Hawthorne. Gang battles have transpired in the Venice area of Los Angeles, between the (Chicano) Culver City 13 Boys and (African American) Venice Shore Line Crips, and the (Chicano) 18th Street Gang and the Black P Stones. There are currently more than twelve neighborhoods in Los Angeles where racialized gang warfare is active and spreading. In Highland Park, the Avenues Gang has engaged in what some observers have described as "racial cleansing," as gang members employ extremely violent tactics, including murder, to drive African Americans from the area. In December 2000, for example, the Avenues Gang gunned down two young black men, Christopher Bowser and Kenneth Kurry Wilson. In June 2006, a rival black gang on East 49th Street near Central Avenue in South Central Los Angeles shot and killed three Latinos, Larry Marcial, David Marcial, and Luis Cervantes. There has been relatively little media coverage of this racialized violence, in part because many African American and Chicano leaders have sought to downplay this discord and behave as if problems between these groups are not as serious as these incidents suggest. In fact, Los Angeles Mayor Antonio Villaraigosa stated that although the assailants of the 49th Street murders are black and the victims Latino, nothing suggested that these crimes were racially motivated.[28]

In addition, as Mexicans continue to immigrate to the United States and reshape America's educational, political, and social landscape, African Americans have had to contend with more intense economic competition, particularly in urban areas and the Southwest. In the aftermath of Hurricane Katrina, for example, the Gulf Coast region played host to the arrival of large numbers of Mexican immigrant workers lured to the area by promises of well-paying jobs and housing. Yet, in New Orleans and throughout the Gulf Coast region, many found themselves mired in poverty without shelter, advocates, or representation. The Advancement Project, the National Immigration Law Center, and the New Orleans Worker Justice Coalition demonstrated how complicated and divisive these issues were when they revealed that African American survivors were often denied employment opportunities, even as migrant and especially immigrant workers secured jobs (in positions that were often quite exploitive and unsafe). Thus, Mexican migrants and immigrants to the United States continue to face manipulation, xenophobia, and racism, even as blacks are encouraged, ostensibly, to compete within an unjust system for economic opportunities with their brown counterparts.[29]

Immigration from Latin America, particularly from Mexico, and increased immigration from Africa have not only challenged America to rethink race and ethnicity, but have forced blacks and Chicanos to acknowledge and reassess diversity within their ranks. Indeed, Mexican Americans and African Americans have never been monolithic groups. Conflicts within the two communities, therefore, have also contributed to the inability of blacks and Chicanos to form lasting alliances, particularly in cities such as Los Angeles, which boasts large numbers of each group.[30] Chicanos and African Americans found it difficult to agree among themselves, let alone with others. The conflicts that developed between individuals and groups reflected, in part, the heterogeneity of each group. Even though many in their respective communities called for solidarity in the face of sometimes overwhelming adversity and racial discrimination, the period between 1970 and the present has brought fragmentation and heightened physical and ideological separatism among the black and Chicano communities.[31]

Although blacks and Chicanos have not formed a sustained alliance, the United States, especially the American Southwest, benefited from the development of two racial liberation movements in the region. "In terms of strategy, tactics, and objectives," Quintard Taylor Jr. argues, "most western protests paralleled those waged east of the Mississippi River. However, many of these protests occurred in a milieu where African Americans were only one of a number of groups of color." As a result, Taylor maintains, "the region's multiracial population moved civil rights beyond 'black and white.'" Perhaps unwittingly, African Americans, Chicanos, and their respective liberation movements forced the region's white population to address race in ways that other parts of the country had not. In Phoenix, for example, Lincoln Ragsdale and Alfredo Gutierrez pressed white city officials to address the racial discrimination and socioeconomic isolation that plagued black and Chicano communities. Both of these groups occupied various sections of central and South Phoenix, where de facto segregation limited their mobility and access to vital social and educational services. Ragsdale and Gutierrez argued independently that the socioeconomic status of both African Americans and Mexican Americans were directly related to racial discrimination and the negative effects of white supremacy. Their appeals worked together, however unintentionally, to put forth penetrating calls for the end of white supremacist politics and racial discrimination in Phoenix. Together, these autonomous pleas constituted a collective outcry for racial equality. White Phoenicians were sometimes forced to respond to these demands, without acknowledging or acquiescing to their bifurcated origins.[32]

Although African American and Chicano leaders and activists have continued to produce spirited and articulate calls for racial equality, their autonomous yet ostensibly linked opposition to white supremacy has not resulted in a unified and sustained coalition. By the end of the dawn of the new millennium, the masses of each group continued to struggle, while leaders from both sides debated the degree to which each group suffered the most. Under this competitive and counterproductive atmosphere, a sustained coalition of black and Chicano activists continued to elude these groups. Nevertheless, hope for such an alliance remains. As long as each group continues to occupy the same space, disproportionately experiences the many ills associated with economic inequality and political marginality, and shares the dream of a more equal and just future, there will exist a common ground upon which a substantive and sustained union can be forged. History has demonstrated that such a union will not be based upon romanticized notions of the past or an uncritical solidarity. Instead, it will be built upon practical prescriptions of cross-cultural collaboration that emphasize action and efficacy.[33]

It has proven difficult for African Americans and Chicanos to break out of the cycle of racial polarization and fragmentation. Many have assumed, incorrectly, that simply because the two groups chafed under the omnipresent corporeality of racial discrimination, that they would be "natural" allies in the fight against white supremacy: a kind of "third world alliance." Both groups will have to make a radical shift in the way they view their most fundamental relationship as human beings, however, to overcome the racial divide that separates them. They will have to, according to historian Richard W. Thomas, first "recognize the organic unity of the human race," and their shared experiences as people who have both suffered under the yoke of racial discrimination. This, Thomas maintains, "cannot occur unless a person is deeply committed to a core set of values and principles" that include unqualified demands for the equal treatment of all persons before the law, and in the areas of education, housing, employment, and health care. If a critical mass of blacks and Chicanos, and any other group, can "reach this stage of commitment," argues Thomas, they will "break free of the cycle of racial polarization and fragmentation and move into a cycle of racial unity" based upon similarities rather than differences.[34]

The election of Barack Obama represented a watershed moment in American history, and it was a major psychological victory for a nation in which the prospect of interracial unity seemed to be an unattainable illusion. For millions of Americans, however, particularly blacks and Latinos, the election renewed their belief in the possibility of positive change and the efficacy of strategic alliances. Despite the distrust and conflict that has often existed between these two groups, 67 percent of Latino voters, many of whom are Chicanos, voted for and helped elect the first African American President of the United States. The inauguration of Obama as president, therefore, is a substantive measure of this seismic shift in American life. He embodies America's promise of interracial cooperation, even between groups such as African Americans and Chicanos, who have had a symbiotic relationship marked by conflict and camaraderie. His ascendency is not a cure-all, as interracial challenges remain. It does, however, offer the water of renewal and unity for a nation, and for these two communities in particular, thirsty for solidarity and advancement. America endures, and the fight for black and brown unity continues.

Notes

1. The Editors of *LIFE*, *The American Journey of Barack Obama* (New York: Little & Brown, 2008), 120–49; David Von Drehle, "Person of the Year: Why History Can't Wait," *Time*, December 17, 2008; Ellis Cose, "Black and White: How Barack Obama Is Shaking Up Assumptions,"

Newsweek, July 16, 2007; Timothy Noah, "Threading the Race Needle: After Obama's Speech on Race, Identity Politics May Never Be the Same," *Slate,* March 18, 2008, http://www.slate.com/id/2186692/ (accessed March 19, 2008); Gallup, "Black or African American? 'African American' Slightly Preferred among Those Who Have a Preference," *Gallup,* Washington DC, September 28, 2009. There is no strong consensus among people of African descent in America for how their socially constructed racial group should be described. In a September 28, 2007, Gallup poll of 2,338 African American adults, a clear majority indicated that they did not care which label is used. Nevertheless, among black people who do express a preference even when given the option of saying it does not matter, Gallup data suggests a slight preference for the term African American rather than black. I have chosen to use the terms "African American" and "black" interchangeably, as both terms, specifically and colloquially, refer to people of African descent. Moreover, my use of the term African American reflects a political consciousness that affirms the current national and historical context from which people of African descent in the United States have emerged. Black is used more generally to indicate the culture, consciousness, and customs of people of African descent in America that form a historically connected, yet heterogeneous group of people whose skin tone, while often dark, may vary drastically.

2. Editors of *LIFE, The American Journey of Barack Obama,* 136; Von Drehle, "Person of the Year." The term "Mexican American" will be used when referring to persons of Mexican descent in the United States prior to 1965. The terms "Chicano" and "Chicana" are used when discussing men and women of Mexican descent after 1965. It was during the cultural and political upheaval of the mid-to-late-1960s that many Mexican Americans adopted "Chicano" and "Chicana," terms that had previously been derisive and abusive appellations. Chicanos and Chicanas gave new meaning to the labels, employed them as declarations of self-determination and dignity, and ascribed to their use an oppositional consciousness. Furthermore, "Latino" will be used to describe people of Latin American descent. I acknowledge that this term is not without problems, however, as it, like the word "Hispanic," can engender confusion—implying, incorrectly, that these terms are something other than rather arbitrary social and political constructions. "Latinos" can be American Indian, black, or white. Indeed, more often than not they are a combination of these, and other, socially constructed races. The word "Latino" has also been used in an effort to deny and obscure indigenous identities within the western hemisphere,

associating both Spanish colonizers and indigenous people, especially the descendants of both groups, as the same.

3. Adam Nagourney and Jennifer Steinhauer, "In Obama's Pursuit of Latinos, Race Plays Role," *The New York Times*, January 15, 2008; Pauline Arrillaga, "Hispanics' Reluctance on Obama Highlights Black-Brown Divide," *New York Sun*, February 11, 2008.

4. Editors of *LIFE*, *The American Journey of Barack Obama*, 174–75.

5. Adam Nagourney, "Obama Elected President as Racial Barrier Falls," *The New York Times*, November 4, 2008; Peter G. Gosselin, "What Helped Obama Win Election Now Could Hurt Him," *The Los Angeles Times*, November 17, 2008; Nancy Gibbs, "How Obama Rewrote the Book," *Time*, November 5, 2008; Mark Z. Barabak, "Barack Obama Wins Presidency, Making History," *The Los Angeles Times*, November 8, 2008.

6. Editors of *LIFE*, *The American Journey of Barack Obama*, 174–75; Nagourney, "Obama Elected President"; Gibbs, "How Obama Rewrote the Book"; Barabak, "Barack Obama Wins Presidency"; Gosselin, "What Helped Obama."

7. F. Arturo Rosales, *Chicano!: The History of the Mexican American Civil Rights Movement* (Houston: Arte Publico, 1996), 1–52; R. Douglass Cope, *The Limits of Racial Domination: Plebeian Society in Colonial Mexico City, 1600–1720* (Madison: University of Wisconsin Press, 1994), 66; Bradford Luckingham, *Minorities in Phoenix, A Profile History of Mexican American, Chinese American, and African American Communities, 1860–1992* (Tucson: University of Arizona Press, 1994), 2–39. On the roots of Mexican American history in the Southwest, also see Thomas E. Skidmore and Peter H. Smith, *Modern Latin America*, 6th ed. (New York: Oxford University Press, 1992); John Charles Chasteen and Joseph S. Tulchin, eds., *Problems in Modern Latin American History: A Reader* (Wilmington DE: SR, 1994). For concise accounts of Mexican American history and the Chicano movement, see Rodolfo Acuña, *Occupied America: A History of Chicanos* (New York: Longman, 1999); Juan Gómez-Quiñones, *Chicano Politics: Reality and Promise, 1940–1990* (Albuquerque: University of New Mexico Press, 1990); Vicki L. Ruiz, *From Out of the Shadows: Mexican Women in Twentieth-Century America* (New York: Oxford University Press, 1999).

8. Arnoldo De León, *Racial Frontiers: Africans, Chinese, and Mexicans in Western America, 1848–1890* (Albuquerque: University of New Mexico Press, 2002), 86–107; Bradford Luckingham, *Urban Southwest: A Profile History of Albuquerque, El Paso, Phoenix and Tucson* (El Paso: Texas

Western Press, 1983), 1–35; U.S. Census of Population, General Character-istics by States, 1870, 1880, 1890, 1900, 1910, 1920, 1930, 1940; Federal manuscript census schedule, Arizona Territory, 1870, 1880; *(Arizona) Territorial Expositor*, June 25, 1880; *Weekly Arizona Minor*, May 13, 1871; *Phoenix Herald*, August 17, 1883; *Phoenix Daily Herald*, May 8, 1896.

9. Shirley J. Roberts, "Minority Group Poverty in Phoenix: A Socio-Economic Survey," *Journal of Arizona History* 14 (1973): 358–59. See also Gordon Connell-Smith, *The Inter-American System* (New York: Oxford University Press, 1962); Federico G. Gill, *Latin American-United States Relations* (New York: Harcourt Brace Jovanovich, 1971).

10. Luckingham, *Phoenix*, 95–96; *Arizona Republic*, June 20, 1934, August 15, 1935, July 23, 1936, September 16, 1938, August 1, 1940; *Phoenix Gazette*, July 20, 1940.

11. Rosales, *Chicano!*, xxi. For a fascinating discussion of the treatment of Irish immigrants by Anglo Americans, and how Irish Americans became "American," in part, by accepting the prevailing racial stereotypes about black people and their alleged inferiority, see David Ignatiev, *How the Irish Became White* (New York: Routledge, 1995). Ignatiev posits that the Irish were initially discriminated against in the United States by Anglo Americans, and that they "became white" by embracing racism; a concept that Ignatiev describes as uniquely American. Ignatiev illuminates the cause of racial conflict between Irish Americans and African Americans, and "draws a powerful connection between Irish 'success' in nineteenth-century American society and their embrace of white supremacy." For an equally captivating history, see Thomas A. Guglielmo, *White on Arrival: Italians, Race, Color, and Power in Chicago, 1890–1945* (New York: Oxford University Press, 2003). Guglielmo argues that while many suffered from racial prejudice and discrimination in America, Italian immigrants, unlike the Irish, were viewed as white on arrival in the "corridors of American power." By classifying instances of discrimination against Italians from the socioeconomic benefits they collected from their recognition as whites, Guglielmo "counters the claims of many ethnic Americans that hard work alone enabled their extraordinary success, especially when compared to non-white groups," particularly African Americans, "whose upward mobility languished."

12. Rosales, *Chicano!*, xxii; George Fredrickson, *A Short History of Racism* (Princeton NJ: Princeton University Press, 2002), 97–137.

13. Rosales, *Chicano!*, xxii; Acuña, *Occupied America*, 328–85; Ruiz, *From Out of The Shadows*, 99–126.

14. Matthew C. Whitaker, *Race Work: The Rise of Civil Rights in the Urban West* (Lincoln: University of Nebraska Press, 2005), 220.

15. *Arizona Sun*, May 9, 1957; Luckingham, *Minorities in Phoenix*, 57, 177; Rosales, *Chicano!*, xxii; Acuña, *Occupied America*, 328–85; Ruiz, *From Out of The Shadows*, 99–126; Action Citizens Committee Paid Political Advertisement, "Peña Supports Opportunity for Underprivileged Youth" (Phoenix: Actions Citizens Committee, 1963); GPCCU, *To Secure These Rights*, 16; Manuel Peña, Testimony on Migrants in Phoenix, *Hearings Before the United States Commission on Civil Rights*, Phoenix, Arizona, February 3, 1962, (Washington DC: Government Printing Office, 1962), 74–75.

16. *New Times*, June 11–17, 1986; Patricia A. Adank, "Chicano Activism in Maricopa County—Two Incidents in Retrospective," in *An Awakened Minority: The Mexican Americans*, ed. Manuel P. Servin (Beverly Hills: Sage, 1974), 246–65.

17. Some of the more illuminating and provocative analyses of Chicano activism can be found in: Lorena Oropeza, *¡Raza Si! ¡Guerra No!: Chicano Protest and Patriotism During the Viet Nam War Era* (Berkeley: University of California Press, 2005); Rudy V. Busto, *King Tiger: The Religious Vision of Reies López Tijerina* (Albuquerque: University of New Mexico Press, 2005); Ernesto Chávez, *'¡Mi Raza Primero!': Nationalism, Identity, and Insurgency in the Chicano Movement in Los Angeles, 1966–1978* (Berkeley: University of California Press, 2002); Armando Navarro, *Mexican American Youth Organization: Avant-Garde of the Chicano Movement in Texas* (Austin: University of Texas Press, 1995); Mario T. García with Bert Corona, *Memories of Chicano History: The Life and Narrative of Bert Corona* (Berkeley: University of California Press, 1994); Gómez-Quiñones, *Chicano Politics*; Carlos Muñoz, *Youth, Identity, Power: The Chicano Movement* (London: Verso, 1989); and José Angel Gutiérrez, *The Making of a Chicano Militant: Lessons from Cristal* (Madison: University of Wisconsin Press, 1998).

18. *Arizona Republic*, October 9, 1970, December 2, 1970; *Phoenix Gazette*, October 7, December 3, 1970, January 13, 16, February 2, 1971; Yvonne Garrett, "Chicano Politics in the Phoenix Metropolitan Area," Typescript, Chicano Collection, Hayden Library, Arizona State University, Tempe (hereinafter cited as CC-ASU), 1–17.

19. *Arizona Republic*, October 9, 1970, December 2, 1970; *Phoenix Gazette*, October 7, December 3, 1970, January 13, 16, February 2, 1971; Yvonne Garrett, "Chicano Politics in the Phoenix Metropolitan Area," CC-ASU, 1–17.

20. Quoted in Luckingham, *Minorities in Phoenix*, 61.

21. *New Times*, June 11–17, 1986.

22. Adank, "Chicano Activism," 246–65; Luckingham, *Minorities in Phoenix*, 60; Quoted in *Phoenix Gazette*, March 21, 1993.

23. *Arizona Republic*, December 13, 1981; U.S. Census of Population, General Characteristics by States, 1970, 1980, 1990; Nicola C. Vaca, *The Presumed Alliance: The Unspoken Conflict Between Latinos and Blacks and What It Means for America* (New York: HarperCollins, 2004), 129. Vaca's account is interesting, illuminating, and provocative, but it also lacks balance and is, at times, critical of African Americans to a fault.

24. Marcy D. Filer quoted in Vaca, *The Presumed Alliance*, 130.

25. Vaca, *The Presumed Alliance*, 132. Also see, Tatcho Mindiola Jr., Yolanda Flores Niemann, and Nestor Rodriguez, *Black-Brown Relations and Stereotypes* (Austin: University of Texas Press, 2003), 43–66.

26. *El Sol*, January 18, February 1, April 12, July 5, 12, August 2, 16, 30, 1991; *Arizona Informant*, September 19, October 8, 1990, April 3, 10, June 5, August 7, November 28, December 25, 1991.

27. *Arizona Informant*, October 8, 1990, April 3, 10, June 5, August 7, November 28, December 25, 1991; Andrew Murr, "Racial 'Cleansing' in L.A.: Federal Prosecutors Say a Powerful Latino Gang Systematically Targeted Rival Black Gang Members and Innocent Black Civilians in a Reign of Terror," *Newsweek*, October 24, 2007, http://www.newsweek.com/id/61950 (accessed October 25, 2007).

28. Murr, "Racial 'Cleansing' in L.A"; Patrick McGreevy, "Triple Killing Leaves Few Clues," *Los Angeles Times*, July 4, 2006; Sam Quinones, "Racially Charged Violence Puts Monrovia on Edge," *Los Angeles Times*, February 4, 2008; Dan Abendschein, "Security on Rise after Five Shootings," *Pasadena Star News*, November 19, 2007; John Spano, "Gang Accused of Conspiring to Kill Blacks," *Los Angeles Times*, July 4, 2006; Ellis Cose, "Black versus Brown: Can the Venerable Black-Latino Coalition Survive the Surge in Hispanic Power?" *Newsweek*, July 3, 2006.

29. Henry Jenkins, "People from That Part of the World": The Politics of Dislocation," Culture at Large Forum with George Lipsitz, *Cultural Anthropology* 21, no. 3 (2006): 469–86; Judith Brownie-Dianis, Jennifer Lai, Marielena Hincapie, and Saket Soni, *And Injustice for All: Workers' Lives in the Reconstruction of New Orleans* (Washington DC: The Advancement Project, 2006), 9–14, 32–38, 50–54.

30. The breakdown of the Los Angeles County population by race/ethnicity and poverty in 2000 was:

Racial/Ethnic Group	Total Population (%)	Beneath Poverty Line (%)
Latino	45.0	24.2
White	31.0	8.5
Asian American	12.0	14.2
African America	9.5	24.4
Indigenous	0.3	22.5
Other/Not reported	2.2	6.2

United Way, *A Tale of Two Cities* (Los Angeles: United Way of Greater Los Angeles, 2003), 11; United Way, *2003 State of the Country Report* (Los Angeles: United Way of Greater Los Angeles, 2003), 12; Laura Pulido, *Black, Brown, Yellow, and Left: Radical Activism in Los Angeles* (Berkeley: University of California Press, 2006), 220.

31. Robin D. G. Kelley, *Yo Mama's Disfunktional!: Fighting the Culture Wars in Urban America* (Boston: Beacon, 1997), 89; Manning Marable, *Race, Reform, and Rebellion: The Second Reconstruction in Black America, 1945–1990* (Oxford: University Press of Mississippi, 1991), 201–2; *El Sol*, January 18, February 1, April 12, July 5, 12, August 2, 16, 30, 1991; *Phoenix Gazette*, May 3, 10, June 2, 15, 1990, February 28, March 29, April 1, 22, September 13, 30, November 11, 1991; *Arizona Republic*, August 30, 1990, January 17, September, 25, 1991; January 27, 1992; Lincoln Ragsdale Sr. and Eleanor Ragsdale, interviews by Dean E. Smith, April 4 and November 3, 1990, Phoenix AZ, Transcripts, Arizona Collection, Arizona State University, Tempe; Lincoln Ragsdale Sr., interview by Mary Melcher, April 8, 1990, tape recording, Arizona Historical Foundation, Arizona State University, Tempe AZ.

32. Quintard Taylor, *In Search of the Racial Frontier: African Americans in the American West, 1528–1990* (New York: Norton, 1998), 292–93; Barry Edward Lamb, "The Making of a Chicano Civil Rights Activist: Ralph Estrada of Arizona" (Master's thesis, Arizona State University, 1988), 122–60; Lincoln and Eleanor Ragsdale, interview by Dean E. Smith; Yvonne Garrett, "Chicano Politics in the Phoenix Metropolitan Area," 1–17; Clovis Campbell Sr., interview by author, August 6, 1996, Phoenix AZ; Kris Aron, "Chicanos Por la Causa: Developing Leadership for the Future," *Phoenix* 19 (1984): 101–2, 130–5; Joe Alvarado, interview, Phoenix AZ, 1977, tape recording, Phoenix History Project, Arizona Historical Society, Central Arizona Division, Tempe AZ; Val Cordova, interview, Phoenix AZ, 1977, tape recording, Phoenix History Project, Arizona Historical Society, Central Arizona Division, Tempe AZ; Charles Lama Jr., interview,

Phoenix AZ 1977, tape recording, Phoenix History Project, Arizona Historical Society, Central Arizona Division, Tempe AZ.

33. Richard W. Thomas, *Understanding Interracial Unity: A Study of U.S. Race Relations* (London: Sage, 1996), 201.

34. Thomas, *Understanding Interracial*, 201; Laura Pulido, *Black, Brown, Yellow, and Left.*

CONTRIBUTORS

Luis Alvarez is associate professor in the Department of History, University of California, San Diego. His research and teaching interests include comparative race and ethnicity, popular culture, and social movements in the history of Chicanas/os, Latinas/os, African Americans, and the U.S.-Mexico borderlands. He is the author of *The Power of the Zoot: Youth Culture and Resistance during World War II* (American Crossroads Series, University of California Press, 2008) and coeditor of *Another University Is Possible* (University Readers, 2010). His publications also include essays in or forthcoming from *Mexican Americans in World War II* (University of Texas Press); *Transnational Encounters: Music and Performance at the U.S.-Mexico Border* (University of Oxford Press); *Latino Studies*; *Aztlán*; *Popular Music and Society*; and *Perspectives*.

Lauren Araiza is assistant professor in the Department of History, Denison University. Araiza received her PhD from the University of California, Berkeley. Her recent publications include "'In Common Struggle against a Common Oppression': The United Farm Workers and the Black Panther Party, 1968–1973" in *Journal of African American History* (Spring 2009). She is currently revising a manuscript for publication entitled *"For Freedom of Other Men": Civil Rights, Black Power, and the United Farm Workers, 1965–1973*.

Robert Bauman is associate professor in the Department of History, Washington State University Tri-Cities. He received his PhD from the University of California, Santa Barbara. His book, *Race and the War on Poverty: From Watts to East L.A.*, was published by the University of Oklahoma Press in 2008. His other publications include "Jim Crow in the Tri-Cities, 1943–1950," which won the Charles Gates Award for the best article published in the *Pacific Northwest Quarterly* in 2005; and "The Black Power and Chicano Movements and the Poverty Wars in Los Angeles" published in the *Journal of Urban History* (January 2007). His current book project is tentatively titled *Religion, Community Organizations and the Long War on Poverty*.

Brian D. Behnken is assistant professor in the Department of History and U.S. Latino/a Studies Program at Iowa State University. He received his PhD from the University of California, Davis. His first book was *Fighting Their Own Battles: Mexican Americans, African Americans, and the Struggle for Civil Rights in Texas* (University of North Carolina Press, 2011.) He is the author of several articles, including "'The Dallas Way': Protest, Response, and the Civil Rights Experience in Big D and Beyond" (*Southwestern Historical Quarterly*, July 2007), which won the H. Bailey Carroll Award for the best article published in the SHQ in 2007.

William Clayson is professor and lead faculty in history at the College of Southern Nevada. He holds a PhD from Texas Tech University. Clayson's publications include *Freedom Is Not Enough: The War on Poverty and the Civil Rights Movement in Texas* (University of Texas Press, 2010) and chapters in *The Peoples of Las Vegas* (University of Nevada Press, 2010) and *The War on Poverty and Struggles for Racial and Economic Justice: Views from the Grassroots* (University of Georgia Press, forthcoming).

Gordon Mantler is lecturing fellow in the Thompson Writing Program at Duke University. Mantler is currently writing a book called *Black, Brown and Poor: Multiracial Politics and the Fight Against Poverty, 1962–1974*. He received his doctoral degree in U.S., African American, and Latino history from Duke in 2008, and a master's in U.S. history from the University of South Florida in 2002. Before that he worked as a daily newspaper journalist for eight years. His honors include a Dissertation Completion Fellowship from the American Council of Learned Societies and Andrew Mellon Foundation.

Jorge Mariscal is professor in the Literature Department, University of California, San Diego. Jorge (George) Mariscal was born in East Los Angeles, California. He received his PhD in Spanish from the University of California, Irvine. He has taught at Grinnell College in Iowa and the University of Wisconsin, Madison, and is currently professor of Spanish and Chicano literature at UCSD, where he has taught since 1986. He is also director of the Chicano/Latino Arts and Humanities Minor program. He has written widely on Latinos in the military, the Chicano movement of the late 1960s, and other cultural and historical issues. His books include *Aztlán and Viet Nam: Chicano and Chicana Experiences of the War* (University of California Press, 1999) and *Brown-Eyed Children of the Sun: Lessons from the Chicano Movement, 1965–1975* (University of New Mexico Press, 2005). His media writings can be found at http://jorgemariscal.blogspot.com.

Lisa Y. Ramos is assistant professor in the History Department, Texas A&M University. She received her PhD in 2008 from Columbia University. Her dissertation, "A 'Class Apart': Mexican Americans, Race, and Civil Rights," examined the impact of racial ideologies and rhetoric on Mexican American civil rights battles in Texas throughout most of the twentieth century. She is currently revising her dissertation for publication. Her research interests include civil rights, U.S.-Mexico borderlands, race and ethnicity, and immigration.

Abigail Rosas is a doctoral candidate in the Department of American Studies and Ethnicity, University of Southern California, studying under George J. Sánchez. She received her BA in Comparative Studies in Race and Ethnicity and Sociology from Stanford University in 2005, and was recently awarded the Huggins-Quarles Award from the Organization of American Historians. Her dissertation investigates the cultural politics and community formation of African American and Latina/o immigrants living in the impoverished community of South Central Los Angeles in the post–World War II period.

Matthew C. Whitaker is ASU Foundation Professor of History in the School of Historical, Philosophical, and Religious Studies, Arizona State University, affiliate faculty in African and African American Studies, and affiliate faculty in the Justice and Social Inquiry program at Arizona State University. He specializes in American history, African American history, the African Diaspora, civil and human rights, social movements, sports history, popular culture, and the American West. He is the author of *Race Work: The Rise of Civil Rights in the Urban West* (University of Nebraska Press, 2005) and the editor of *African American Icons of Sport* (Greenwood, 2008). His forthcoming books include *Over Jordan: A History of Modern Black America* (Harlan Davidson) and *Icons of Black America* (ABC-CLIO). His recognitions include the 2003 Bert M. Fireman Prize from the Western History Association, the 2005 Dan Shilling Public Scholar award from the Arizona Humanities Council, and the 2005 Journal of the West award for best article of the year. In 2010 Whitaker was given ASU's Parents' Professor of the Year Special Recognition award, and in 2008 he was one of five partners who were given the Excellence in Diversity award by the National League of Cities for their work on the local Healing Racism Community Dialogue Series.

Daniel Widener is associate professor in the Department of History, University of California, San Diego. His research and teaching interests include the politics of culture, the American political left, and comparative race and ethnicity. His first book, *Black Arts West: Culture and Struggle in Los Angeles*, was published by Duke University Press in 2010.

INDEX

In the Justice and Social Inquiry series

*The Struggle in Black and Brown: African American
and Mexican American Relations during the Civil Rights Era*
Edited and with an introduction by Brian D. Behnken

Hurricane Katrina: America's Unnatural Disaster
Edited and with an introduction by
Jeremy I. Levitt and Matthew C. Whitaker

To order or obtain more information on these
or other University of Nebraska Press titles,
visit www.nebraskapress.unl.edu.

CPSIA information can be obtained at www.ICGtesting.com
Printed in the USA
BVOW020613051111
275242BV00002B/2/P